ANZAC DAY:
The Undying Debt

The Author

Janice Pavils was awarded a Doctor of Philosophy degree from the University of Adelaide in August 2005. Her research centred on Australian identity as expressed through the commemoration of Australian war dead. After completing her PhD Janice travelled to Europe, in particular to England, Germany and the Western Front, furthering her research on Anzac Day and the Australian soldiers who gave their lives.

ANZAC DAY:
The Undying Debt

J. G. PAVILS

LYTHRVM

LYTHRUM PRESS • ADELAIDE

Lythrum Press
54 Currie Street
Adelaide SA 5000

www.lythrumpress.com.au

Published 2007

Cover painting Egils Pavils
Designed and typeset by Michael Deves

Publication of this book has been supported by the
History Trust of South Australia

National Library of Australia
Cataloguing-in-Publication

Pavils, J.G. (Janice Gwenllian), 1941- .
Anzac Day: the undying debt.

Bibliography.
Includes index.
ISBN 9781921013126 (pbk.).

1. Anzac Day - History. 2. Anzac Day sermons - History. 3.War memorials - Australia - History. 4. World War, 1914–1918 - Casualties - Turkey - Gallipoli Peninsula - Anniversaries, etc. 5. World War, 1914–1918 - Campaigns - Turkey - Gallipoli Peninsula - Anniversaries, etc. I. Title.

940.46794

CONTENTS

Foreword – *Bill Gammage* *vii*

Preface *ix*

Acknowledgements *xi*

Abbreviations *xiii*

Chapter 1 'Honouring the Debt' 1

Chapter 2 Sacred Ground 21

Chapter 3 'The One Day' 43

Chapter 4 'Diggers and Slackers' 61

Chapter 5 Widening the Ranks 77

Chapter 6 Harefield and the Remembrance Connection 99

Chapter 7 God Save Australia 118

Chapter 8 Australian Britons 139

Chapter 9 Balancing the Ledger 155

Chapter 10 The 'Pilgrimage Trail' 175

Epilogue 192

Notes to the Text 195

Select Bibliography 228

Index 234

FOREWORD

Anzac Day is Australia's only public day begun in sorrow, its only secular day shared with another country, New Zealand, and its only national day arising from individual hearts and minds across the nation. It still reflects its diverse beginnings: what happens on the day, when, who does it and who watches it varies from town to town, state to state. Once it varied even more, as each community struck its own balance of grief, wartime recruiting, honouring the dead and the returned, and celebrating the day's growing legend.

Janice Pavils has seen an enduring thread through all these rituals: a sense of debt. *Anzac Day: The Undying Debt* shows how powerfully that sense was felt in the beginning, and argues why it should remain in future. Janice writes of South Australia, particularly Adelaide, tracing the day's changes in feeling and ritual by exploring all its forms – the dawn service, the march, the fund-raising, the sports, the memorials in stone and bronze, wood and paper.

Her book is a model for the rest of Australia. All Anzac Day's questions are here. Should it be a public holiday? If so, on the day or the nearest Monday? Who should be allowed to march? Who should conduct the services? Should they be religious? Should sport or fund-raising be allowed? Who should lay wreaths at memorials, and to whom? Should memorials be commemorative (a shrine or a monument), or useful (a hall or a hospital)? These have been contentious questions since 1915, and they can rankle still.

The differences and the consensus reflect Anzac Day's distinctive place in Australia and New Zealand, and perhaps in the world. Most public holidays are imposed from the top; this is a people's day. Almost everyone feels able to say what it should or should not be. Only committed research, clear vision, and great narrative skill could tell such a story. Janice Pavils tells it richly and abundantly. If you want to understand Australia, read this book.

Bill Gammage

Australian National University

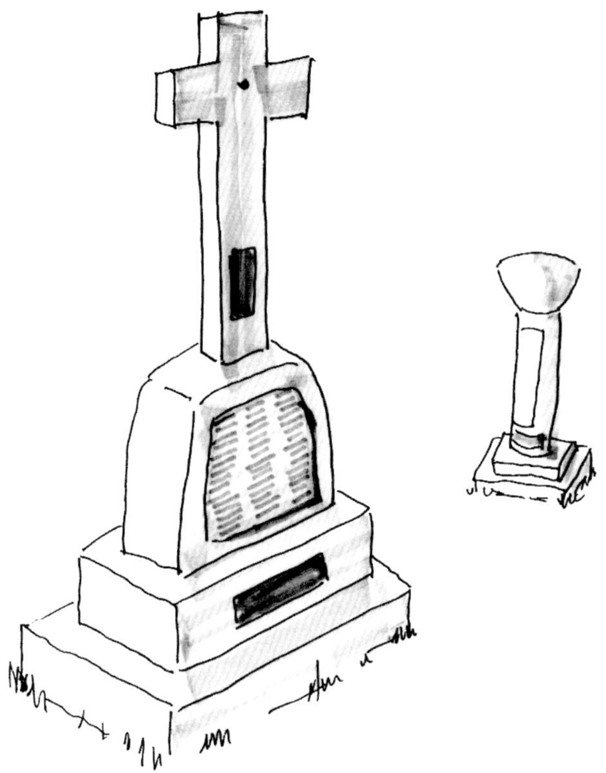

Rosewater Women's Memorial

PREFACE

In March 2001, while on our way to Semaphore for a walk along the beach, my husband, Egils, parked the car at Rosewater because I wanted to record the details of a memorial in the corner of the oval that housed the local football club. While I jotted down the memorial's details and Egils sketched the memorial, a man who came from a house fronting the oval, interrupted our work and demanded to know what we were doing. That man was Ron Hoskin, a former Port Adelaide Councillor, who kept a watchful eye on the memorial and nearby drinking fountain in an effort to guard against vandalism. Having established our credentials, Ron invited us into his home and gave me a copy of his self-printed book *Early Recollections of Ron Hoskin*, which was a local history of Alberton and Rosewater. When I asked if he knew what had happened to the honour rolls in the old Methodist Church on Grand Junction Road, Ron could not tell me. However, he did tell me about the honour rolls that had been in the old Rosewater Council Chambers further along Grand Junction Road. Waving vaguely in the direction of Ottoway Ron told me the honour rolls were now hanging in the Council building at 'The Junction'. Further enquiries led me to the Junction Community Centre in the old Congregational Church Building and the 'Rosewater Womens Memorial 1914–1919 Roll of Honor' [*sic*]. A plaque attached to the 'Roll of Honor' stated that it had been

UNVEILED BY HIS EXCELLENCY THE GOVERNOR
SIR ARCHIBALD WEIGALL K.C.M.G.
APRIL 15th 1922
AND ERECTED AS A TRIBUTE OF PRIDE
BY THE WOMEN OF ROSEWATER
IN HONOR OF THE MEN
WHO ENLISTED FROM THE DISTRICT
IN THE GREAT WAR 1914–1919
LET THOSE WHO COME AFTER SEE TO IT
THAT THEIR NAMES ARE NOT FORGOTTEN

This is my personal effort to follow the Rosewater women's instructions and tell the story of those who gave up their lives in the service of their country and of the efforts of South Australia ex-servicemen and women to keep alive the memory of war dead and war serving Australians.

Janice Pavils

Note on spelling

Throughout this book current spelling conventions have been adopted. In the early part of the twentieth century 'honour' was more usually spelt as 'honor', but to avoid inconsistencies of usage the modern spelling has been used here, except where inscriptions have been quoted exactly. Other current conventions have similarly been adopted.

Antecedent bodies of the Returned & Services League, South Australian Branch (League)

Formed as the Returned Soldiers' Association South Australia in December 1915 (RSA).

In July 1917 the Returned Soldiers' Association South Australia became the Returned Sailors' and Soldiers' Imperial League of Australia, South Australian Branch.

In 1941, the Returned Sailors' and Soldiers' Imperial League of Australia, South Australian Branch became the Returned Sailors', Soldiers' and Airmen's Imperial League of Australia, South Australian Branch.

In 1966, the name changed to the Returned Services League of Australia South Australian Branch.

In 1990, it became the Returned & Services League of Australia (S.A. Branch) Inc.

ACKNOWLEDGEMENTS

A South Australian History Fund 2005/06 publication grant enabled the publication of this book.

Primarily, I must thank Dr Vesna Drapac, for her encouragement to develop my recently examined PhD thesis into a draft manuscript. Above all, I appreciate her interest in my research and her support for I followed a path less travelled in relation to Anzac Day.

My thesis 'Anzac Culture: A South Australian case study of Australian identity and commemoration of war dead' would not have been possible without a solid historiographical foundation. Therefore, I acknowledge a debt to all historians involved in the international identity/memory/history debate and the remembrance of war dead. In particular, to the work of Jay Winter, George L. Mosse, John Gillis, and Ken Inglis. I owe a further debt to Ken Inglis and Annette Becker. Their work on soldiers' memorials, faith and war dead enriched my understanding of the mourning rituals carried out on Anzac Day. The work of Jennifer de Freitas, provided insight into both religious and secular aspects of pilgrimage and the resultant sense of communitas, while Adrian Gregory's work on Armistice Day was another source of understanding. I have taken up the challenge extended by Geoffrey Moorhouse in 1992, in *Hell's Foundations*, and investigated part of the 'Anzac legacy' within South Australia. I also owe a personal debt to the examiners of my doctoral thesis for their comments on my work.

Many other individuals have provided assistance to enable the completion of the thesis that provided the basis for this book.

First of all my thanks go to Ken Inglis for acting as my 'Mr Smith' by providing access through the National Library of Australia to his collection of papers and newspaper cuttings. The extent of my work would not have been possible without the help of the RSL State Secretary, John Spencer who allowed research into RSL South Australian Branch Minutes, together with the use of a computer and library facilities.

Margaret Hosking, History Research Assistant at the Barr Smith Library and Sandra Morton of the Port Adelaide Library, local history section, both gave freely of their time when asked for assistance, as did Archivist Robert Thorton of the Adelaide City Archives.

William Pearce, Hon Archivist, Adelaide High School took time to answer my queries concerning the Harefield Flag, while ex-POWs Ralph Churches and Bill Schmitt as well as Ex-Port Adelaide Councillors, Rex Searle and Ron Hoskin, willingly supplied detailed answers to all my questions.

Mr Simon Berry, Managing Director, Berry Funeral Directors, set time aside to provide me with details concerning the funeral of the Unknown Australian Soldier, while Brian Samuels of the South Australian Department for Environment & Heritage supplied a copy of the 1967 RSL Survey of South Australian War Memorials.

I received further assistance from Tony Chaplin at the RSL, Bill Seager at the South Australian Maritime Museum, Kate Walker of Unley Museum, David Ennis at the Repat Museum, the Rev George Potter, Secretary, and Colin Watson of the Uniting Church Historical Society, and Alan Thyne, at the Uniting Church, Alberton.

I must also acknowledge support in the way of documentation supplied by the Department of Veterans' Affairs through contact with Robert Healy in Canberra and Wayne Stidston, Commemorations Project Office in Adelaide.

The Rev Andrew Gandon, Mr Hedley Mortimer and Mr Patrick Whiteman of St Mary's Parish Church, Harefield and Rev Tim Sedgley, of St Mary, Walton on Thames, kindly provided information from the United Kingdom.

David Schubert read through and commented on the draft manuscript for this book. I would also like to thank Michael Deves for his guidance and advice during the publication of this book. Any mistakes are my own.

The following kindly granted permission to quote from or use other sources. Adelaide City Archives, Advertiser Newspapers Pty. Limited, National Archives of Australia, The Returned and Services League (S.A. Branch) Inc, Decie Denholm, Ralph Churches, Norman G. Manners, Heather McLaren, Bill Pearce, George Potter, Bill Schmitt and the family of Edwin Broomhead.

Last, but certainly not least, I must also thank Egils Pavils who provided invaluable technical computer and photographic support together with his artistic talents. He has been my travelling companion and fellow pilgrim throughout this project.

ABBREVIATIONS

ACT	Australian Capital Territory
AD Committee	Adelaide Anzac Day Committee
ADCC	Brisbane Anzac Day Commemoration Committee
AIF	Australian Imperial Force
AWM	Australian War Memorial
CBD	Central Business District
CMF	Citizens' Military Forces
Ex-POWs	Ex-prisoners-of-war
League	Returned & Services League of Australia (S.A. Branch) Inc.
MBE	Member British Empire
MC	Military Cross
NSW	New South Wales
POW	Prisoner-of-war
RAAF	Royal Australian Air Force
RAF	Royal Air Force
RAN	Royal Australian Navy
RAR	Royal Australian Regiment
RSA	Returned Soldiers' Association of South Australia
RSL	Returned & Services League of Australia
RSS & AILA	Returned Sailors', Soldiers' & Airmen's Imperial League of Australia
RSSILA	Returned Sailors' and Soldiers' Imperial League of Australia
RSSILA SA	Returned Sailors' and Soldiers' Imperial League of Australia South Australian Branch
SA	South Australia
State Memorial	State National War Memorial
TS-OH	Their Service Our Heritage
VP Day	Victory Pacific Day
WDL	Wattle Day League
WWI	World War One
WWII	World War Two

'Prologue' of war, the State National War Memorial, North Terrace, Adelaide. The figures of the student, the farmer and the girl symbolise youth.

Dedicated to all those Australian service men and women

who lie in marked and unmarked war graves overseas including:

LIEUTENANT WILLIAM FRANCIS LYON DODSON
10TH BATTALION, AUSTRALIAN INFANTRY, AIF
WHO DIED BETWEEN 19 AND 20 SEPTEMBER 1917 AGED 29.
BURIED HOOGE CRATER CEMETERY, IEPER, WEST-VLAANDEREN, BELGIUM.

Husband of Lilian Schaumberg Dodson.
Father of Hazel Doreen and Doris Lilian Dodson.
Son of George William and Margaret Mabel Dodson
of Rosewater South Australia.
Brother of Alfred Edward, Mabel Marian, George and
Sergeant Aubrey James Dodson No. 782, 27th Battalion.

FLIGHT SERGEANT 417348 ALFRED SHURROCK DODSON
467 SQUADRON RAAF WHO DIED ON SATURDAY 28 AUGUST 1943 AGED 19.
BURIED DURNBACH WAR CEMETERY. BAYERN, GERMANY.

Son of Alfred Edward and Gwenllian Mary Dodson
of Henley Beach South Australia
Brother of Alfreda Mabel, Gwenllian,
Warrant Officer Class 2 George Evan Dodson SX29981 (S30506)
2/1 Field Ambulance,
Lieutenant Aubrey James Dodson SX5631
2/3 Machine Gun Battalion ex POW and
Corporal William Dodson SX23702 (S9552) 2/6 Armoured Regiment.

CHAPTER 1

'HONOURING THE DEBT'

Leon Gellert was a South Australian poet who served at Gallipoli. His poem 'Anzac Cove' describes the landscape of blood and bones resulting from the Gallipoli Landing. The last two lines of his poem draw attention to the impact of Australian deaths on overseas battlefields, for Gellert ends the poem with the lines: 'There's an unpaid waiting debt:/ There's a sound of gentle sobbing in the South'. South Australian community groups reacted spontaneously to the news of war dead and wounded after learning of the Gallipoli Landing on 25 April 1915. William Sowden, editor of the *Register*, and various women's groups organised patriotic fund-raising days for wounded soldiers and recognised a 'Debt of Honour'. Repayment of the 'Debt of Honour' began in 1915, Violet, Wattle and Anzac Day being just three of the patriotic fund-raising days held that year in recognition of the 'unpaid waiting debt'.

Initially, 1915 editions of the *Register* and the *Advertiser* newspapers raised the subject of 'honouring' the dead and 'paying a debt of honour' in articles reporting on patriotic days, a debt that John Howard now terms a debt of gratitude. 'Roll of Honour' casualty listings began appearing in May 1915, listing the growing numbers of war dead. The commemoration of war dead was taken up by returned soldiers' organisations in terms of 'honouring' the debt to the 'Army of the Dead' and 'human wreckage' that resulted from the Great War. In 2000, the Department of Veterans' Affairs funded 'A Last Debt' seminar dealing with aged care needs in the Veteran community.[1] In this day and age Australians do not think of Anzac Day in terms of debt repayment, despite fundraising conducted by the Returned & Services League's (RSL) Anzac Day Appeal each Anzac Day. The RSL, as a non-governmental welfare organisation, relies on community generosity on Anzac Day. Funds raised from the sale of Anzac badges provide essential care for all ex-servicemen and women and their dependants. The debt acknowledged in 1915, grew, increased by the death and sacrifice of Australian servicemen and women during the Second World War, the Korean War and Vietnam War. The Australian Government still acknowledges the debt owed to ex-servicemen and women. Nowadays we also include the service and death of Australian service personnel in peacekeeping missions such as Timor, the Solomon Islands and Indonesia.

Documents written during the Great War and immediately afterwards imply that because those who served Australia fighting overseas had sacrificed their lives for King and country, those who stayed behind in Australia profiting from the 'work' performed overseas owed ex-servicemen and women a debt. This debt was acknowledged not only to those who paid the ultimate price with the sacrifice of their lives, but extended to the injured and disabled, together with those who served overseas, sailors, soldiers and nurses, as well as their mothers, sisters, wives, children and lovers. The acknowledged debt was one of blood sacrifice supposedly made to save Australia and the Australian way of life for those left behind when the service personnel, both men and nurses, travelled overseas. Australians were British subjects then. In theory, Australians enlisting in the Australian Imperial Force, (AIF), responded to the call of King and country, their patriotic war service as Australian servicemen and women ultimately served the British Empire.[2]

Anzac Day emerged from various patriotic days held throughout the state during the period of the Great War. The 'Anzac Day Committee' inaugurated the first day formally labelled 'Anzac Day' in South Australia in 1915 as a day intended to raise funds for 'Wounded Soldiers'. This first Anzac Day took place on 'Eight Hours Day', celebrated as a holiday, on Wednesday 13 October 1915. Adelaide City Archives hold letters that provide details of those Anzac Day arrangements. In a letter dated 6 September 1915, Mr Fred L. Seager of West's Pictures, advised the Town Clerk that instead of the usual Eight Hours' Day Procession a Committee planned to raise funds for wounded soldiers on 13 October and wanted to advertise the day with 'sandwich men in the streets'.[3] According to Mr Seager's letter, theatrical Managers and other leading citizens planned the special day as a day with 'purely patriotic and philanthropic' objectives. On 29 September 1915, a second letter arrived for the Town Clerk, this time sent from the Trades Hall and signed by T. B. Merry, Secretary, on 'Anzac Day (Eight Hours' Celebration)' letterhead. Mr Merry, under the direction of the Anzac Day Combined Committee, requested permission for the Anzac Day Pageant to follow a route from the Trades Hall in Grote Street to Gawler Place. The Town Clerk received a third letter signed by L. J. Powell, as Hon Organiser on 'Anzac Day, October 13th, 1915' letterhead. This letter came from the 'Committee Rooms, Royal Exchange', and applied for permission to use Victoria Square, in the city centre, and Creswell Gardens, next to the Adelaide oval, for supplying refreshments on Anzac Day.[4]

With Adelaide City Council permission granted, from the beginning of October the *Register* and the *Advertiser* advertised 'This space is reserved for

Anzac Day announcements, watch it daily'.[5] On 13 October, the *Register* reported on the day's appeal under the sub-heading 'The Anzac Celebration'. According to the *Register* no gift or sum of money was too great for the 'Soldiers' Fund' for the fund had to grow with recruiting figures. The Soldiers' Fund was not for charity 'but to liquidate a liability which came into existence on the day that the Australian and New Zealand Army Corps landed on Gallipoli'.[6] The next day the *Register* published reports on the spectacular procession that included soldiers, patriotic tableaux, trade union displays and concert parties. The *Register* gave details of the entertainment that took place at the Adelaide Oval where two trams rushed together along special rails laid on the oval and crashed head on. Further events on the oval included a balloon ascent and kite flying. There was praise for 'Labour's Loyalty' in putting patriotism before politics by giving up the Eight Hours Day holiday and helping to raise an amount of over £2,500. The report continued:

> For all time, then, Anzac, with its thrill of heroic reminiscences, will have a fixed place in South Australian history, and will, at the same time, record the admirable spirit of self-denial on the part of the workers. Only war would have inspired an act which so worthily sacrificed the identity of a great movement. It showed how real and how robust was the loyalty of Labour, that it should have retired into the background and given all that wonderful talent of organisation, unique splendour of display, and fine monument of enthusiasm, to the noble humanitarianism of the Wounded Soldiers' Fund.[7]

South Australians spontaneously observed Anzac Day as disability support for wounded soldiers. Storylines in the *Advertiser* of 14 October 1915 are those of 'Soldiers and Police, Another Serious Riot, Disgraceful Scenes in the City, Two Arrests made'.[8] In South Australia Anzac Day remains a binary of mourning and celebration, being both an acknowledgement of death and sacrifice, as well as a celebration of life and survival.

However, Anzac Day in October 1915 was not the first attempt to recognise publicly the 'debt of honour' believed owed by South Australians for the war service of the men at Gallipoli and nurses in the Dardanelles area. The first casualty lists appeared in the *Register* and the *Advertiser* on Monday 3 May 1915. The same day in the *Advertiser*, the Minister of Defence, Mr Pearce, made a statement indicating that the Department was under pressure from the friends and relatives of those fighting, who wanted news from the battlefront. Recognising that war conditions caused time lapses in compiling casualty lists that some saw as the 'callous treatment' of distressed relatives, Pearce asked people to curb private feelings to enable the Australian people 'to suffer their private griefs without adding to the difficulties and dangers of our men on active service'. By the end of May 1915 'The War' was dominating daily news: the Commander-in-Chief of the Australian Forces in the Dardanelles, General Bridges, had died at sea from wounds; the *Lusitania* had been torpedoed; and twenty-five casualty lists had been published. Accompanying the lists were photographs of South Australians killed and wounded, together with biographies obviously prepared in haste.[9] As a direct result of the growing number of casualty lists, the South Australian community observed Violet, Australia and Wattle Day during July and September 1915.

Violet Day recognised the debt owed by Australian society and encompassed the sacrifice of both those killed overseas and the sacrifice of Australian women. Mrs Alexandra Seager, who co-ordinated the first South Australian Violet Day in memory of war dead, was nicknamed 'Little Mother' by soldiers. Seager was honorary organiser of the Adelaide Cheer-Up Society, which cared for troops while still in Australia.[10] In an endeavour to highlight the significant impact casualty lists were having, Violet Day combined mourning rituals and fund raising by including hymns and the 'Last Post' in a service held at the Soldiers' Memorial on the corner of North Terrace and King William Street. Erected to commemorate the valour of Citizen Soldiers, South Australians now call this memorial the 'Boer War Memorial'. Highlighting the significant impact the casualty lists were having on bereaved relatives, the Cheer-Up Society applied to the Town Clerk asking for the City Council's approval for the society to hold a Violet Day 'in memory of the Australian Soldiers who have died for this Country in the war. The Ladies of the Society to sell Violets in the Streets'.[11] The Violet Day 'demonstration' took place on 2 July 1915. In this instance, violets were a symbol of grief and token of remembrance. South Australians sought to repay the debt to the killed and wounded by purchasing violet 'buttonholes', and placing floral wreaths around the soldiers' memorial as a substitute communal headstone.

The spontaneous demonstration of Violet Day as a form of grief management provides evidence of state-wide solidarity for the relatives of war dead. Mrs Seager, whose youngest son was killed at Gallipoli, organised Violet Day in an endeavour to show those who were in mourning for men killed in the Dardanelles and Egypt, that even though things appeared to be going on as normal in South Australia, with the usual sport, pleasures, and business, that was not necessarily the case. According to the *Advertiser*, thoughtful South Australians were aware 'that there were many homes darkened by the shadow of death'. In 1915, most Australians would recognise this 'shadow of death', as an excerpt from the 23rd Psalm in the *Bible*.[12] Violet day enabled South Australians to demonstrate a shared sense of community sorrow to those grieving for war dead.

In Adelaide and the larger South Australian towns, people prepared to show their acknowledgement of that debt by the purchase and wearing of violet buttonholes as a token of sympathy. On Friday 2 July 1915, from 8.30 in the morning as the first workers arrived in the city, women dressed in white, sold violets tied with purple ribbon on which was printed 'In Memory' with a representation of the Christian cross symbolising sacrifice. The sale of buttonholes suitable for both men and women continued until evening. Mrs Seager organised the printing of thirty thousand purple ribbon mementoes. Helping to meet demand some violets arrived from Victoria. Applications for the mementoes from leading country centres amounted to one thousand from Gawler, five hundred each from Mount Barker, Burra, Bute and Laura while three thousand went to Port Adelaide. The Kadina Banking and Currency Museum has a photograph of a bouquet of violets sold by the Burra Cheer-Up Society for £384. Women travelled up and down in the trains from Glenelg, selling mementoes and flowers. The *Register* reported that in their thoughts, South Australians laid the memorial tokens on the graves of brave men in Gallipoli and Egypt. Violet Day was seen as a 'sacred obligation' to show that burial sites marked by 'little mounds and rough-hewn crosses', were not forgotten.[13] The practical purpose served by the sale of violets was to provide a place for the returned wounded soldiers to meet, and somewhere for the troops currently undergoing battle training to be entertained before their departure at the Cheer-Up Hut on the banks of the Torrens.

Signifying the importance of the Gallipoli campaign, the Governor, Premier and Military Commandant made speeches from the steps of the soldiers' memorial, while the Police band supplied the music for hymn singing. The *Advertiser* reported that the Governor, Sir Henry Galway, addressed the crowd and said:

> If any day is to be chosen for Australia's day I think it should be April 25, when the Australian troops landed under the most hellish fire at Gaba Tepe. (Applause.) Those heroes will hand down the finest traditions to their sons and their son's sons, and still further on. The troops have sent back a tremendously fine example for all young men. (Applause.) Today we not only honor the dead, but our hearts go out with the deepest respect and sympathy to those who are mourning the loss of their nearest and dearest. The British Empire will never be able to repay the debt owed to the women for their calm, self-sacrifice in this great struggle. (Applause.) They have given everything uncomplainingly. (Applause.) We are as proud of our women as of our men. (Applause.) It is not for me to say more, except to pay my personal tribute to the fallen, and to say how proud I am that I should be closely connected with Australia during this crisis.[14]

Violet Day buttons, sold in 1916, 1917 and 1919 by ladies of the Cheer-Up Hut in memory of the 'fallen brave'.

Wattle Day League buttons, sold during the Grear War to fund the purchase of ambulances for the 'front'.

The Australasian Soldiers obelisk, South Terrace, Adelaide, originally erected in Wattle Grove by the Wattle Day League.

The Cross of Sacrifice, Light Oval AIF cemetery, West Terrace, Adelaide

The South Australian Governor recognised a debt for women's sacrifice and the symbolic importance of 25 April to the Australian nation less than three months after the Gallipoli landing.

When observing patriotic button days, known in later years as 'badge days' South Australians linked the debt with Australian identity. Adelaidians were so eager to recognise the debt owed to wounded soldiers that they called a meeting of prominent citizens to organise 'Australia Day', which was observed on 30 July 1915. Members on the organising committee included representatives from theatrical and other entertainments, the Cheer-Up Society, the Trades and Labor Council, the Wattle Day League and the Belgian Fund. The sum targeted for fund raising was £100,000 and at the time of the public meeting organisers claimed to have already raised half of that amount.[15] On 31 July 1915, the *Register* claimed the pageant of patriotism a magnificent success for raising £104,457, reporting that 'the duty of those who are staying at home is to provide for the sick and the wounded'.[16] As money raised for war funds on 'Australia Day' was organised nationally by Mr Hugh Ward, Managing Director in Sydney for J. C. Williamson Ltd, South Australians showed a willingness to acknowledge that the 'debt of honour' extended into the national sphere.[17]

A women's group associated with the Australian Natives Association, the Wattle Day League, also used the patriotic community spirit of the war years to raise funds providing amenities to the men in the trenches at the front. Those eligible for membership of the Wattle Day League were 'Australian born women and the wives of members of the Australian Natives Association, whether Australian born or not.' In a booklet outlining the history of the Wattle Day League, W. J. Sowden states the reason for the formation of the Wattle Day League was 'the private desire to have a body of ladies working to advertise the objects of the Australian Natives Association, outside its own membership.' One specific object of the Wattle Day League was to 'encourage the planting and conservation of the wattle as a matter of practical as well as sentimental policy', together with the desire to inaugurate a celebration of Wattle Day throughout the Commonwealth in the same way Canadians observed Maple Day. Sowden in his outline history of the wattle blossom celebration listed as one of the objects of the Wattle Day League, the desire that all people, 'rich and poor, high and low, well or ill – should proclaim themselves as Australians and Australian Britons'.[18] Although this sentiment appears to indicate a desire to promote an Australian sense of identity, the desire was for a dual identity in the sense that the identification was that of 'Australian Britons'.

Political reformer and freelance journalist who worked closely with Catherine Spence, Mrs Jeanne F. Young, Hon Secretary and Organiser of the Australian Wattle Day League, South Australian Branch, wrote to the Town Clerk on 12 August 1915 seeking permission for the Wattle Day League to plant a Wattle Grove in the South Park Lands. In her letter, Young credited Mr Walter Torode, a builder of Unley and Wayville, as originator of the idea 'to commemorate the landing of the Australian troops in Gallipoli on April 25th'.[19] Consequently, on 7 September 1915, the Wattle Day League organised a memorial day in the South Parklands on Cohen Avenue at 'Wattle Grove' when they erected an obelisk where floral tokens could be placed by the mothers and relatives of the men killed in the assault at the Dardanelles. Before the Grove's official opening by civic officials, the *Register* reported the speech of Mr Meincke, the Australian born son of Danish and Cornish immigrants. Meincke felt it necessary to tell the gathering of workmen that despite his German name, he had patriotic pride in his British citizenship, going on to acknowledge that the volunteer work of those assembled, in a humble way, honoured the sacrifice of 'brave sons and brothers' overseas.[20] (Later Meincke changed his German name and adopted an Anglo-Saxon one. He went on to become a suburban Mayor and Member of Parliament.) On Wattle Day the Governor-General, Sir Ronald Munro Ferguson unveiled the obelisk, a forerunner of numerous soldiers' memorials in Australian cities and townships. the *Advertiser* quoted Sir Ronald as saying:

> Certainly the Wattle Day League has done much in giving us a national emblem. From the war to Wattle Day a great deal has helped us to strengthen and unite the national life of Australia. I find it a great honour, representing his Majesty's Australian Forces, to have attended at the ceremony of unveiling this memorial of the landing at Gallipoli, which will ever be a tribute to the gallantry of our troops, to the record they have established, and to the wonderful manner in which they have maintained the tradition of the British Empire.[21]

Celebrations of Wattle Day took place throughout South Australia at Kapunda, Kadina, Wallaroo, Petersburg, Port Wakefield and Gawler as well as at the Wattle Grove. The main patriotic work of the Wattle Day League was that of supplying ambulances to the front. In this way the Wattle Day League provided a practical service for wounded soldiers.[22]

Therefore, the initial reaction of Australians was to organise patriotic fund raising days providing help and support for wounded soldiers. Community groups also organised quasi-religious or civic memorial services that acknowledged the grief of those whose family and friends had died overseas. A further reaction was the inauguration of a community organisation specifically designed to provide supporting services for returned soldiers. One antecedent body of the Returned & Services League of Australia (S.A. Branch) Inc. was the Returned Soldier's Association of South Australia, (RSA), an association that subsequently became the Returned Sailors' and Soldiers' Imperial League of Australia South Australia Branch. The inaugural meeting of the RSA, held 8 December 1915, elected Mr William Sowden, as President of the association. At a general meeting held 22 December 1915, a motion carried appointing Mrs Seager as a Vice President.[23] Thus, the first response to Australia's participation in the Great War within South Australia, was the spontaneous use of grass roots organisations to acknowledge community suffering and raise money for wounded soldiers, followed by the inauguration of a specific group to help returned ex-service personnel.

In 1916, the Brisbane Anzac Day Commemoration Committee (ADCC) put forward a plan suggesting the national observation of Anzac Day on the first anniversary of the Gallipoli Landing. South Australian authorities co-operated with the Brisbane ADCC celebrating Anzac Day on the anniversary of the landing on 25 April. The Brisbane ADCC asked that the observance be 'as far as practicable, Australasian'. They also advised His Worship the Mayor:

> It will be noted that so far as Queensland is concerned, the Day is to be kept with solemnity and with avoidance of anything approaching jubilation or carnival. For this reason, no attempt is being made to raise funds for any purpose, it being felt that a valuable factor will be added to the building up of our people by an effort to make them realise there are other things of importance in the creation of national character. Of course, Queensland does not presume to impose its views on any other State.[24]

The Brisbane ADCC forwarded a 'Plan of Observance of Anzac Day. Tuesday, 25th April, 1916.' setting out three objectives:

> The Commemoration of our fallen heroes;
> The remembrance of our wounded;
> The recognition of the gallant courage displayed by Australia's sons, in fighting for the preservation of liberty and civilisation.[25]

Adelaide City Archive files also contain details relating to a public meeting held in Brisbane on 11 January 1916, which 'originated with and was carried out by the Queensland Recruiting Committee', where a committee was appointed responsible for arranging the celebration of Anzac Day on the first anniversary of the Landing at Gallipoli.[26] Brisbane was the first ADCC to endeavour to harness the instinctive or spontaneous combustion of parochial ideas concerning grief management in each state, into a national observation, using the anniversary of the Gallipoli Landing as a decisive or defining moment.

Moving the South Australian celebration of Anzac Day from October, to 25 April, acknowledged the federal nature of Anzac Day, rather than the provincial nature of a limited South Australian observance. Ignoring the request of the ADCC in relation to fund raising, in Adelaide, under the authority of the State War Council the Premier, Hon Crawford Vaughan, published a souvenir booklet outlining the celebratory events of Anzac Day 1916. A donation of the proceeds from the sale of the booklets went to the Australian Soldiers' Repatriation Fund. Wounded soldiers were the beneficiaries of the fund raising efforts. The booklet was a compilation of information relating to events held throughout the Empire in the observance of the first anniversary of the Gallipoli landing. The souvenir, compiled from Adelaide daily press reports, included messages from King George V and the Prime Minister of Australia, the Right Honourable W. M. Hughes, in London. The meaning of the word 'ANZAC' was explained, along with descriptions of the official ceremony at Queen Victoria's statue, and events at St Peters Cathedral, the Town Hall, Wattle Grove, the Cheer-Up Hut, and Mitcham Camp. As part of the commemoration, the Albert Bells pealed from the Town Hall, the Police Band played 'Dead March', from 'Saul' and buglers played 'Last Post'. Amid the celebrations the Governor's address took time to record 'respectful sympathy to those who mourn their loss', while the Premier noted 'unhesitatingly the womanhood of the land had responded to the clarion call of duty as splendidly as had their manhood.'[27] With events taking place at both Wattle Grove and the Cheer-Up Hut, it would appear that in less than a year since their own patriotic days, the members of the Wattle Day League and Cheer-Up Society deemed it more appropriate to shift the focus of commemorative observances from Wattle and Violet Day to Anzac Day.

Memorial days, imbued with the significance of ANZAC, Australia, wattle and violets, were only a few of the spontaneous patriotic days held throughout the duration of the war. There were so many different organisations wanting to conduct patriotic button days or raise money for the troops, that a separate body 'Council of Control of Patriotic Street Sales, South Australia, a Branch of the Commonwealth Button Fund', regulated the days and times the various groups held button days and fund raising activities. 'Belgian Flag Day' for the Belgian Relief Fund and 'Rose Day' organised for the Wattle Day League Motor Ambulance Fund had already taken place in April 1915, before the publication of Australian casualty lists. During September, as well as Wattle Day raising funds for Motor ambulances, 'French Flag Day' raised funds for the French Red Cross. Although the Adelaide Town Clerk's Office Index of Letters Received between 1916 and 1917 lists the only patriotic button day for October as Anzac Day, in the following month of November the Cheer-Up Society held a 'Cheer-Up Button Day' and the YMCA Army Department held a further 'Active Service Button Day'.[28] Likewise, in April 1916 and 1917, the City of Unley organised a 'Gallipoli Day', held at the Unley Oval, which was in aid of the Red Cross and Trench Comforts Fund.[29] All these events took place, as well as the celebration of Anzac Day on 25 April.

In 1918, the Wattle Day League chose not Wattle Day, but the anniversary of the Gallipoli Landing, as the appropriate day for commemoration of war dead. On 25 April, again at the suggestion of Mr Torode, the Wattle Day League arranged for the placement of a simple stone cross on the flattened top of the obelisk in Wattle Grove recognising both the Christian attribute of sacrifice and the significance of 25 April to Australians.[30] Newspaper reports proclaiming the success of the landing on the Dardanelles resulted in the erection of the obelisk following traditional examples of erecting memorials on battlefields such as the Lion Mound at Waterloo. Wattle Grove was a symbolic battlefield or metaphor for the Dardanelles, given that the Wattle Day League described the obelisk as representative of the cliffs Australians had climbed at Gallipoli.[31] The addition of a cross on Anzac Day indicates recognition of the Allies' withdrawal from Gallipoli and the sacrifice of those who remained buried there.

The Returned Sailors' and Soldiers' Imperial League of Australia, South Australian Branch, (League), on behalf of ex-service personnel, maintained a projection of group identification, working to gain recognition of the service debt within other Australian community organisations, with particular focus on Anzac Day during 'Anzac Week' thus promoting a culture associated with Anzac Day. By 1918, the League set up a Building Fund Appeal for a residential club to raise money to provide a place where returned soldiers could meet in a homely atmosphere, away from the public houses and billiard saloons. Receiving permission from the State War Council to raise money in support of the Building Fund Appeal between the dates of 15 to 30 April, the League set about organising a procession. The procession left from Gouger Street, not on 25, but Friday the 26 April at 11 am, then proceeded 'along King William Street, Currie Street, then Morphett Street, Hindley Street, Rundle Street, Pulteney Street to North Terrace.' In conjunction with the procession the button day was not the only means of raising money as in the vicinity of the Soldiers' Memorial, the League of Loyal Women ran a Market Fair, the stalls of which were erected on 25 April, itself. It is easy to see the purpose of this Anzac procession was to draw attention to the Building Fund Appeal and raise money for returned soldiers rather than a church parade in memory of fallen comrades. The League gained permission for another procession on 20 April ensuring fund raising activities came to the notice of the public during the period of greater significance, 'Anzac Week' itself. Further extending efforts consistent with fund raising rather than commemoration, a carnival took place on the banks of the River Torrens on Saturday 27 April.[32] Anzac Week extended fund raising activities for Anzac Day. Subsequently the League purchased a hotel in Angas Street with funds raised through the Building Fund Appeal. The League set the hotel up as the RSL Club Rooms, part of which was residential. The old residential club building was demolished in 2001.

Military participation in the Anzac Day parades held on Wednesday 25 April 1917 and Thursday 25 April 1918 encouraged recruitment. However, in 1918 it also endorsed and reinforced the premise of repaying a debt, for the Australian Military Forces co-operated in League fund raising activities.[33] Brigadier-General J. K. Forsyth, CMG, Commandant of the District Headquarters at Keswick Barracks issued a Special District Order on 20 April 1918, designed to aid the League's Building Fund Appeal. Forsyth advised that a parade of Returned Soldiers, Citizen Forces and AIF Troops would be held on 26 April in aid of the Button Day Appeal for the Returned Sailors' & Soldiers' Residential Club.[34] With the Armistice and return of veterans, the make-up of the parades or processions changed, there being no need to foster recruiting in 1919 when the League held a pageant on 'Gallipoli Day', Friday 25 April, and a memorial service on Sunday 27 April 1919. Of the patriotic button days held within the State and City of Adelaide during the Great War, only three patriotic days, ANZAC, Wattle and Violet Days continued for any length of time after service personnel returned to South Australia. Other patriotic days faded in significance, unable to compete with the symbolism of Anzac Day or rise to the challenges and changes taking place within Australia. With the passing of time, different cultural practices eclipsed Wattle Day and Violet Day. Nevertheless, the ritual of placing wreaths around the obelisk in Wattle Grove on Wattle Day, the ritual of hymn singing and the 'Last Post' enacted around the soldiers' memorial on Violet Day and the Anzac Day procession on 13 October 1915 all herald the nascent rites of an emerging Anzac culture.

Signing the Great War Armistice extended the rituals of Anzac culture developed at grass roots level on Gallipoli, Wattle, Violet and Anzac Day to include and encompass the Empire on Armistice Day. ANZAC, Wattle, Violet and Gallipoli patriotic button days developed from Australian initiatives. Anzac Day became 'Australia's Day' in the sense it was a special day, a public holiday, for remembering Australians and New Zealanders buried overseas. In contrast Armistice Day, a commemorative day, currently observed as

Remembrance Day, did not begin in Australia as a patriotic day set aside for fund raising in aid of wounded soldiers, but as a memorial day instigated by King George V in 1919. The King's proposal set aside two minutes at eleven o'clock, on the eleventh day of the eleventh month on the first anniversary of the Armistice, as a time in which to remember the Empire dead of the Great War with the observance of silence.[35] Journal articles published by the League, reflect an aura of pathos as South Australians, tried to come to terms with the 'Army of the Dead', and the wounded 'Human Wreckage', some of whom stayed in hospital for the rest of their lives, ultimately dying from wounds inflicted in overseas battles.[36]

Peace was a time to celebrate life and survival, but at the same time, few Australians could forget the dead left overseas and the bereavement of their loved ones. In 1920, the official organ of the Returned Sailors' & Soldiers' Imperial League of Australia (South Australian Branch), the *Diggers' Gazette*, reported on the burial and funeral procession of the Unknown Warrior in Westminster Abbey, London, as a tribute to the Common Soldier. At the instigation of the King, the whole Empire observed the 'silence'. As reported in the *Diggers' Gazette*, 'in South Australia citizens of all classes bowed their heads in unison with those across the seas.' Afterwards, the Soldiers' Mothers' Band laid wild flowers on the graves of the eleven soldiers buried in the West Terrace cemetery. The memorial obelisk in the Wattle Grove was still in use, but eleven graves in the Adelaide cemetery provided another focus of closure for those mourning the death of family members, for that cemetery contained the graves of soldiers who had died since returning to South Australia from overseas.[37] Armistice Day symbolically commemorated Empire Dead. The League, through the *Diggers' Gazette* encouraged practical support with fund raising designed to help the war torn regions of France as well as Australian ex-servicemen and women.

The red poppy linked to Flanders fields by the poem of Colonel John McCrae, became a further symbolic floral memorial to the dead of the Great War. Soldiers' organisations throughout the British Empire and Allied countries, including the RSL, passed resolutions at international conventions recognising the poppy of Flanders fields as an 'international memorial flower to be worn on Armistice Day.' The *Diggers' Gazette* reported a consignment of one million poppies was expected to arrive in Sydney around 20 October 1921. These were not fresh flowers as those used on Wattle and Violet days, but imitation poppies made by war orphans living in the devastated regions of France and Flanders. The poppies sold for the sum of one shilling as a means of raising money both for France and for the purposes of the RSL in Australia.

Initially the RSL remitted five pence from the sale of every poppy to France. At the instigation of the Federal Secretary, the RSL asked State Branches to assist by requesting the Lord Mayor of Adelaide and the mayors of other municipalities to reserve Armistice Day for the sale of imitation poppies. In a further departure from the sale of the other floral emblems used as tokens of remembrance, the League was to have sole responsibility for distribution of the poppies. 'Millie', author of an article in the the *Diggers' Gazette* entitled 'In Flanders Fields where Poppies Grow' wrote:

> It is largely for the benefit of those war orphans that the League is arranging to sell the poppies throughout Australia. In addition, it is hoped that this red poppy will be a reminder to those in Australia who have almost forgotten what a deep debt of gratitude the Empire owes to those who now lie beneath the soil on which the red poppy blooms.[38]

With the coming of peace and the return of the veterans, the 'debt of honour' became a 'debt of gratitude'.

On Anzac Day 1921, the Australian Prime Minister, Hon W. M. Hughes, addressed a large crowd of returned sailors and soldiers at the Melbourne Cricket Ground. Hughes said during his address that the Australians of every city and hamlet throughout the Commonwealth commemorated 'not only the imperishable end of the greatest war of all time, but the inauguration of a new era in the history of this Commonwealth and of the Empire'. Hughes went on to say that the 'Army of the Dead' exceeded the number of those assembled to hear him speak and spoke of the many homes mourning the loss of loved ones. To Hughes Anzac Day was a day symbolic with triumph but also mindful of the great sacrifice made in purchasing that triumph, he asked the crowd pray for those who mourned and to prove by the exercise of their 'liberties' that they were not 'unworthy of the sacrifice by which those liberties had been purchased'.[39] But, despite the Prime Minister's words, the Australian Government was selective about which returned servicemen it considered worthy of medical and financial support.

Miss Clegget was a South Australian who worked for the benefit of returned soldiers suffering from tuberculosis that the Government declined to help. Clegget wrote to the Controller of Stores at the GPO in 1921 asking for help in fund raising activities for the Tubercular Soldiers Aid Society. The Government accepted that some returned soldier's tuberculosis resulted from war service; these soldiers were 'lucky' enough to be treated and cared for at the War Veterans Home, Myrtlebank. Specifically, Clegget's concern was for those TB returned soldier sufferers whose illness authorities judged to be 'pre-war existent' or whose illness did not manifest itself within two years from date of discharge, for the Government would not support them. In spite of difficulties, Clegget raised money to improve conditions for the TB returned soldiers at Bedford Park Sanatorium, where accommodation was isolated hillside huts, described as 'wooden chalets'. Fund raising also provided reading material, and alleviated the plight of the TB returned soldiers' families by giving help and Christmas gifts to wives and children otherwise left destitute. Clegget took up the debt abrogated by government authorities.[40] Despite the refusal of the postal department to grant her 1921 request for help, and a request in 1925 to sell badges, Clegget, persisted with fund raising proposals.

On the 12 November 1926, Miss Clegget requested permission from the Post Master General Department to place 150,000 'crests',on postal articles. The PMG eventually granted permission to Clegget to put the crests on the back of articles, for the crests were already printed and ready for sale at one penny each. 'The Optimist', official organ of the Tubercular Soldiers Aid Society, in 1929, published a record of the Society's relief work at the Angorichina Hostel.[41] The relief work of the Tubercular Soldiers' Aid Society, begun on farming land at Bedford Park, also took place in the remote Flinders Ranges, 'half-way between Parachilna and Blinman, in the Parachilna Gorge', where TB returned soldiers received recuperative help on land donated by J. Lee and W. H. McFarlane of Angorichina Station.[42] After the return of ex-service personnel to Australia, Miss Clegget honoured the debt owed to TB returned soldiers by alleviating their suffering and family distress.

The maintenance of Wattle Grove became a burden to the Wattle Day League as the focus of commemorative activities shifted, and remembrance rituals began taking place in other locations throughout Adelaide. With the return of peace, the Wattle Day League sought permission for more parkland in recognition of the League's President, Sir William Sowden. However, the Wattle Day League had neglected the trees planted to 'honour the debt' during the war years. In August 1923, the Adelaide City Council found the obvious neglect of the Grove unacceptable. The Council refused to release more land and curtailed further enlargement of the wattle plantation. The Soldiers' Mothers' Band held Anzac Sunday memorial services at Wattle Grove in 1925 and 1926. The hymns 'O God our help in ages past', 'Lead kindly light', and 'Nearer, my God to Thee', which had become the mainstay of Christians seeking solace during the war, continued to be a comfort. Speeches given during the memorial services maintained the theme and tenor of the war years, acknowledging the debt owed to the wives and mothers of the men of the AIF for their suffering during the war, as well as that of the debt owed to the men. Further neglect of the grove ultimately led to the removal of the obelisk from

Cohen Avenue in the South Parklands, in October 1940, to Lundie Gardens, opposite the Trades Hall on South Terrace, where it remains today.[43]

Rhetoric during the war had been of undying remembrance, of heroic deeds, memorials, and work for returned men, but in reality, the bodies of some of the ex-servicemen lay in paupers' graves, neglected and weed ridden, in different parts of West Terrace cemetery. Under the title 'Dishonouring the Dead, Neglected Soldiers' Graves', the *Diggers' Gazette,* in 1921, reported that the promises made to the 'gallant lads' who volunteered to take up arms, had been forgotten. The Government of South Australia, 'alone of the Governments of the Empire' allowed burial of the country's saviours in paupers' graves. The League, negotiated for a grant of land known as 'Light Oval', which was situated adjacent to the cemetery, intending to exhume all the bodies of the returned soldiers and bury them in a fitting manner at that location.[44] Early records relating to Anzac Day ceremonies held by both the League and Adelaide City Archives, exhibit evidence that mourning rituals were an important feature of Anzac Day, that those who had given their lives had little else to give and therefore had given their all.

Newspaper reports of Anzac Day services during the later period of the WWII underline the importance of commemorative services in memory of war dead and refer to prisoners-of-war. In the aftermath of the Second World War *Back,* magazine of the RSL, published a cartoon by Goodchild in the *News*, referring not to the debt owed to war dead but delivering an 'Account Rendered' for War Reparations on behalf of ex-POW and Dependents for the 'Siam Railway and other Death Jobs'.[45] The RSL added the WWII 'account rendered' to the original 'debt of honour' and lobbied Local, State and Federal Government on behalf of the ex-service community.

Although the national commemorative initiatives of Anzac Day and Remembrance Day supported by the RSL continued, the 1960s and 1970s saw the decline and eventual demise of two of the original South Australian remembrance initiatives instigated by women. In 1960, the League State Board discussed funeral arrangements for Miss Clegget but the President advised he could not agree to recite the 'Ode'. However, the Board did reach an agreement to drape Miss Clegget's coffin with the flag. Subsequently, the State Board recommended the termination of Angorichina Hostel, with the result that by 1970 the TB Soldiers' Aid Society prepared to close down the association's facilities in the Flinders Ranges.[46] The defunct Cheer-Up Society ceased to exist in 1963, when it presented funds totalling over five thousand pounds to assist in the establishment of an infirmary at the War Veterans Home, Myrtlebank. Violet Day observances consisted of a service at the Adelaide

Town Hall with children's choirs providing choral items. Takings from the commemorative collection donated to the AIF Cemetery Trust, enabled the continued upkeep of the AIF section at West Terrace. By the mid 1960s, concurrent with the period of the Vietnam War, Violet Day, now labelled Violet Memory Day, reached its 50th commemoration service, the momentum of the day itself fading in collective memory. The State Board of the League received advice in May 1971 that a Violet Memory Day Service Committee meeting had agreed to discontinue the service. However, the committee decided to continue the observance of Violet Day with the memorial ritual of placing wreaths on both the Cross at the AIF cemetery and the State Memorial.[47] Australians had changed. They had loosened formal British ties while widening the net of Australian citizenship to embrace other cultures. Changes within Australian society in relation to patriotism, and spirituality hastened the decline of Violet Day. Rituals formerly observed in school assemblies such as saluting the flag, honouring the monarch, singing the national anthem and acknowledging the self-sacrifice of earlier generations of Australians at Anzac Day and Armistice Day ceremonies with a silence, ceased in some Australian schools. The death rate of ex-servicemen and women was exceeding that of over one thousand a year and calls for assistance in arranging burials and erecting memorial headstones continued as the burden of honouring the debt became heavier each year.[48]

In contrast to the debt accepted by the Australian community as owing to those who served the nation during WWI and the account rendered after WWII for the war service of ex-POWs, the war service of those Australians who served in Korea and Vietnam went largely un-appreciated. Korea, subsequently labelled 'The Forgotten War' elicited very little attention within Australia, while the Vietnam War was the cause of controversy. It was not until Saturday 3 October 1987 that some Vietnam Veterans took part in a Welcome Home Parade in Sydney.[49] The 1987 parade, 'honoured the debt' metaphorically, for 'the debt' remained un-acknowledged at the time of service. By the end of the century, the 'debt of honour' acknowledged as owing to those Australians who served the nation at the time of the Great War on behalf of a grateful nation, had become a debt of gratitude to all veterans.

Despite the demise of Wattle and Violet Days and the waning significance of Armistice or Poppy Day until its revival in the 1990s during the time of the Keating Labor Government, the observance of commemorative ceremonies on 25 April, Anzac Day, continued because the League's Anzac Day Committee made decisions acknowledging and adapting to changes within the Australian nation. Adjustments made by the League in the organisation of Anzac Day marches and commemoration services, endeavoured to accommodate differences within the Australian community and ensured the Day's survival. The South Australian Anzac Day march changed its route, its format, its ideology to fit into the prevailing and evolving identity of the Australian nation. As we have seen, changes are evident in the first year of the observance, in 1916, when the South Australian community changed its original idea of celebrating Anzac Day on Eight Hours Day, and adopted some of the suggestions of the Brisbane ADCC. During the period from 1916 to 1920, Anzac Day was a combination of returned soldiers, not only from the Great War, but also from the Boer War, serving military, and militia. Anzac Days during the war were not only a time of patriotic exhibition from the military and returned men and women, but also of the wider service groups within the community. Although Anzac Day was used as a means of raising money to provide a place of entertainment and comfort for returning and embarking servicemen, it was also used as a patriotic example of empire loyalty and acknowledgement of suffering within the South Australian community. An acknowledgement that only widened with the return of the men and the knowledge that the many dead lying overseas outnumbered those taking part in the parades at home.

Anzac Day also encompasses a sense of Australian identity in the observance of a memorial 'dawn service' timed to elicit a sense of anticipation, in the birth of a new day, bonding participants at the memorial service to the men who made the dawn landing at Gallipoli in 1915. This hyperbolic ceremony attunes modern Australians into recognising the heightened sensibilities of a dawn battle, and the debt owed for the sacrificed lives of earlier generations, especially when the service takes place surrounded by the resultant graveyards of Gallipoli, Europe and Asia. RSL documentation credits the introduction of the first Australian Dawn Service to Rev Arthur Ernest White, Church of England clergyman, in Albany, Western Australia on 25 April 1923. Rev White left Australia with the men of the First AIF in November 1914. White chose Albany for the inaugural Dawn Service because it was there that some 'ANZACS' who remained in graves overseas had their last sight of Australia. Dawn services conducted in South Australia originally took place on Anzac Day in memorial gardens at Unley. After the dedication of the State National War Memorial (State Memorial) on North Terrace, focus shifted from suburban Dawn Services to the main observation of the Dawn Service in Adelaide.[50] Christian liturgy used in grief management rituals evolved into an Anzac Day liturgy used at civic memorial services, not only statewide, but also nationally and internationally at Gallipoli, Villers-Bretonneux, Kokoda, Hellfire Pass, Bali and London. I include Bali because John Howard utilised the last verse of a 'letter' to the Australian troops on Gallipoli 'We're All Australians Now', by 'Banjo' Paterson, to justify the wearing of a sprig of wattle in the grief management of the Bali terrorist attack during a national day of mourning on 20 October 2002. Anzac culture continued the acknowledgement of the 'debt of honour'. The spirituality inherent in commemorative services observed as a dimension of Anzac Day takes place at soldiers' memorials on sacred ground. As we shall see, in 1922, the South Australian Anzac Day march concluded at a surrogate burial site that incorporated the Cross of Sacrifice and Stone of Remembrance used in overseas war cemeteries.

CHAPTER 2

SACRED GROUND

Australian group responses made to honour Australian war dead led to the development of rituals forming the basis of morning Anzac Day grieving rites on 'sacred ground'. The rituals of Anzac Day that take place before noon are predominantly those of mourning, developed to substitute and encompass Judaeo-Christian funeral rites adapted throughout Australia to portray a community sense of Australian remembrance. The essence of spirituality in the rites conducted during the morning of Anzac Day at the Dawn Service and Service of Remembrance assuage grief, endeavouring to bring a sense of acceptance or closure, particularly to the relatives of war dead, because of the absence in Australia of a corpse over which to conduct formal funeral services. Tanja Luckins records that on Tuesday afternoon 25 April 1922, in Woolloomooloo, New South Wales, Governor-General Lord Forster unveiled a memorial fountain erected by the women of New South Wales. Luckins writes 'the memorial drinking fountain was a women's war memorial', and that the fountain, together with the nearby wharf gates were 'part of a mnemonic landscape ... intended to assist, memory'.[1] In Adelaide, South Australia, on the morning of the same day, South Australian women arranged the dedication of a Women's Memorial to the Fallen of the Great War. Memorial days encompassing funereal, spiritual rituals, developed not only in Australia but also throughout the British Empire and other Allied Countries at memorials built on sacred, or within hallowed ground. With death, battlefield cemeteries became sacred ground. Sacredness compounded in an analogy with the 'translation of saints', the removal of a saint's remains from one place to another. The Imperial, now Commonwealth War Graves Commission exhumed the bodies of war dead from their original hastily dug burial sites in battle areas, and subsequently interred them within the war cemeteries of Europe, the Middle East and Asia.

In Australia, memorials imbued the ground upon which they stood with a sense of sacredness, despite the absence of bodies. As discussed in Chapter 1, 'Honouring the Debt', during the Great War the Wattle Day League added a cross to the obelisk in Wattle Grove. After the war, some communities adorned their memorials with an effigy of a Digger hewn from white stone. 'Digger' memorials symbolised the bodies or ghosts of the army of the dead. With peace and the signing of the Armistice, a combination of women's organisations, St Peters Anglican Cathedral, and veterans' organisations in Adelaide, sought to bring to their various memorials a sense of spirituality or sacredness by the erection of a cross. The women's group in particular, found comfort in the use of designs that shadowed the overseas graves of Australian war dead. Although the three groups all decided to erect a memorial cross, the women's group were first to obtain copyright of Sir Reginald Blomfield's design for the 'British Cross of the Great War', erected initially in Wiltshire, then in European war cemeteries.[2]

Attending funeral services for loved ones operates as an act of closure. Symbolism displayed on headstones preserves people's sense of identity. Tending the grave, keeping them tidy and placing flowers on or near headstones acts as a visible act of remembrance. After the Great War, American next of kin had a choice whether they left American war dead lying in overseas graves or arranged with the American government to bring the bodies of their men home for burial as heroes. Australians, as members of the British Empire, did not have that choice and were therefore unable to bring the bodies of war dead home. Of all Australians killed overseas during the First World War, only the body of General Bridges, exhumed from Alexandria, received transportation back to Australia for re-burial in the grounds of Duntroon, Canberra in September 1915. The body of General Bridges remained the only Australian body brought back from World War I (hereinafter WWI), battlefields until 1993. In that year the body of an unknown Australian soldier was exhumed from Adelaide Cemetery in France, returned to Australia, given a State funeral and entombed in the Hall of Memory at the Australian War Memorial.[3]

Australian community groups sought to alleviate the distress of war-caused bereavement with the establishment of memorials for Australian war dead lying in overseas cemeteries. The bodies of Empire dead lay buried with comrades and given identical headstones showing no preference to rank, class, creed, or distinguished service, although relatives could choose an identifier symbolising religion, such as a cross, or a Star of David. Senator G. F. Pearce, Minister of State for Defence, in *Where the Australians Rest* (1920), published descriptions of the many cemeteries overseas where Australian war dead lay buried. Among European cemeteries named in the publication are Tanks Cemetery, Hooge Crater Cemetery, and Ypres Town Extension Military Cemetery. Jerusalem Military Cemetery, situated on the western slope of the

Mount of Olives, faced the 'Holy City', while the bodies of some wounded who died away from the battle fronts lay in cemeteries in England at Harefield, Brookwood and Lark Hill. The 'Glorious Dead' received further recognition and commemoration at the Cenotaph at Whitehall, the memorial erected not to a division, brigade, company or battalion but to the '1,000,000 soldiers and sailors who died that Liberty might live.'[4] While Soldiers saluted the London Cenotaph, civilians showed their respect to Empire war dead by baring and bending their heads. Soldiers and civilians alike treated the London Cenotaph as sacred ground.

Once erected, Australian soldiers' memorials intended to provide a sacred site for mourning and remembrance, received as a label the term 'war memorials'. In contrast, the French call monuments to the fallen, *monuments aux morts*, saviours of their own land.[5] Whether a question merely of semantics or the Australian tendency to devise shorter 'nick-names', designating effigies and monumental structures 'war memorials' led later generations of Australians to regard them as a commemoration of war itself. Because a number of Australian monuments also included the names of ex-servicemen and women as well as war dead, some Australians failed to recognise the memorials' main function of symbolising the overseas burial sites of thousands of individual Australians. Australians were so far away in distance from the war graves and cemeteries in other countries that, what in effect Australian collective memory now terms 'war memorials', became communal headstones representing absent corpses, memorials to common sacrifice, where grieving relatives could place tokens of remembrance. Memorial days became part of Anzac culture, a collective display of bereavement and remembrance throughout the Australian community. Had the memorials been described as 'peace memorials' or more truthfully 'sacrificial memorials', later generations of Australians may well have avoided some mistaken assumptions in relation to the intended purpose of mourning ceremonies held before noon on Anzac Day. Attending services at memorials in remembrance of those who had made the 'supreme sacrifice' became part of the patriotic function of showing Australian loyalty to the British Empire, and thereby British Australian identity, in a display of grief, which forced recognition of family and Australian sacrifice in the maintenance of British interests.

Ken Inglis published a study of 'War Memorials in the Australian Landscape' *(Sacred Places)* in 1998. In writing about Adelaide memorials, Inglis referred to the Cross of Sacrifice as a women's memorial, Memorial Drive as a public work, and discussed the South Australian State Memorial in a chapter entitled 'Capital Monuments'.[6] I will not duplicate his work in relation to the State of South Australia, but in order to outline the intended purpose of the memorials' originators, deal with debates concerning principal soldiers' memorials within the city of Adelaide, memorials that have become the focus of Anzac Day and Armistice or Remembrance Day services. Soldiers' memorials designed in the form of monumental structures include the Cross of Sacrifice and the State Memorial. Memorial Hospital is an example of a memorial within the utilitarian, institutionalised category dedicated with the intention of 'honouring the debt'. The Adelaide City Council built 'War Memorial Drive' as a substitute for extensive peace celebrations. [7] Collective memory no longer recognises the original purpose of some monuments and utilitarian memorials built after the signing of the Armistice, but documents held in Council and Church archives reveal their intended purpose.

South Australian women planned to erect the first official Women's Memorial within an Australian city for they wanted to provide a communal space in which to conduct funeral and mourning rituals designed to commemorate war dead. After the conclusion of hostilities ending World War I, in March 1919, the Adelaide League of Loyal Women's organisation set about organising a general and executive committee for 'The Women's Memorial to the Fallen of the Great War'. Mrs C. R. J. Glover, the wife of the Lord Mayor, was instrumental in organising the first meeting of the Women's Committee in the reception room of the Town Hall; the project began under her administration and she was President of the General Committee. With the formation of committees, the objective of the Adelaide Women's Memorial Fund was to follow the example of English women who organised the memorial that the Adelaide women believed to be the only extant Women's Memorial at that time, the Lion Mound at Waterloo.[8]

Civic leaders readily utilised the Waterloo memorial, as one example of fulfilling a 'debt of honour' owed to war dead. Adelaide's Mayor, Mr A. A. Simpson, referred to the Lion Mound at Waterloo in Belgium on 13 September 1915, in a memo submitted to an Adelaide City Council works and Highways Committee regarding a 'memorial to the heroes of Gallipoli'. Simpson envisaged a memorial too big for North Terrace because he believed that any memorial should list the names of the dead on bronze tablets around the base, like the Citizen Soldiers' memorial for the 'heroes of the South African War'. The Mayor suggested a memorial like the Waterloo memorial in Belgium.[9] The Adelaide Women's Memorial established by the Women's Memorial Fund adapted Western traditions for Australian purposes in fulfilment of the women's desire to recognise their 'Glorious Dead' and be a 'link in the Imperial chain of Crosses' known as the British Cross of the Great War.[10] The concept was born primarily because there was no suitable site in Adelaide available to carry out western traditions of mourning and closure for South Australian war dead buried overseas.

Temporarily, churches compiled rolls of honour or honour boards, as did many schools and the work places where men and women had left employment to serve overseas. Local honour boards in the hallowed space of Christian churches acknowledged the debt owing for sacrifice called for from Australian churches. Sir Josiah Symons, speaking at the dedication of the Upper Sturt Church memorial on 2 April 1916, said that mothers had a 'sacred duty', in a spirit of love and self-sacrifice, to encourage their sons to go to war. Mothers, Symons said, should tell their boys 'Go and do likewise.'[11]. Rolls of honour and honour boards recognised the debt owed, but did not satisfy the need to play out acts of closure. Women in particular still lacked a gravesite to care for, or a site on which to place material tokens of remembrance in the form of floral wreaths. The parents and relatives of some British Soldiers travelled across the English Channel to visit battlefields and gravesites as described by Vera Brittain in *Testament of Youth* (1933). In France where a great proportion of Allied men's bodies lay buried, relatives of the French dead wanted the bodies of French war dead brought home to local burial plots. Some French families were prepared to 'steal' the bodies of their men, against the wishes of their government.[12] The bulk of South Australian bereaved knew there was no likelihood of their travelling overseas to visit the grave of loved ones in overseas war cemeteries.

In an attempt to remedy the situation in Adelaide, a public notice placed in daily newspapers by the Lady Mayoress invited women of all ages and descriptions to work together in an effort to construct a place in Adelaide suitable for women to mourn their dead.[13] The *Register* reported that Miss Dorothy Gilbert, elected as honorary secretary, made a 'moving and scholarly address' at the first general meeting and outlined the object of the memorial as:

> To enable us, the women of this State, to erect as a memorial to those who have sacrificed their lives in this war, something which in its beauty, its permanence, and its symbolism, shall express what we can never put into words for the men who went out of our own homes, out of our everyday lives, carrying our hearts with them, and have left us with a memory, an ideal, and an outlook on life very different from that which was ours before the war.[14]

The Women's Memorial Fund required Adelaide City Council permission and approval, together with copyright designs from overseas to convert the envisioned idea of a memorial into a material edifice suitable for commemorative purposes. The Women's Memorial Fund first requested from the

Relatives of British war dead could choose a religious symbol, such as a cross or Star of David, for the headstone of fallen soldiers.

Cenotaph, Whitehall, London, the memorial to one million soldiers and sailors who died during the Great War.

Cross of Sacrifice, Women's Memorial, Pennington Gardens, Adelaide, originally erected in memory of men who died serving overseas during World War 1.

St Peter's Cathedral cross, Adelaide, in memory of all who served in World War 1.

Darwin Defenders wreaths, Women's Memorial, Adelaide

'Prologue' of war, the State National War Memorial, North Terrace, Adelaide. The figures of the student, the farmer and the girl symbolise youth.

'Epilogue' of war, North Terrace, representing the consummation of sacrifice. The winged spirit symbolises 'womanhood' and her sacrifice of son and lover

Council, a site on North Terrace outside the Art Gallery, on which to erect their memorial. After the publication of an article on war memorials in *The Times* by Mr Herbert Baker, the Executive Committee contacted Baker thus initiating protracted negotiations with both him and the Adelaide Council. Baker suggested the space the women required was not on a boulevard surrounded by the noise of tramlines and a busy city, but a space near the spiritual heart of the city, namely the cathedral. Placing the memorial in a garden near the cathedral would help the women attain the 'atmosphere of peace and reverence' necessary for the formation of a sacred place.[15]

Subsequently, while working on the development of New Delhi, India, Baker devised an open-air cathedral in a garden setting planned to provide the peace and tranquillity the South Australian women required for their memorial.[16] Delay occurred while the women sought permission from Sir Reginald Blomfield and Sir Edwin Lutyens, for copyright to existing Empire memorials. Purchasing the necessary copyright enabled the women to achieve their desired objective. A memorial garden that surrounded the exact reproduction of the two monuments, so that anyone entering the garden would feel that somewhere, on some battlefront, the man they personally knew was lying under the shadow of the cross, facing the stone, just one of almost a million British dead who gave their lives for the Empire.[17] The shadows cast by the Adelaide Cross of Sacrifice and cenotaph, symbolically represented the shadows cast by Blomfield's British Cross of the Great War and Lutyen's 'Altar of Remembrance' erected by the Imperial War Graves Commission in overseas war cemeteries.

South Australians of both genders saw 'The British Cross of the Great War' as a suitable symbol signifying the commemoration of Australian war service. It was not only the women working to honour the fallen of the Great War who wished to erect the same cross in Adelaide as that in overseas cemeteries for the purposes of remembrance and mourning. The same form of remembrance crosses stands in the AIF section of West Terrace cemetery. Another two crosses stand in Centennial Park cemetery, one in Derrick Garden of Remembrance the other in a section reserved for those members of the forces who died while still in Australia. The Cathedral Memorial Committee of St Peter's Cathedral also wanted to erect the same cross in the grounds of the Cathedral. The Women's Memorial Fund discovered the Cathedral Memorial Committee's intentions in the midst of conducting negotiations with the Imperial War Graves Commission, and copyright negotiations with Blomfield.[18] Eventually, the Cathedral Memorial Committee resigned all rights to Blomfield's cross in favour of the Women's Memorial Fund. The Cathedral Memorial Committee altered the shape of their cross to that of a Celtic cross, and also bowed to the women's wishes and placed the Cathedral cross on the North Adelaide side of the Cathedral where it stood sentinel in what eventually became an asphalt car park.[19] The women's committee objected to the same cross being erected by the Cathedral in 1920, because the Cathedral congregation intended to remember all those who enlisted for war service, whereas the cross in Pennington Gardens was specifically raised to honour the dead, for the men who had made the 'supreme sacrifice'.[20] Discussion took place concerning women who had died while on overseas' service. Debate centred on whether nurses should also be included within the memorial aspects signified by the Cross of Sacrifice. After research found only three South Australia nurses died, the Women's Memorial Fund General Committee decided that their cross was only to be in memory of the men who had fallen in the Great War.[21] Another source of contention among community groups was the right to conduct memorial services on significant dates.

A number of community groups tried to organise fund raising and memorial functions on symbolic dates during the period immediately after the Armistice. The inevitable clashes resulted in the Women's Memorial Fund and League coming together on Anzac Day, 25 April, which both organisations viewed as the most appropriate day for remembrance rituals. The Women's Memorial Fund sought permission from the Council to hold a silent appeal in Adelaide streets on Monday 26 April 1920. In an effort designed to double the memorial funds already raised, the Committee intended that women should proceed in a procession to Pennington Park, wanting to facilitate the placement of offerings of money and flowers at the memorial site. The League already had permission from the Council for fund raising between 24 and 26 April therefore the women postponed their arrangements, deciding to lay the foundation stone of the Women's Memorial on 4 August, the anniversary of the outbreak of war.[22] One can discern the evident passion caused by the frustration of trying to arrange memorial functions on significant dates without clashing with other community groups, and the conflict within the women's ranks in correspondence directed to the Council and in the Minutes of the Women's Executive Committee. The Women's Executive Committee made a decision to hold the foundation stone ceremony on 4 August, and decided at the following meeting held on 22 April, to make 'collecting bags' of purple material and 'to bespeak at once large quantities of violets'. The Executive Committee therefore not only usurped the day on which the usual Violet Memory Day ceremonies and fund raising took place, but also moved to ensure supplies of violets.[23] These decisions forced the Cheer-Up Society to change the date of Violet Day to a day in July to avoid further conflict, despite Mrs Seager's assurances to the public, published in the *Register*, that the observance of Violet Memory Day would take place on 4 August.[24] The decisions made by the Executive Committee of the Women's Memorial to the Fallen in the Great War, to avoid clashing with the League fund raising activities, placed the fund raising plans of the Cheer-Up Society at a disadvantage. As early as 1920, Adelaide women working for the memorial garden, adjudged their plans, and the fund raising efforts of the League during Anzac week, to be more deserving than the usual observance of Violet Day on 4 August.

The Executive Committee of the Women's Memorial took steps to consolidate their decisions. Following instructions from the Executive Committee, Dorothy Gilbert wrote to the Lord Mayor, requesting confirmation in writing of the Council's implied permission, given on 12 April, to transfer a women's procession from 26 April to 4 August. Gilbert also requested the clarification of three separate points concerning matters planned for 4 August. One, permission to organise a women's procession, two, permission to lay the foundation stone of the memorial and three, confirmation of the permission already given to collect funds on 4 August at the memorial gardens. As requested, the Council wrote to the Committee of the Women's Memorial Fund granting the first two points and confirming the third.[25] A letter published in a local newspaper from 'A Sorrowful Onlooker' criticised the Women's Memorial Fund for their perceived mistakes. First, they forgot most women had already helped with memorials to their sons in the schools and churches to which their sons belonged. Second, there would have been no injury to the community, or Adelaide, if both the Women's Memorial Fund and the Men of the Church of England had erected crosses. Another perceived mistake was that the Women's Memorial claimed 'Violet Day as their particular property', despite the Cheer-Up Society having observed Violet Day for five years since 1915. Continuing the 'Sorrowful Onlooker' asked, 'would it not have been wiser, from woman to woman, to have asked the original movers regarding Violet Day to co-operate?'[26] As in other allied countries, the ramifications of grief management extended throughout all classes of the community, enabling those groups with access to the civic power base to achieve their objectives.

Individual names were important to the women, the names of those they wanted remembered being placed under the foundation stone of the Cross in Pennington Park East before its unveiling in 1922, in an urn covered in the Union Jack. The names in the urn included those of Allied, British and French fighters received the day the foundation stone was set in place.[27] A Crusader's sword, especially imported from W. Bainbridge Reynolds Ltd, London, became the focal point of the tall stone Cross of Sacrifice.[28] The Cross of Sacrifice looked down the gardens laid out in the form of a cross to the 'apse', where Baker suggested placing the 'Altar of Remembrance' or 'War Stone' designed by Sir Edwin Lutyens, designer of, among other memorials, the London Cenotaph and the Australian National War Memorial in France at Villers-Bretonneux.[29] Carved on the Altar of Remembrance was the verse chosen by Kipling from the book of Ecclesiasticus, 'Their name liveth for evermore'. Baker suggested the rest of the garden should become a 'garden of remembrance'.[30]

Originally the intention of the Women's Committee for the Fallen of the Great War was to provide a sacred place or open-air cathedral in which every religion would be free to participate in the service proceedings, including Jews and those who did not wish to take part in Christian ceremonies.[31] The *Advertiser* reported in 1922, that as requested by the Federal and State Governments, memorial services took place in Churches and at the Synagogue, on the Sunday and Saturday preceding Anzac Day. Catholic response was such that Catholics needed no special day to remember the dead, as priests raised prayers and masses each day for the souls of the dead. Even so, the officiating Catholic priest acknowledged it was a solace to know that 'their separated brethren who worshipped in other places were also meeting that day to offer their prayers to the great Father of all'. As Australians, Catholics offered 'deep sympathy to the sorrowing mothers, wives and sisters of their gallant dead.' On the same page, the *Advertiser* reported that at the Synagogue the Rabbi 'stressed the importance of making Anzac Day a day of special conciliatory service'.[32] Christian and Jewish clergy expressed and reinforced Australian identity acknowledging Empire service and sacrifice as part of Anzac week religious services.

Women working for the erection of the Women's memorial strove to include all faiths and sects in official commemoration ceremonies. Chaplains officiating at the unveiling of the memorial cross on Anzac Day 1922 were from the Church of England, Methodist, Church of Christ, Presbyterian and Congregational churches. The Women's Memorial Fund extended an invitation to the Rev Father Murphy of Yorketown to take a portion of the service, which he declined owing to his appointment to the Mt Gambier parish.[33] Significantly, minutes record debate concerning the choice between a utilitarian or symbolic memorial. The Committee of the Women's Memorial to the Fallen in the Great War decided to build a memorial 'in the nature of a shrine, rather than a work of art pure and simple' or a utilitarian or institutional memorial such as Memorial Hospital or War Memorial Drive.[34] As an exam-

World War II Memorial, North Terrace, Adelaide, records the names of those who made the supreme sacrifice during the Second World War.

Memorial erected in the Memorial Reserve, North Terrace, Adelaide, in memory of servicemen who paid the supreme sacrifice in the Malay Peninsula, Korea, Borneo and Vietnam conflicts.

ple of an institutional memorial, Memorial Hospital, on Avenue Road, next to Pennington Gardens does not convey a message to the general public that it exists because of the donations of Methodist men, women and Sunday School children as a memorial to remember the dead of the Great War, while still serving the living. However, documents held by the Uniting Church Historical Society provide evidence that the Methodist Church intended the hospital as a utilitarian memorial. An outline of the scheme produced as 'The Memorial Hospital Souvenir, 1919', under the title of 'Our Memorial Hospital', stated:

> The Hospital in its ultimate development promises to be one of the finest of its kind in Australia, and as the intention is that it shall be dedicated as a memorial to more than 1,000 young Methodists who made the supreme sacrifice in the Great War, it can well be realised that the enthusiasm behind the movement is great and worthy of the inspiration which gave rise to it.[35]

The souvenir also asks 'Is our Debt Understood as well as Remembered?' It continues:

> On all hands there is this desire to express in tangible and symbolic form the gratitude of the living to the dead. We wish to pay our debts, and this in no mean spirit, but lavishly, promptly, handsomely.[36]

Interestingly, the Women's reasoning that in the future an institutional or utilitarian memorial would become forgotten as a memorial, might become a burden to future generations, or suffer neglect has been verified.[37]

Concluding the Anzac March with mourning rituals under the trees at the Women's Memorial solved the problem of various groups clashing over Anzac Day commemoration practices. On 15 December 1921, the Anzac Day Celebration Committee of the League took matters in hand, writing to the Women's Memorial Fund offering to end the 1922 Anzac Day parade at the Cross of Sacrifice thus beginning a ritual that still forms part of South Australian Anzac Day observances.[38] Before unveiling the Cross of Sacrifice in 1922, a women's procession, accompanied by the Salvation Army Band, preceded the League procession, accompanied by the League's official band and Scottish pipers. At the conclusion of the Anzac March 4,000 returned men took part in the memorial service.[39] The Order of Service included three hymns, one of which, 'The Supreme Sacrifice - O Valiant Hearts', currently continues as part of the order of service. Other items continuing in modern Anzac Day orders of service are the 'Last Post', 'Reveille' and the national anthem.[40]

The next year the Altar or 'Stone of Remembrance' designed by Lutyens, otherwise described as the 'war stone' or 'cenotaph' was unveiled on Anzac

Graves (above) and plaques (below) at Derrick Gardens, Centennial Park Cemetery, Adelaide. The flags were placed by schoolchildren during Anzac commemoration services.

Day, complementing the Cross erected by the Women's Memorial Fund for the Fallen in the Great War. The *Advertiser* reported on 19 April 1923, that in its rough state, the granite for the Stone of Remembrance weighed 7 tons. Four huge draft horses hauled the 'jinker' carrying the stone.[41] The five and one half ton 'cenotaph' stands at the base of the memorial garden, however the Cross of Sacrifice is the focus of the spiritual rituals that conclude the formal part of the Anzac Day remembrance service. The *Register* reporting on the Women's Memorial described the walk to the memorial as a pilgrimage:

> To lay flowers on the graves of the dead is the last offering of love, the first instinct of the living. And all through South Australia are women who will never lay one wreath for their sons except at this cross – for those who they love sleep under the poppies, or in burning sand, or on the grey coasts of Gallipoli. Do you wonder that women of South Australia made a memorial of their own?[42]

The captain of the English eleven, Mr G. C. MacLaren laid a wreath in the form of a rising sun at the cross on Armistice Day 1922, a French Admiral paying a tribute on behalf of the fleet.[43] Just as the London Cenotaph provides a site for conducting various remembrance rituals, the Adelaide Cross of Sacrifice provides a focus for the rituals of remembrance organised by members of the ex-service community such as the Darwin Defenders and Vietnam Veterans and on Armistice Day as well as Anzac Day.

The mnemonic garden of remembrance is rich in symbolism. Herbert Baker suggested enclosing the cruciform shaped garden within a hedge. The plant chosen was the olive, a symbol of peace. In 1923, the Women's Fund requested the Council plant rosemary, the herb of remembrance, along the edges of the garden's pathways.[44] By the 1960s, in the opinion of the War Graves Commission, the Women's Memorial, needed repairs and maintenance. With this chore undertaken by the State Government, and ongoing maintenance provided by the Adelaide City Council, the religious service concluding the Anzac march of ex-service personnel was able to continue within the 'sacred' precinct.[45] In 1972, the War Graves Commission agreed to maintain the plaque on the Cross of Sacrifice in Pennington Gardens.[46] In 1986, the League discussed the replacement of rose plantings with the Council's Landscape Architect. Spirit of peace roses now line Baker's apse; red and white roses fill the garden beds Baker suggested should be 'arranged like the rows of graves facing the altar or war stone'.[47] In co-operation with the League, the Adelaide City Council has maintained the Women's Memorial as an important site within Anzac culture and improved the symbolic mnemonic garden to the standard set by the Commonwealth War Graves Commission.

In contrast, War Memorial Drive in Adelaide does not provide a focus for an expression of Anzac culture on sacred ground. The Committees of the combined Women's Memorial Fund distinguished between those killed and those enlisted, raising funds for the 'cross of sacrifice' in honour only of those killed overseas, while the Church of England Cathedral raised the Cathedral cross in memory of all who enlisted. Veteran organisations also recognised a debt owed to all who served overseas, working to distinguish the graves of veterans by lobbying for separate areas and marked headstones, or plaques, that named each individual deceased veteran, distinctively maintaining Australian ex-service identity on hallowed ground even within Australian cemeteries. Individually recognising the names of war dead or war serving was not the object of Lord Mayor of Adelaide Mr C. R. J. Glover who, when the Council considered the question of celebrating the 'restoration of peace', in 1919, initiated a peace memorial, now named 'War Memorial Drive'. The idea for this carriageway and walk on the northern bank of the River Torrens gained popularity when members of the public voiced complaints over plans to celebrate peace over three days with 'excessive expenditure on illuminations and decorations.' The *Register* deemed boisterous displays inappropriate in deference to the feelings of parents and relatives of the 8,000 South Australians killed. Glover donated five hundred pounds as a contribution towards the construction of the first portion of War Memorial Drive, which began opposite Pennington Gardens at Avenue Road and followed the banks of the River Torrens to Frome Road. The first section opened officially by Sir Henry Galway on 30 October 1919, at which date the Secretary for Colonies raised the office of Mayor of Adelaide to the degree of Lord Mayor. The plaque erected at the opening, specifically mentions Glover as a donor jointly with 'citizens'. With completion of the final section of the drive between Frome Road and Hackney Bridge in 1925, the first plaque naming the drive needed updating and replacing. Replacement of the first sign enabled Mr Glover to take delivery of the original plaque for his personal museum.[48] 'Memorial Drive' does not recognise the war service of named individuals.

Although War Memorial Drive along the banks of the River Torrens began as a celebration of peace and a utilitarian memorial in remembrance of those soldiers who had died, it does not imbue a sense of sacred ground or even feelings of remembrance. In reality, the carriageway is a Council memorial designed to enhance and beautify the City of Adelaide. Although the reason given for the drive's construction is that of remembrance of the fallen, the plaque attesting to the memorial's significance recognises the contribution of the serving Lord Mayor of Adelaide at the time of the signing of the Armistice and the desire of Adelaidians to enjoy the benefits of peace. Hurriedly constructed during Glover's period in office, with the drive's conclusion, industrial and manufacturing companies used the memorial carriageway in an effort to by-pass traffic congestion. Therefore, the Council passed By-Law No XLIV restricting the Drive's use, forbidding wagons, lorries, trolleys, drays, transport engines, traction engines, motor-buses, motor char-a-bancs, motor lorries or motor vans, road trains or any other commercial vehicle on any portion of War Memorial Drive.[49] Restricting commercial use made the Drive a space set aside for the purpose of recreation, a utilitarian memorial celebrating peace bought at the expense of individual Australians' personal sacrifice.

Veteran's organisations sought to record personal sacrifice and acknowledgement of debt in burial plots set aside as AIF Gardens of Memory. The League asked church leaders to take up collections on Anzac Sunday, as fund raising for the upkeep of soldiers' graves in West Terrace cemetery. The Soldiers' Welfare Combined Recommendations Committee initiated a movement that raised funds set aside for the layout and subsequent maintenance of the site in the West Terrace Cemetery for a 'Soldiers Burial Ground'. Negotiations made with the League ensured the proper maintenance of the graves, the objective being to create not just a burial ground, but also a sacred garden of memory. The Electricity Trust provided free lighting for the 'Cross of Sacrifice' situated in the 'garden cemetery', giving an added sense of spirituality to the AIF section of West Terrace Cemetery.[50] Not all South Australian veterans lie buried in West Terrace cemetery. Many chose cremation or burial in local cemeteries throughout Australia. Eligible veterans are entitled to services provided by the Office of Australian War Graves located within the Department of Veterans Affairs. With the passing of time, there being no further land available at West Terrace, other cemeteries have set aside land for veteran burials, in particular at Derrick Gardens in Centennial Park Cemetery for the burial of WWII ex-servicemen and women. There are service graves in other cemeteries at Cheltenham and Enfield. Viewed as hallowed ground rather than sacred, the graves receive extra attention, especially from schoolchildren, during times of remembrance ceremonies such as Anzac Day and Remembrance Day.[51]

League Councillors felt it was the duty of the public, not the Returned Soldiers, to arrange the erection of a State memorial, recognising the major problem of the 'War Memorial Committee' was the fact the committee was too big and unwieldy. Suspension of standing orders during the 24th State Council Meeting of the League in June 1926 enabled discussion of the then proposed State memorial by State Councillors. The League discussed possible utilitarian memorials with members speaking against proposals for an arch, the city bridge, a hospital, a war museum or a hall. Mr Butler resolved the debate moving a motion carried unanimously that the memorial be in the form of a 'Shrine of Memory'.[52] The involvement of Parliamentarians and the decision to run a competition to choose the form of the memorial resulted in Anzac Day rituals developing before the completion of the official State Memorial. At the corner of North Terrace and Kintore Avenue in what was the domain of Government House, the memorial envisaged by the League as a 'Shrine of Memory' was eventually built to honour South Australians who enlisted during World War I. Originally, the Government offered a one-acre block for the purpose of the memorial, but the actual size of the land set aside for this purpose was only half the amount first mentioned. Of great importance to the League was a 'permanent record of the men who paid the supreme sacrifice' but the small amount of land set aside constricted the size of any shrine built within that designated space.[53] The winning architect of the memorial competition, Mr Laybourne Smith, designed sculptured figures to occupy the centre of the front and rear facades of the memorial. Raynor Hoff, born and trained in England, sculpted the figures representing the 'Prologue' facing North Terrace, with 'the Epilogue of war', on the reverse. Hoff's sculptured figures on the reverse of the Adelaide memorial represent the 'consummation of sacrifice.' The winged 'Spirit' symbolises 'Womanhood', and her sacrifice of son and lover: she supports a limp figure, a naked man, representing a dead hero. The passive 'Epilogue' did not raise the degree of controversy caused by 'The Crucifixion of Civilization', a plaster model of a nude woman on a cross, which Hoff designed for the Anzac Memorial in Sydney.[54] What did cause much debate within League circles however, was the fact that Laybourne Smith's design allowed no room for listing names on the outside of the edifice. Placing the names of those killed along the interior subterranean walls of the structure solved that problem.[55] Ultimately, placing the names in the interior of the memorial, which the League envisaged as a shrine, created a larger problem for the League: desecration.

Built as the official State Memorial on what the *Advertiser* described as 'no man's land', the memorial is the subject of Parliamentary legislation. For the League to have any influence on the use and treatment of the State Memorial, they must negotiate through State and Local Government bodies. The South Australian Government provided free railway passes enabling veterans from country areas to attend the opening of the State Memorial on Anzac Day in 1931. The Governor unveiled the memorial on the sixteenth anniversary of ANZAC, a time described as 'the most memorable Anzac Day celebrated in Adelaide.' The *Advertiser* believed up to 75,000 people participated in the unveiling ceremony, with 10,000 taking part in the annual procession and noted the presence of an amazing number of youth, representatives of the Scouts, Guides, Wolf Cubs, Brownies and Junior Legatees. League minutes record that the League 'had to give way' to the All Australian Exhibition and the Boy Scouts' rally.[56] Describing the events of Anzac Day the *Advertiser* reported:

> To them [youth] the spirit of Anzac was directed, years ago it seems now, so that they might carry on a tradition so hardly won. Their grand array must have added sparkle to misty eyes and braced up shoulders which are drooping now, tired and feeling the burden of having given the best years of their manhood.[57]

Read in hindsight, that statement carries an ominous sense of prediction, or premonition of the forthcoming service of these youngsters soon caught up in the turmoil of the Second World War.

After the official dedication of the State Memorial, the League had a continual problem trying to establish its spiritual dimension as a 'shrine'. In September 1931, the Attorney-General, W. J. Denny, wrote to the Adelaide City Council requesting that the Council take over the maintenance of the memorial, a request the Council declined in October 1931. With Armistice Day fast approaching in November 1931, the Hon M. McIntosh raised questions in the House of Assembly about the unkempt, uncared for state of the memorial reserve. The *Advertiser* published articles decrying the 'Neglected War Memorial Site Weeds Three Feet High'. Council eventually formally agreed to maintain the memorial reserve but refused responsibility for the memorial itself. Within a year League sub-branches complained about general public apathy shown towards the memorial and the lack of respect in general, urging an educational campaign to cultivate a spirit of respect like that engendered by the Cenotaph in London. Debate at League Conference centred specifically around concern associated with young people eating their lunch on the steps of the memorial, because the League wanted respect for the memorial to be that of a sacred or hallowed ground.[58] As a result, the League lobbied State Parliament and the City Council in an effort to stop desecration of the memorial. At a City Council meeting, Councillor Johnson proposed a motion for a caretaker in an effort to stop the use of the memorial's interior chamber as a urinal.[59] Unlike the imposing symbolism of the Melbourne Shrine, which stands at the apex of a rise imparting an aura of visual importance, the Adelaide memorial stands on level ground, not on a constructed mound as recommended by Mayor Simpson in 1915. The memorial in Adelaide provides a striking vista, within the gardens along North Terrace, but in my opinion, Mr Herbert Baker's doubts about the advisability of siting a memorial on North Terrace, reservations he had expressed in his letter to the Women's Memorial Fund in July 1919, were correct. The ambience of busy North Terrace, complete then, with a tram line, and part of the bustling CBD, did not offer the sense of serenity of a shrine, but attracted attention as a space within which to enjoy fresh air and sunshine when escaping from business offices during the lunch hour.

Council efforts to protect the memorial were unsuccessful. When the League persisted with efforts seeking to enhance the significance of the State Memorial and impose a greater sense of reverence for war dead, the Adelaide city Council passed By Law LXIII on 23 January 1950, designed for the memorial's protection. Plans drafted for the erection of a notice board warning those using the steps of the memorial as a substitute park bench that they were liable to prosecution, went to the designer for his comments. Laybourne-Smith objected to the erection of a large notice board because it would spoil the line of sight of his architectural artwork and requested that any sign be as inconspicuous as possible.[60] A subsequent Council recommendation dated 19 November 1951 reads:

> It has been decided that a copy of the Bylaw dealing with the National Soldiers' Memorial is to be erected on an ordinary post in an inconspicuous place, adjacent to the Memorial following opinions from Mr Laybourne Smith and the Returned Sailors', Soldiers' & Airmen's Imperial League of Australia. The previous proposal to display the Bylaw in a metal frame in a prominent place has been abandoned.[61]

The League did not achieve the degree of community reverence that it wanted for the 'sacred ground' of the State Memorial.

Although the State Memorial for Great War dead was unveiled on Anzac Day, dedication of an additional memorial recording the names of those who made the 'supreme sacrifice' during the Second World War took place on Remembrance Day, 1956. Messrs Woods, Bagot, Laybourne-Smith and Irwin designed the WWII memorial, situated at the rear of the War Memorial Reserve, which records the names of 3,275 South Australians who died serving their King and Country during that war. After a Royal Salute and the hymn 'God of our Fathers, known of old', the Governor, Sir Robert George, unveiled the memorial. The ceremony included the 'Last Post' and 'Ode of Remembrance', the hymn 'Lead kindly light', 'Reveille', the 'Song of Australia', and national anthem with musical accompaniment by the Salvation Army Citadel Band.[62] Correspondence held in Adelaide City Archive files records that the beauty and significance of the State Memorial remained compromised by persons committing acts the League and some other South Australians considered sacrilege. During the period of the Vietnam War, in March 1963, the Town Clerk initiated a survey that recorded the age of persons sitting on the memorial steps. The survey illustrated that the majority of those cautioned were teenagers, suggesting that younger Australians were unaware of the memorial's symbolic significance to the veteran community.[63] In August 1964, Constable no 1533, questioned a middle-aged Lithuanian woman who refused to move from the memorial steps when asked to do so by an Inspector. The woman admitted she knew her actions constituted an offence. Subsequently women police dealt with the matter and the woman was committed to the Institution for the Insane at Parkside.[64] Even with the WWII memorial structure dedicated to South Australian war dead added to the memorial reserve in 1956, some South Australians who were either unaware or unwilling to recognise the memorial's spiritual and symbolic representation of the personal sacrifice of earlier generations of Australians, continued sitting on the memorial steps. During the 1990s, skateboarders utilised the memorial steps as a launching pad. Currently a third memorial to remember war dead from Asian conflicts stands in the memorial reserve, a memorial used by Vietnam Veterans to commemorate the battle of Long Tan.

The State Memorial remains a significant site for Anzac Day and Remembrance Day rituals. As we shall see in chapter 6, the memorial also provides a venue for multicultural commemorative rituals, a ceremonial site for indigenous, Anglo-Celtic, and new ethnic Australian cultural groups to commemorate war dead.[65] Currently, Dawn Service at the State Memorial heralds the start of Anzac Day with that memorial providing the starting point of the Anzac march later in the morning. The foresight of Adelaide women and the planning ability of Mr Herbert Baker, ensured that the Women's Memorial to the Fallen in the Great War, designed in the form of an open-air cathedral in a 'Garden of Remembrance', achieved a greater degree of ambience associated with sacred ground. Another reason for the continued spiritual significance of the Women's Memorial was the offer from the League to assist the Women's Memorial Fund on the occasion of the unveiling of the Women's War Memorial on Anzac Day 1922. On 25 April 1923, the League arranged the conclusion of the Anzac Day procession at the Cross of Sacrifice. The Cross of Sacrifice, in the garden of remembrance designed to represent the graves of South Australian war dead buried overseas, continues to provide a setting for spiritual rituals of remembrance associated with Anzac culture on the morning of Anzac Day.

When the South Australian annual Anzac Day march arrives at Pennington Gardens some veterans disperse, having already attended Requiem Mass at St

Xavier's Cathedral or taken part in mourning rituals for dead comrades at Dawn Services. Others gather with families around the Cross of Sacrifice until they, too, have taken part in remembrance rituals played out in the singing of hymns, prayers, the bugle calls of 'Last Post' and 'Reveille', the 'silence' and National Anthem. Official mourning rites on sacred ground completed, Anzac Day offers an opportunity for making a further statement of Australian identity, providing a public holiday for an Australian celebration of survival in the participation of sporting events and veteran reunions. However, before South Australia could set aside Anzac Day afternoons for charity sporting events and veteran reunions, Anzac Day had to become a public holiday. Credit for the institutionalisation of Anzac Day as a South Australian public holiday lies with the RSSILA South Australian Branch and State politicians debating the *Holidays Act Amendment Act* in 1922.[66]

CHAPTER 3

'THE ONE DAY'

As we have seen, the Brisbane Anzac Day Commemoration Committee initiated the national institutionalisation of the 'Day', in 1916. The League took responsibility for the institutionalisation of South Australia's Anzac Day in 1921 when it urged the Premier to declare Anzac Day a South Australian public holiday. The eventual outcome of League and Parliamentary debates concerning Anzac Day was a cultural change from the Great War recruiting aims of the military that Michael Reardon outlined in 1979.[1] Anzac Day is now 'the One Day' of the Australian year observed as a binary of sacred mourning as well as a celebration of life. Adelaide women and the ex-service community developed South Australian Anzac Day remembrance rituals carried out Anzac morning on sacred ground. The other side of the Anzac binary, the celebration of life and survival, which most overtly takes place on Anzac Day afternoon, also occurs at reunion dinners and concerts held over Anzac Week. Anzac Day, as part of Anzac Week, became the focus of fund raising activities for the relief of distressed ex-servicemen and women as well as a means of raising funds for a building appeal.

The *Holidays Act Amendment Act* assented to 21 December 1922, the same year as the dedication of the Women's Memorial to the Men who fell in the Great War, governs the observance of Anzac Day in South Australia.[2] The title of this Chapter, 'The One Day', is taken from the *Diggers' Gazette* of 7 April 1921, and Hansard records of 1922 South Australian parliamentary debates that predate Alan Seymour's play and novel about Anzac Day, *The One Day of the Year* by four decades.[3] In South Australia, the League worked to ensure the voluntary support and compliance of industrial and commercial organisations in the observance of Anzac Day, rather than legislate to make the 'Day' a 'close holiday', as in New Zealand and some other Australian States.[4] Anzac Day afternoon developed into a time for maintaining contact with other Diggers at family functions, public houses and sporting venues.

During the twenty years between the two World Wars, other states passed various Acts to make Anzac Day a public holiday throughout Australia. The limitation of Anzac Day observance in each Australia State is officially controlled by the different Acts passed by each State Parliament, which vary according to State legislation enacted over a series of years, namely Western Australia 1919, Queensland 1921, New South Wales 1924, Victoria 1925, and according to Graham Seal, by 1927 in Tasmania. Western Australia allowed theatres to open with hotels, shops and factories closed all day and all racing and competitive sport prohibited. By 1937, the Queensland Act did not allow theatres to open, with hotels and shops remaining closed all day. Subjected to the *Bank and Bank Holidays Amendment Act*, Anzac Day in New South Wales received the same treatment as Easter Monday, with theatres and hotels open in the afternoon and shops closed all day, but allowing a military tattoo. In Victoria, Anzac Day was the equivalent of Sunday, with hotels, shops, and warehouses closed all day, sporting and racing prohibited, with a few theatres opened only at night. In Tasmania, shops closed all day, hotels opened after 12 noon and theatres opened at night. Carnivals controlled by the League and devoted to schoolchildren took place throughout the State in the afternoon. In 1937, the Federal Capital Territory was completely different from the States. At Duntroon, a 9 o'clock service took place at the grave of Major General Bridges, with a later service arranged by the Commonwealth Government held on the steps of Parliament House. The main service and parade organised by the Canberra Branch of the RSL was held at 11.30 am at Albert Hall. After the completion of the Australian War Museum, Anzac Day morning activities occurred at that venue.[5]

During the 1920s, the League, and South Australian politicians laid down the foundations of current South Australian Anzac Day functions. At the third State Council Meeting of the League held in September 1920, a motion was carried that 'Anzac Day should be set aside as a day of rejoicing and that the nearest Sunday should be a day of mourning and sorrow.'[6] In February 1921, the *Diggers' Gazette* advised readers of the decision made at the Fourth State Council Meeting, to stop holding button days on Anzac Day. Instead, a sub-committee of metropolitan councillors planned Anzac Day events and reported to the State Board. The meeting further decided that Sub-sections would have the power to hold district services on Memorial Sunday. By March 1921, the *Diggers' Gazette* advised readers of the decision to hold a memorial service on Anzac Sunday at Elder Park, of an Anzac dinner on Saturday night and football matches on Anzac Day itself.[7]

Under a heading of 'Anzac Day', the *Diggers' Gazette* of 7 April 1921, set out a case in favour of observing Anzac Day as a national holiday:

> It is greatly to be regretted that the Government cannot see its way to make Anzac Day a national holiday, for it is the one day of the whole year which returned soldiers look

> upon as the most glorious in its history, when Australia created for itself a name which will live for all time. It will probably be urged that at the present time Australia has more holidays than has any other country in the world. This is possibly so, but even assuming that we have more holidays than are good for us (and this we are not prepared to admit), there is no reason why one of our numerous public holidays should not be cut out in order to allow Anzac Day to become a national holiday.[8]

The *Diggers' Gazette* justified a national holiday on 25 April, not because the feat of arms at the Gallipoli landing was any greater than subsequent battles, but because sentimental interest meant the day was 'sacred' in the military history of Australia.[9]

The League was successful in having 25 April declared a public holiday for the next edition of the *Diggers' Gazette,* published 21 April 1921, praised the Premier for recognising Anzac Day as a public holiday saying:

> The Premier did well in recognising Anzac Day a public holiday, following direct representations made to him by the League. It can now be hoped that for all time the 25th April will be celebrated in a fashion well worthy of the great historical event in Australian history, which took place six years ago.[10]

The *Diggers' Gazette* reminded readers that, regretfully, some of the men who made 25 April a 'sacred day', were in need of help and that others who served the Empire 'saving civilisation' need assistance themselves. Underlying the twofold purpose of Anzac celebrations the *Diggers' Gazette* described them as, first, the commemoration of the day 'Australia attained its military manhood', and second, a memorial service for 'gallant dead'. Sunday memorial services commemorated war dead, whilst Monday, the day of the procession, was a day of rejoicing set aside for the reunion of ex-servicemen.[11] The League added another dimension to mourning rites for war dead and fund raising functions for distressed soldiers. Ex-servicemen and women attended reunions as part of the rituals of Anzac Day, as a celebration of their survival and return home to Australia.

The May edition of the *Diggers' Gazette* described the Anzac Day celebrations from 23 April until the conclusion of the sports programme on Anzac Day 1921, as passing off 'almost without a hitch', and gave credit to the League writing:

> Practically from beginning to end, from the time of the re-union dinner until the conclusion of the football match on the Monday, the whole affair was under the sole charge of the Returned Soldiers' League. It speaks volumes for organisation and efficiency that so successful a military undertaking as the parade of soldiers through the streets of Adelaide should have been carried out entierly [sic] by soldiers, the majority of whom, six years ago, were raw recruits.[12]

The numbers of those attending the annual 're-union dinner' filled the Exhibition Hall, while the procession of approximately 2,500 soldiers, exceeded all expectations and the attendance at memorial services was good. In addition to the Sunday service at Elder Park, the Catholic service at St Francis Xavier's cathedral was overcrowded and St Peter's congregation overflowed the Anglican cathedral. During the service at the Synagogue, the Rabbi noted that in most of Australia, Jewish soldiers outnumbered the average quota of enlisted 'eligibles'.[13] When undertaking the organisation of Anzac celebrations in 1921, the League injected a spirit of enthusiasm into the proceedings and demonstrated the latent potential inherent in the State Board's administrative ability to work for the common good of the League membership.

Although non-party political, the League endeavoured to work for ex-servicemen and women by gaining greater access to the institutional power base. The Board received a ruling from the League Council concerning policy for the 1921 South Australian general election. One policy was to supply each AIF candidate with a list of questions and publish their answers in the *Diggers' Gazette*. Mr C. P. Butler, DSO, Liberal Candidate for North Adelaide and Vice-President of the Returned Soldiers' League, wrote:

> I do not wish the impression to go abroad that returned men want any special privileges or favours other than the carrying out of promises made to them when they enlisted. The really genuine returned soldier does not desire or expect any favours for having done his duty, but he does expect a grateful country to grant him the means of re-establishing himself in civil life if his war services have left him physically fit, so that he can prove himself as good a citizen in peace as he was a soldier in war.[14]

Subsequently, the *Diggers' Gazette* reported that only three Digger or soldier candidates were successful, Messrs I. McMillan, H. S. Hudd, M.C., and W. J. Denny, MC, mentioned in Chapter 3 as the 1931 Attorney-General.[15] The League viewed the election results as disappointing and afterwards saw a need to include more items of general interest in its official publication. Specifically the *Diggers' Gazette* set out to publish more articles designed to appeal, not only to the nurses who were part of the League, but also to the mothers and sisters of Diggers, in an endeavour to achieve a greater degree of patronage for the publication and promote League objectives.[16]

The League continued working to achieve the support of the family unit by providing greater opportunities for family entertainment on Anzac Day afternoons. At the fourth Annual Sub-Branch Conference of the League, held 15 and 16 September 1921, Messrs Smith and O'Connor, members of the Islington Sub-section, moved and seconded a scheme designed to bring Diggers and their families together for 'one day' with AIF sports and a picnic somewhere in or near Adelaide on Anzac Day.[17] The motion was lost, when an amendment carried that left the matter in the hands of the Entertainment and Anzac Day Committee. Members of the Islington Sub-section had initiated discussion centred on the appropriate family arrangements for the celebration of Anzac Day. At the eighth State Council Meeting of the League, the Council expressed a sense of alarm, because the Chairman of the Chamber of Commerce and Manufacturers and the Chairman of the Stock Exchange had articulated a desire to cut out Anzac Day as a public holiday.[18] With the public holiday status of Anzac Day threatened, the League asserted its right to arrange and carry out Anzac Day celebrations, as well as maintain the 'Day' as a public holiday.

According to John Robertson: 'South Australia had generally celebrated Anzac Day on the nearest Sunday' and a proposal to reduce the number of public holidays 'opened the door to an Anzac Day holiday.'[19] That statement is a simplification of the South Australian situation for although in some years memorial services did take place on Sundays, the procession, fund raising, and reunion dinners took place on different days. Three Australian born Diggers in the South Australian Parliament successfully argued the case for the observance of Anzac Day as a South Australian public holiday, when the Parliament acted to establish uniformity in respect of public holidays among the Australian States. On 15 December 1922, William Joseph Denny, born in Adelaide, argued that 'Anzac Day should be the one day of days in Australian history', during debate concerning the South Australian *Holidays Act Amendment Act*, (No 1547).[20] The Chief Secretary (Hon J. G. Bice, a blacksmith) introduced the Act in an effort to establish uniformity in respect of public holidays among the Australian States. A similar Act, the result of a recommendation of the 1918 Premiers' Conference, had lapsed at the end of the 1920 Parliamentary session. The 1922 Act, which sought to bring the schedule of public holidays into line with other states by striking out the holidays for the King's Accession and the Prince of Wales' Birthday, passed after a second reading. In the House of Assembly, Denny asked, 'Are you going to insert Anzac Day instead?' Son of a publican, Denny, a solicitor, was educated at Christian Brothers' College and the University of Adelaide and worked as a clerk until he became editor of the Catholic *Southern Cross* in 1896. In 1898, he served as a Councillor on the Adelaide City Council, winning the West Adelaide seat in the House of Assembly in 1900. Admitted to the Supreme Court in 1908, he served as Attorney-General and Minister for the Northern Territory in 1910–1912. The *Holidays Act Amendment Act* returned from the House of Assembly to the Legislative Council with an amendment adding a new clause, 2a, declaring the 25th day of April (Anzac Day) a public and bank holiday.[21]

Voicing a premonition, which proved to be correct in relation to racing, football and other sports, the Hon D. J. Gordon, a South Australian born journalist and deacon of the Port Adelaide Congregational Church, objected to the amendment on the grounds:

> If there is one day in the year, in addition to Good Friday and Christmas Day, that ought to be regarded as a holy day and not as a holiday it is Anzac Day … If there is one day in the year that should be set aside for remembrance it is April 25, and my idea is that the Sunday nearest to it should be observed for that purpose. If we make it a public holiday it will not be long before the racing authorities fix a race meeting for that day, and not long before football matches or other sports in season will be carried out. The whole populace will be engaged in keeping high holiday on the anniversary of the day when thousands of Australians were laying down their lives for this country.[22]

A Committee consisting of the Chief Secretary, together with D. J. Gordon and W. G. J. Mills, a stud sheep-breeder, decided against the Assembly amendment to observe the day as a public holiday arguing: 'Anzac Day should be regarded as a sacred day and not a day of pleasure.'[23] However, the Assembly insisted upon its amendment that Anzac Day be a public holiday. With the Legislative Council further insisting on its disagreement, the Chief Secretary requested a conference with the Assembly. The resulting recommendation being: 'that the House of Assembly do further insist on the amendment and that the Legislative Council do not further insist on its disagreement thereto.'[24] Subsequently the Chief Secretary moved:

> That the recommendation of the Conference be agreed to.
>
> This was the only possible course that was left to us in view of the further information received at the Conference that the Commonwealth Government had for the last two years observed Anzac Day as a public holiday, and that the Prime Minister of the Commonwealth had agreed to issue a proclamation making a public holiday of Anzac Day.[25]

Gordon reluctantly conceded the up-to-date practical lesson, a result of unification in the form of Federation:

> No matter how the State legislated in respect of Anzac Day, no matter what the expression of public opinion is in South Australia, the Prime Minister, by merely issuing a proclamation, can override any such legislation. He can stop all the wheels of Commonwealth activity in this State. Under the proclamation of the Commonwealth Government Anzac Day can be filled with festivities, football matches, and every other sport, with fireworks at night, and the bulk of the people will forget all about the great lesson that the day should teach. I very much regret the position, but it is inevitable.[26]

The South Australian Legislative Council, agreed to Denny's amendment because of decisions made by the Australian Prime Minister allowing Commonwealth Government employees a holiday on Anzac Day.

In the House of Assembly, Mr McMillan, born in Mannum and a Digger who represented the Albert District, read correspondence dealing with Anzac Day. One example was a telegram received from General Monash, which supported Anzac Day as a public holiday. A further communication, received by the Rev T. Percy Wood of Strathalbyn, was from the Churches of Christ Evangelistic Union that set out a unanimously carried resolution:

> (a) That Anzac Day be known as Australia's National Day, and be observed only on April 25th, and that it be gazetted by Commonwealth and State Governments as a statutory public holiday. (b) That the day be observed in such a manner as to combine the memory of the fallen with rejoicing at the birth of Australia as a nation. That the morning be observed in a strictly solemn manner, and the afternoon be devoted to sports and carnivals of a national character, designed to inculcate into the rising generation the highest national ideals. Horse racing and gambling to be strictly barred.[27]

Continuing, McMillan reminded honourable members that in 1921, during Anzac morning, hotelkeepers had voluntarily closed hotels, and intended to do the same on future Anzac Days. A further letter from the general secretary of the RSSILA revealed Commonwealth and State Ministers had adopted a resolution that:

> [I]rrespective of the day on which it falls, Anzac Day should be observed on the 25th April each year, and that the holiday should be a uniform one throughout the States.[28]

McMillan, concluded his speech in support of the amendment of Anzac Day as a public holiday by stating:

> All the different women's organisations, which did such fine work in the war, are in sympathy with this movement. If there is one day in the calendar worth a place in the list of statutory holidays I claim that it is Anzac Day.[29]

Denny advocated 'South Australia should set an example to the other States regarding Anzac Day' explaining Anzac Day should not be a day of sorrow and mourning alone, because the first anniversary of Anzac Day in France and Egypt had been celebrated with divisional sports, as well as services conducted by the padres.

The Attorney-General, Sir Henry Barwell, still sought to impress upon Members of Parliament the necessity of observing Anzac Day on Sunday to preserve its sacred nature.[30] In answer, McMillan referred to William Burke, a murderer executed for suffocating his victims:

> It is a deliberate attempt on the part of the Chamber of Commerce to burke the Returned Sailors and Soldiers Imperial League of Australia, the loyal bodies associated with that association, such as the women workers who did such noble and good work throughout the war period and since, and who are carrying on that good work at the present time by their tender and loving care of the maimed, ill, and distressed soldiers … It is the one day in the calendar that Australians should look up to with respect, and I implore this Committee to insist on the amendment.[31]

Mr Hudd, an Adelaide-born chocolate manufacturer and another Digger, regretted the disagreement between the two Houses, seeing the amendment as an opportunity for South Australia to 'take a lead on a question which I am certain would be followed by the other States'. The Attorney-General eventually moved agreement to the recommendation with the result that South Australia embraced the celebration of Anzac Day as a public holiday despite the objections of the Chamber of Manufacturers.[32] The successful South Australian soldier candidates of the 1921 general election helped establish Anzac Day as a public holiday.

The Chamber of Manufacturers' argument for a 'silence' on 25 April, rather than a public holiday, was one of obvious self-interest. Had Parliamentarians adopted the stance of the Chamber of Manufacturers and Anzac memorial observances taken place only on 'Anzac Sunday' at church services, it is unlikely that Anzac culture would have revived to the extent that it did during the 1980s and 1990s. The advent of Sunday trading heralded the devolution of Sunday sacredness. Increased numbers of Australians profess to practice no religion at all. If the Legislative Council had persisted and made Anzac Day a holy day like any other Sunday, 'the one day' would now be a day for trading and commercialisation just like any other Sunday in post Christian Australia. By having either the luck, or perhaps the foresight, to treat Anzac Day as 'sacred', in the same manner as the other religious high holidays of Good Friday and Christmas Day, the mornings of Anzac Day have retained the idealism and the sacrosanct nature that the soldier candidates sought, on behalf of the League, in 1922. The Act became one of a series of acts cutting British Empire ties and in doing so, replaced those ties with a new sense of Australian identity. The adoption of Anzac Day as a public holiday in the place of the King's Accession Day and Prince of Wales' birthday reinforced the popular notion that Australians obtained recognition as a nation among other nations, on the slopes of Gallipoli, rather than with the adoption of the Federal Constitution in 1901. Although the new public holiday reinforced Australian identity, debates surrounding the manner in which Anzac Day should be celebrated mirrored arguments in Britain concerning the observation of Armistice Day.

League minutes record some of the debates surrounding the observance of Anzac Day giving insight into the various ways in which veterans felt the public holiday should proceed. At the twelfth State Council Meeting of the League in May 1923, veterans favoured the option of sacred mourning rites until noon and national sports in the afternoon. Messrs Menzies and Lawrence moved and seconded a motion suggesting a service at 11 am, with the afternoon of 25 April devoted to sports, because they felt that with services held on the Sunday before Anzac Day, as they had been earlier in the year, the 'Day' itself would develop into a holiday, and lose its significance. The Rev T. P. Wood moved an amendment believing there was no possibility of improving upon the last Anzac Day, but the motion lapsed for want of a seconder. Messrs Dalziel and Lawrence then moved, and seconded, an amendment to the effect that on Anzac Day, processions should proceed to, and pay tribute at the various monuments erected in honour of war dead. Subsequently, the rest of Anzac Day should 'be devoted to rejoicing at the achievement of the Australian soldier in raising Australia to a state of nationhood'. The motion further left the recognition of Anzac Day itself in the hands of Sub-Branches. The amendment carried and the motion was lost.[33] By 1923, the League had resolved that Anzac Day should begin with processions to monuments representing communal headstones, for commemorative or 'grief management' rituals, and close with afternoon rejoicing.

Australian newspapers featured reports of international Anzac Day events. Recognition of Anzac Day took place in London, with services at the Cenotaph, Australia House and the church of St Clement Danes. In 1925, the *Advertiser* reported extensively on British, Anzac Day events. Australian cadets in Sheffield telegraphed the High Commissioner for Australia in London, Sir Joseph Cook, who had served as Australian Prime Minister in 1914, advising him that they joined with him in spirit at the Anzac memorial service.[34] Workmen at the Australian Pavilion, Wembley, observed two minutes silence at 11 o'clock, as they bowed their heads and stood in memory of Anzac Day. Describing the ceremony of remembrance the *Advertiser* stated:

> There were remarkable scenes at the Cenotaph. The High Commissioners [of Australia and New Zealand] had to struggle through a vast crowd in order to place wreaths on it in honour of Anzac Day. Thousands of men and women from Yorkshire and from Wales had arrived to attend the Cup final, and wearing football colours, they ranged on both sides of the road. All were reverent and quiet, in contrast to their previous hilarity and excitement in journeying through the streets in charabanc and afoot. They doced [*sic*] their weirdly-coloured hats, and there was a sudden silence and 'cease fire' of rattles with the hushing of clamorous voices more impressive than any organised

demonstration of respect. The crowd waited all the morning with bunches of flowers, including scores of buttonholes plucked impulsively from the lapels of their coats and dresses, which were laid at the foot of the Cenotaph.[35]

Subsequently, Sir Joseph Cook, addressed discharged Diggers at Australia House and attended a memorial service conducted by the Bishop of Rockhampton at St Clement Danes church.[36] In 1938, Australian cricketers, together with a large crowd, lined up before the Cenotaph, while two members of the Australian team, Messrs Bradman and McCabe, laid a wreath at the base. Fifteen hundred people attended a Service of Remembrance at St Clement Danes church. Several of the cricketers, led by Messrs W. H. Jeanes and D. Bradman, sat in the front pew during the memorial service. Bradman referred to the solemn thoughts evoked by the team's Anzac Day visit to the Cenotaph. 'We hope trouble is far away', he said, 'but if the occasion arose, Australia would again stand shoulder to shoulder with the Empire.' To the *Advertiser* it was a sad reminder that this was the first team to visit England since the war that did not include a member of the AIF eleven.[37] Although Bradman alluded to the international situation and the possibility of another war, the *Advertiser's* comment was a reference to the increasing age of Great War veterans. As we shall see in Chapter 6, even though the United Kingdom does not observe Anzac Day as a public holiday, in London and at other English localities, Britons and Australians still conduct Anzac Day remembrance services.

In Australia during the 1920s, organisations in New South Wales representing ex-service personnel, were still actively arguing the case for the observance of Anzac Day as a public holiday. In April 1923, the RSL clashed with the Chamber of Manufacturers, the RSL President, Mr L. C. Eliott, declaring in Sydney:

[T]hose members of the Chamber of Manufacturers who only wished their doors to be closed for three minutes on Anzac Day, had either a very poor memory or a very paltry idea of nationalism. Last year the publicans decided to close their doors during the church services, and of their own volition would do the same this year without Government intervention. Anzac Day was a most important day to Australians as on that 'day' they mourned the loss of their 'heroes,' and celebrated the birth of Australia as a nation.[38]

Subsequently the *Advertiser* reported that the Sydney Retail Traders' Association and Butchers' Association had decided to close their shops on Anzac Day. An article on the same page advised that with news reaching New Zealand that shops in some Australian States would remain open on Anzac Day:

> It is considered in many quarters [of New Zealand] that Australia easily forgets her glorious dead. Shops and hotels will be closed. The same procedure will be observed throughout New Zealand, and the annual observance is likely to continue so for all time.[39]

The same year, the Prime Minister, Mr Bruce, instructed that flags flown half-mast on Anzac Day during morning ceremonies commemorating the fallen, were to fly from the masthead after noon.[40] Although the Prime Minister's instruction related to all States, as we have seen the commemoration of Anzac Day did not occur uniformly within Australian States for in some States specific businesses were unable to open, while some forms of entertainment were barred on Anzac Day.

Having achieved the institutionalisation of Anzac Day as a public holiday in South Australia, the League rejected attempts to enforce the observance of Anzac Day as a 'close holiday'. In 1930, a motion submitted through Council by the Prospect Sub-Branch, suggested Anzac Day should be made a 'close holiday'. Mr Menzies, a Vice President, argued the sacredness of Anzac Day would be lost if race meetings took place on Anzac Day, but a number of sub-branches, particularly those in rural areas, used the 'Day' for fund raising functions for the relief of distressed Diggers. When eventually put to the vote, the motion for a 'close holiday' was lost.[41] The following year Prospect Sub-Branch once more brought up the subject of a 'close holiday', this time conjointly with Yorketown. The President, Mr W. F. J. McCann, argued that it was really a question of education, that what was required was the same sentiment prevailing at the end of the war. McCann saw no objection to afternoon functions, providing the funds raised were for charitable purposes. In conclusion, the Conference reaffirmed the method of observing South Australian Anzac Days and urged that the League should make every effort to prevent attempts by organisations or individuals to exploit the afternoon for profitable purpose.[42] The State Board encouraged voluntary observation of Anzac Day rather than initiate further legislation that would enforce a close holiday.

The League worked with organisations representative of commercial, industrial and professional bodies to keep the mornings of Anzac Day 'sacred', lodging protests against some Anzac Day activities. In May 1933, the League resolved to advise the Licensed Victuallers' Association that if their members did not obey the instruction to close hotels before noon, that the League, 'may be compelled to move for a close holiday.' At the following meeting, the State Board resolved to lodge a protest against the State Bank for holding a picnic on Anzac Day.[43] The State Board further considered withholding custom from any baker or shopkeeper infringing an agreement made with the Master

Bakers curtailing Anzac Day bread supplies. In 1937, a petrol station donated profit made from the sale of petrol on Anzac Day, to the Distress Fund. The League refused to accept the donation under those circumstances. The President, and Immediate Past President, ordered the return of the cheque to the Prospect Sub-Branch, which had originally received the cheque.[44] Characteristic activities held on Anzac Day and supported by the League, were charitable sporting events that took place in country areas, and military sports held in Adelaide. Sub-Branches of the League held fund raising events in country areas on Anzac Day during the 1920s and 1930s, the *Advertiser* advising readers of functions in Anzac Day articles.[45] The League was actively engaged in negotiations with community organisations, while it monitored activities and worked to maintain the 'spirit' of Anzac Day throughout the State.

Travel arrangements made through the League enabled veterans from all over South Australia to attend Anzac functions in Adelaide. As revealed in 'Sacred Ground', in 1931, ex-members of the AIF, Navy, and Nurses, received an offer of free rail tickets on State and Commonwealth Railways, for the unveiling of the State Memorial. Some veterans travelled from as far away as Parachilna, Port Augusta, Quorn and Alice Springs. The railways allowed free travel to enable veterans to farewell the Governor Sir Alexander Hore-Ruthven in 1932, and on the 20th anniversary of the Anzac landing in 1935. These concessions were indicative of conditions in other Australian states for in March 1937, the Department of the Interior, Canberra, received advice that special fare concessions in connection with Anzac Day celebrations also operated in Queensland, New South Wales and Victoria.[46] Australian Commonwealth Archive records show the recurrence of free travel from country areas to Adelaide on Anzac Day from 1936, the South Australian Centenary year, until 1970, with only two exceptions. The League abandoned the usual Anzac celebrations during 1942 and 1943, because of war conditions.[47] Veterans travelling to Adelaide during Anzac week could take advantage of free travel to attend other functions.

Military sports were organised in Adelaide, where various battalions competed for the Anzac Day shield between 1931 and 1937. Troops from Moonta, Gladstone, Jamestown, Orroroo, Victor Harbor, Goolwa, and Strathalbyn, participated in sporting competitions on Anzac Day, for the maintenance of physical fitness. Bad weather caused problems for the military sports at Wayville and a trotting meeting on the night of 25 April 1938, the *Advertiser* reporting:

> The unhappiest result of the rain was the cancellation of the military sports which were to have been held at the Showground in the afternoon and the trotting at night

in aid of the Soldiers' Distress Fund, for which a State-wide appeal is being made.[48]

Nevertheless, twelve thousand people attended a pageant held at Wayville on Saturday 23 April the net proceeds going to the Soldiers' Fund. The *Advertiser* printed lists of donations to the Distress Fund Appeal, which included the Stock Exchange, Government Departments, law firms, primary and high schools as well as individuals. The Sailors and Soldiers' Distress Fund established 23 September 1937, had the support of a large section of the South Australian community in 1938.[49]

Even so, the League and Australian Military Forces both effected alternative actions in respect of fund raising events and athletic competitions the following year. Although, the 'Distressed Diggers Fund' received a small donation from the 4th Military District Military and Athletic Competitions Association when the sports were cancelled in 1938, the State Board took out Pluvius insurance in 1939 and following years.[50] The Australian Military Forces policy regarding sports provided conditions for members' physical fitness, however, by the year 1939, another objective in relation to military sports emerged. An advertisement was prepared for broadcast on 5AN radio and insertion in the *News* and the *Advertiser*, that announced it was the policy of the Defence Department to 'encourage recruiting' as well as 'provide means to obtain physical fitness for its members.'[51] The League took action that ensured the Distress Fund received monies budgeted for the relief of distress, irrespective of the detrimental effects of inclement weather on afternoon and evening activities.

Although some Australians during different periods since the 1920s associate Anzac Day predominantly with the public face of veteran reunions complete with revelry, two-up and boisterous, drunken celebrations, there was little reference to this type of behaviour in the *Advertiser* Anzac Day reports between 1915 and the 1950s. However, League minutes of the Sixteenth Sub-Branch Conference held 13 and 14 September 1933, record that the State Board had definitely decided to cease holding the Anzac reunion social because of the damage caused to the prestige of the League by the uncontrollable conduct of some of the men 'towards their guests'. Despite cancellation of the Anzac Social at the Keswick Drill Hall, the State Board desired that as many reunions as possible be held on Anzac Eve.[52] Behind the scenes, League minutes record how hard the State Board worked to maintain the symbolism and significance of Anzac Day while at the same time fostering public acceptance and repayment of the 'debt of honour'.

After the Second World War, the League remained vigilant, guarding the spirit of 'the one day', but diverted some proceeds from charitable fund raising events into the provision of a utilitarian memorial. League minutes in February 1946, record a letter received from the Trustees of the Sailors and Soldiers' Distress Fund advising that they were not willing to give up the Anzac Day Appeal in favour of the League's Building Appeal for a 'living memorial'. The League offered the Distress Fund the proceeds of Poppy Day in lieu of Anzac Day, and decided to approach the Government with a request for licences for additional charity and race meetings in November. Later the same month, the State Board considered a resolution from the Prospect Sub-Branch proposing the observance of Victory Pacific (hereinafter VP) Day as a public holiday. The Board considered the proposal undesirable and decided to take no further action. League minutes in December 1946, record that a letter from the Retail Storekeepers' Association asked 'that Anzac Day should always be observed on a Monday', instead of 25 April, but to veterans Anzac Day remained sacred, the Board advising the retail association that the League was 'definitely not in favour of their suggestion.'[53] The League jealously guarded the sacrosanct nature and fund raising potential of Anzac Day, against all those who intentionally or unintentionally encroached upon the established written and unwritten confines of the day.

In 1948, the League continued its support of the Legacy Club despite an attempted intrusion upon the League's Anzac Day fund raising efforts for the Sailors and Soldier's Distress Fund. A delegation from the Legacy Club met with the State Board in January 1948 to discuss the Legacy Club's Appeal, which was due for finalisation on 16 April. However, in April, the League received advice that the Kooyonga Golf Club had arranged a fund raising competition in aid of Legacy on Anzac Day itself. Consequently, the League resolved that a letter be sent to the Legacy Club pointing out to them that Anzac Day was 'the one day of the year' which had always been, in sport and public life, regarded as solely devoted to the Sailors' and Soldiers' Distress Fund. The League drew attention to the fact that Legacy was breaking a rule regarding Anzac Day fund raising, a rule that had been maintained for nearly thirty years. Despite the League's censure, the minutes recorded 'complete and utter sympathy with Legacy'.[54] Although the League's decision to prevent fund raising activities on behalf of Legacy appears harsh, it is important to note that when the delegation met with the board in January, Legacy had pointed out that they did not wish to encroach on the League's usual arrangements. The Legacy Club was aware of the League's proprietary claims regarding the 'ownership' of 'the one day'.

Answers to implied criticism of Anzac Day rituals and reunion activities appeared in the 1950s, in South Australia publications. On 28 April 1953, the *Advertiser* published an article entitled 'Victoria's Anzac Day Defended', in which the Victorian RSL President, Mr N. D. Wilson, answered criticism over Victoria's failure to fall into line with South Australia, with an 'observance' in the morning and sport in the afternoon. Wilson stated:

> Opening the hotels would sabotage an observance that is as near perfect as it can be ... With experience of methods in other States, Victorian returned servicemen, with few exceptions prefer to retain what they have.

Under a sub-heading 'Proof', the article continued:

> In other States, the hotels open at 1 p.m. but the criticism against the opening is far more trenchant and widespread than it is against the closing here.
>
> I have press cuttings to prove that.
>
> A suggestion that the march should be held in the morning is designed only to get the principal event of the day over as quickly as possible so that it shall not interfere with trade.[55]

The 'sacred' nature of Victoria's Anzac Day was under threat by commercialism, however, whilst defending criticism against 'light heartedness' in South Australia the League's publication sought to impress upon readers the spirituality inherent in the remembrance of overseas war graves.

During 1959, *Sentry-Go* endeavoured to justify the 'Day's' activities with an article entitled 'Here's Why Anzac Day Means So Much to Him'. Although ending with a reference to 'men and women who had the spirit of Anzac in them', the article deals only with the Anzac Day activities of men. *Sentry-Go's* article claimed that under the cloak of light-heartedness, Anzac Day was a day of memories, and that along with the marching men, many more 'fellows' marched along with them metaphorically. Criticism that Anzac Day was a day for making 'whoopee', and glorified war to encourage service recruitment, was described as 'just utter rubbish!'[56] Nevertheless, despite Wilson's earlier criticism of South Australian Anzac Day commemoration and claims regarding the preference of Victorian members for a closed whole-day commemoration, *Sentry-Go* reported in 1960 that:

> The Anzac Day observance plebiscite vote in Melbourne was overwhelming for a close observance till 1 p.m., with restricted entertainment for the rest of the day. Forty per cent. of the RSL's 70,000 members voted – 21,933 for a change and 8,576 against ... After 33 years of a closed whole-day commemoration, the RSL has changed to a half-day commemoration.[57]

Traditional South Australian Anzac Day functions continued steadfastly after the Korean War, when demobbed, professional soldiers who had served in Korea were entitled to join the League membership.

During the 1960s, the League worked hard all year, particularly during Anzac Week and on Anzac Day afternoons, to ensure the success of the Anzac Appeal. Using the medium of charity speedboat meetings, racing, trotting and football events, which the League advertised in the 'department store columns' of the *Advertiser* each Anzac Day, the League raised money used to relieve distress among ex-servicemen and women.[58] Beneficiaries of the Anzac Appeal, were the War Veteran's Home at Myrtlebank, the WWII Services Welfare Fund, the AIF Cemetery Trust and the Sailors' & Soldiers' Distress Fund. Representatives of the South Australian State Board attended Anzac Eve reunions, and endeavoured to ensure that any festivities ended at midnight on Anzac Eve, with businesses remaining closed until at least 12 noon on Anzac Day.[59]

Overt criticism of veteran behaviour during Sydney Anzac Day commemoration ceremonies appeared in Alan Seymour's play *The One Day of the Year*, which the Adelaide Festival Board banned from the 1960 Festival of Arts. Major General Hopkins successfully prevented its production as part of the Festival because he considered the play derogatory to ex-servicemen. However, the Adelaide Theatre Group premiered Seymour's play on 20 July 1960.[60] Well known for disparagement of Anzac Day veteran reunions, the play used Anzac Day activities to highlight the 1960s 'generation gap'.[61] The play depicted in vivid detail, the character of the working class 'larrikin' and returned ex-serviceman, Alf Cook. Seymour underlined the generation gap between the older generation of Australians who claimed Anzac Day as a 'sacred' day, and a younger generation of Australians who considered the spirituality of morning ceremonies hypocritical, because of the revelry associated with afternoon Anzac Day reunions and sporting events.[62] Hughie talking about Anzac Day told Wacka that Wacka had been 'brought up on the speeches' saying what Anzac Day was supposed to be. In contrast Hughie knew Anzac Day to be 'A great big meaningless booze-up' and nothing more.[63] However, after the publication of the photographs, which he took on Anzac Day, Hughie admits to feeling like 'a priggish, hysterical kid' who only thought he understood Anzac Day.[64] In October 1961, League minutes referred to *The One Day of the Year*, when the League received a letter regarding the play from the Council of Adult Education.[65] Superficially, Seymour's play *The One Day of the Year* was a brutal criticism of Anzac Day afternoons, of Australian workers, of Australian leaders and Australian culture in general, but the play did attempt to depict the reasoning behind Anzac Day rituals.

Anzac Day observances remained a subject of scrutiny at the time of the

Vietnam War for in subtle ways the executives of community groups reduced the commitment of their organisations to the Anzac Appeal as anti-war sentiment grew within Australia. The Football League stopped paying a percentage of charity match takings into the Anzac Day Appeal and instead nominated a set figure donation while the Royal Agricultural & Horticultural Society decided not to grant any concessions for future charity trotting meetings at Wayville.[66] At the State Board meeting in 1972, League Secretary, Mr K. W. Hoffman, pointed out that some unions had caused difficulties on Anzac Day, by forcing a long weekend with a holiday Monday on 24 April. Further problems developed over wine and bottle shops hours of opening, with the League requesting the closure of such outlets on Anzac Day, during the same hours as those advocated by the Australian Hotels Association. It is worth noting that the League demanded Sub-Branches and clubrooms remain closed during the same period.[67] With Violet Memory Day commemorative services discontinued, the League relied on Anzac Day and Poppy Day for charity fundraising.[68] In the aftermath of the Vietnam War, Anzac Day no longer commanded the same respect evident after World War II.

Alan Seymour's novel, *The One Day of the Year,* published in 1967, heralded a metaphorical revival of the 'Day', for Seymour, has Alf Cook's son Hughie ask, 'In all our talk against that day, did we ever visualise an alternative? If it were destroyed, wiped out, what would replace it?'[69] In the 1960s, the drunken behaviour of some veterans who returned home from Anzac Day afternoon functions obviously inebriated was not recognised as a possible manifestation of Post Traumatic Stress Disorder related to the revival of traumatic memories while in the company of other Diggers.[70] Seymour's play and book stirred conservative South Australians into action. Minutes dated 22 April 1974, reveal that the League wanted an interview with the Minister for Education and planned to discuss flag procedures, the National Anthem and the book *The One Day of the Year*.[71] The League was aware it had a generational problem and acknowledged the challenge posed by waning community support. As we shall see, the League made administrative changes designed to include a younger generation of Australians in commemorative activities and fund rasing promotions, changes that ensured the continuation of the Anzac Appeal.

In 1979 Philip Kitley researched Anzac Day on a deeper level than that of Alan Seymour and drew on anthropological literature describing reunions in terms of afternoon 'rowdyness', quoting V. W. Turner's notion of 'communitas', which was: '[e]ssentially communitas is a relationship between concrete, historical, idiosyncratic individuals.' Kitley acknowledged Ken Inglis's suggestion there was 'a significant tradition of larrikinism in the AIF', reasoning 'that the larrikin spirit is still abroad.'[72] In reality, veteran reunions are part of Anzac culture, an opportunity to renew social contact with a group of former Diggers. In a parody of the 'Ode' to war dead recited on Anzac Day, 'Age shall not weary them/ nor the world condemn', the world did condemn the larrikinism and rowdiness of veterans, and age wearied surviving WWII Diggers, Korean and Vietnam Veterans, just as it did WWI Diggers.

Definitely not confined to 'the One Day of the Year', League minute books provide evidence that planning and preparation for Anzac Day and the Anzac Appeal begin in December. Discussions related to planning for the current year take place each month up until April, while the State Board receives reports in relation to Anzac Day in May, June and July. State Board minutes sometimes contain a reference to Anzac Day and its relative concerns every month of the year.[73] In retrospect, Alan Seymour contributed to the retention and renewal of Anzac culture because his play and novel provided the League with an impetus that lifted League members out of a period of apathy. RSL South Australian Branch leaders addressed perceived problems with the RSL's media image and the problem of smaller Anzac Appeal funds by adopting new strategies.[74] The following two chapters, 'Diggers and Slackers' and 'Widening the Ranks', illustrate in greater detail, the administrative changes the League made to media broadcasts, fund raising and community support programmes in order to sustain and renew the progressive spirit of Diggers in periods of decline. The League's efforts with regard to the organisation of remembrance services for the commemoration of war dead, fund raising for distressed ex-servicemen and women, and reunions held on Anzac Day enabled the 'Day' to survive into the 21st century still reflecting an image of the Australian Digger as a dimension of Australian national identity.

CHAPTER 4

'DIGGERS AND SLACKERS'

In November 1919, in the first edition of the *Diggers' Gazette*, the League delineated a policy relating to politics:

> Without being party political we can be critical. We can discuss any and every subject in its political sense, and seek to find the solution of all those complex problems that beset us in these momentous days of reconstruction.[1]

Historians have previously recorded some of the activities of the Returned & Services League of Australia and its antecedent bodies (hereinafter RSL). In 1966, G. L. Kristianson noted that some of the Australian population disagreed with the RSL's conservatism and found support among other Australians who had critical attitudes towards the RSL based on generational changes.[2] David Hood's 1994 doctoral thesis discussed RSL conservatism and change before the Second World War.[3] Historians generally accept the conservatism of RSL activities. I am not concerned with RSL conservatism but with RSL decisions related to repayment of the 'Debt of Honour,' Anzac Day and Anzac culture. M. McKernan and M. Browne edited *Australia, Two Centuries of War and Peace* published in 1988. In Chapter 8, 'The Power of Anzac', Marilyn Lake wrote of RSL pressure on governments to keep recruiting campaign promises. Lake concluded that in responding to the apparent power of the Anzacs, Australia's repatriation policy focused on ex-servicemen's discontent concerning civilian 'eligibles', 'slackers', Bolsheviks, women or coloured workers.[4] However, the 'discontent' of the League did not extend to all 'eligibles' and concern for those of the unemployed within the ex-service community included women and children of war dead and war serving. The League also lobbied for citizenship rights on behalf of indigenous ex-servicemen. The emergence, consolidation, decline and renewal of Anzac Day mirrors Australians' changing perception of Australian identity.

During the period between the First and Second World Wars, especially during the depression, the League found that the Government and community readily forgot the debt of honour taken up during the Great War. The League was 'strictly non-political, or rather, non-party, in its constitution', and saw itself as an organisation in the 'vanguard of progress' looking to the future: it used the strength of its membership numbers within the state to concentrate efforts towards overcoming some of the problems faced by repatriated ex-servicemen and women.[5] The implied strength of the League to mould its own destiny lies in the use of the *Diggers' Gazette* in 1921 as a forum for electioneering by 'Digger Candidates'. Although non-party political, the League believed 'Digger Candidates' more likely to protect the interests of returned veterans, than 'slackers'. As discussed in 'The One Day', the League allowed ex-soldier parliamentary candidates for the 1921 South Australian election a forum in the *Diggers' Gazette*. In March 1921, in an article entitled '"Slacker" Parliamentary Candidates', the *Diggers' Gazette* reported League policy as willing to advertise only returned soldier candidates, although not necessarily advocating Diggers vote for them. The article described 'slackers' as those who were 'eligible to go to the war, but who failed to do so', arguing that as 'slackers' did not act in their country's interest 'at the time of her hour of greatest need' they would not act responsibly 'in minor matters of public interest'. Eligibles who were unable to go to the front because of physical disability or other valid reasons did not rate the classification of 'slackers'.[6] Mr Vaughan, a previous South Australian Attorney-General, felt it necessary to publish a 'Personal Explanation' after having aspersions cast against his character in relation to his overseas service. One of his political opponents claimed that Vaughan took a comfortable headquarters job in England, when in fact Vaughan explained he was with the 'footsloggers' in the French trenches. Vaughan went on to declare:

> I am in a position to fully protect in Parliament the interest of returned men, and to obtain the complete fulfilment of the public promises held out to them on enlistment – promises which till now have been only partially and inadequately fulfilled. I maintain that returned men should have the right, with other sections of the community, to direct representation in Parliament, and I am satisfied this can only be obtained by substituting for the present system of voting the system known as proportional representation, for which I stand. The Digger spirit is too valuable a national asset for us ever to allow its direct influence to be lost in those public affairs which are under the control of Parliament.[7]

The League sought returned-soldier representation in Parliament to present a case for veterans to gain recognition that the 'debt of honour' still required repayment in an effort to secure the promises made to soldiers during the period of the Great War.[8]

As we shall see, decisions made by the RSL and the League contained the expression of social unrest within Australia. During the interwar years, the

Repatriation Department reduced and cancelled pensions in Australia. The Depression exacerbated the problem of unemployment among the ex-service community, which resulted in protests on Anzac Day against unemployment. The Returned Sailors' & Soldiers' Imperial League of Australia (hereinafter RSSILA), reacted to the problem of unemployment by setting up employment bureaus to assist veterans, war widows and dependants in finding employment. When reporting on the 1928 procession of returned men as the largest for some years the *Advertiser* stated:

> As the long procession swung down King William-street to the strains of the bands cheers broke from the crowd. When the head reached Victoria-square a number of the unemployed sang 'The Red Flag' and 'Solidarity for Ever', as the troops passed by. It was noticed that many of those so singing wore returned soldiers' badges.[9]

Unemployment continued to cause concern the following year. Under the sub-heading 'Unemployed Returned Soldiers' the *Advertiser* reported that:

> Between the returned men and the citizen forces a body of unemployed returned soldiers had joined in the procession and they, in company with the units of the AIF, gave 'Eyes Right' as they passed his Excellency, who returned the salute. At their head they carried a banner on which was printed, 'Unemployed Returned Soldiers. We had a job in 1914–1918. Why not now?'[10]

Some veterans entitled to march with the Diggers in the Anzac Day procession chose to remain on the sidelines. The *Advertiser*, when reporting on the 'march' in 1932, noted that '[t]hose whose bitterness with existing conditions had prevented them marching were sorry they had not marched.'[11] The *Advertiser* provided no evidence of regret on the part of the ex-servicemen who did not march, but the inclusion of the above statement suggests that a degree of bitterness existed amongst the ex-service community because promises made during the Great War were reneged.

The South Australian Sub-Branch Conference and the League attempted to reduce unemployment amongst veterans, reacting to the building of the Australian War Memorial in different ways. In 1933, the South Australian Sub-Branch Conference passed a resolution against the building of the Australian War Memorial in Canberra, which was described by one delegate as a 'useless edifice', for the Conference considered the memorial a waste of funding given the thousands of unemployed returned soldiers seeking work. The Conference resolution was in direct opposition to the previous stance taken at the National Congress. The League's State Board suggested a solution and requested that the RSL Federal Office approach the Federal Government to ask for a limitation regarding those employed in connection with the construction of the War Memorial: the confinement of employment to ex-servicemen.[12]

Further extending the idea of the availability of specific employment for ex-servicemen only, League minutes record protracted dealings, beginning in 1935, relating to 'absolute preference in employment' for returned ex-soldiers and the proposed Anzac Highway memorial from Adelaide to Glenelg.[13] Negotiations resulted in the League signing an agreement with three local councils, Unley, West Torrens and Glenelg, together with the State Government, that gave preference to unemployed returned soldiers seeking to work on the re-construction of Anzac Highway.[14] Despite controversy over preference for ex-servicemen and letters to the *Advertiser* disagreeing with the preference clauses, with the help of Members of State Parliament and Local Government Councillors, the Agreement eventually became part of a Bill ratified by the Parliament.[15]

The RSSILA took steps to reduce unemployment among ex-servicemen. In 1937, the RSSILA *Official Year Book* reported on Preference in Employment.[16] By 1938, the *Official Year Book* advertised the services of the RSSILA's own employment service bureau, which operated throughout Australia, to help 'all ex-servicemen and their kin whenever and wherever possible'.[17] The RSSILA *Official Year Book 1939* advised employers:

> If you have a vacancy for a professional man, for an artisan – a job of any description – get in touch with the League, which will be happy to meet and satisfy your requirements immediately.
>
> Dependable men with all variety of professional qualifications and attainments and hard-working experts in every trade are registered from day to day.
>
> Also there are Soldiers' Widows, with many qualifications, seeking employment. Girls and youths, the children of ex-servicemen, are registered, too.
>
> Males and females – of every age, who because of their service in war or who, as wives and children, have been sadly touched by war, must be specially privileged in the matter of employment.
>
> The employer who is a returned man owes it to his comrades of 1914–1918 that they or their folk shall have a first consideration!
>
> The employer who is not an ex-serviceman or woman owes it to the great record of those who served that they and their dependents shall have a special preference – surely?[18]

In the same *Year Book* the South Australian Branch gave details of employment and advised:

> During the 11 months ended 30/11/38, 578 position [*sic*] were obtained through the Employment Bureau. At present 907 ex-servicemen are on the books compared with 1,080 at January 1st, 1938 – a decrease of 173. One full-time and one part-time officer

look after the interests of the unemployed. Registrations are made at the Bureau, Kintore Avenue, Adelaide.[19]

The League extended the bonds of 'diggerhood' forged during the Great War into peacetime activities by forming employment bureaus in response to the Anzac Day protests of the unemployed among the ex-service community.[20] Because the League believed that Diggers had readily defended and identified with Australian interests, it looked to Diggers in Parliament to deal with reconstruction and repatriation problems and absolve the debt of honour incurred during the Great War.

The Defence issue of the RSSILA *Official Year Book 1939* listed 'Diggers in Parliament'. Of the ten Diggers in the Senate, two 'Digger Senators' represented each state of Queensland, Victoria, New South Wales and Western Australia, with one 'Digger Senator' representing each State of Tasmania and South Australia. There were twenty-two Diggers in the House of Representatives. Two from Queensland, nine from Victoria, eight from New South Wales, with one each from Tasmania, South Australia and the Northern Territory. Although there were only two South Australian Diggers in the Commonwealth Parliament that was on a par with Digger representation from Tasmania and Western Australia. Individually in the State Parliaments New South Wales had 22, Victoria 21, Western Australia 19, and Tasmania 15, a total of 77 Diggers. One Tasmanian Digger was the Leader of the Opposition while another was Minister for Lands.[21] On a national basis, South Australia had the smallest number of Diggers in State Parliament.

By the end of the Interwar period, there was a larger representation of 'Diggers' in the South Australian Parliament than the three ex-soldier candidates, namely, Denny, McMillan and Hudd, elected in 1921. The *Official Year Book 1939* records nine 'Diggers' in the South Australian Parliament. The nine 'Diggers' being the Premier Hon T. Playford, a fruit grower, two Members of the Legislative Council Hon E. D. A. Bagot and C. R. Cudmore, together with MPs Hon A. W. Christian, J. A. Lyons, J. McLeay, C. J. D. Smith, H. D. Michael and Hon R. J. Rudall, Lawyer, Commissioner of Crown Lands.[22] With Diggers in parliament the League had achieved some measure of preferential employment on behalf of ex-servicemen, for in the section of the Year Book allocated to the South Australian Branch, under the heading 'Preference', appeared the following:

> A State Regulation approved by the Executive Council with regard to Preference in Employment to ex-Service Men provides:
>
> 1. Where only one workman is required, a vacancy shall be filled by a Returned Soldier if available and suitable.

> 2. When two workmen are required a vacancy shall be filled by one Returned Soldier, if available and suitable, and one civilian.
> 3. Where more than the abovementioned are required, the vacancy shall be filled by approximately one-third Returned Soldiers, if available and suitable, and two-thirds civilians.[23]

Preferential employment extended to members of the Australian ex-service community assisted repayment of the 'debt of honour' owing to Australian war dead and war serving.

Although officially Australians were British subjects, the *Official Year Book 1939*, considered the issue of dual nationality. Despite concern with this issue, European migrants to Australia who sought RSSILA membership and identification with the 'Anzacs' in the lead up to WWII achieved League membership status if naturalised British subjects. The 'Defence Issue' of the *Official Year Book* looked at the question of nationality stating that 'Southern Europeans and refugees from Germany and other European nations' were flooding into Australia. The Year Book saw inevitable complications in the 'little communities' springing up in Australia. Writing that in the past Australia and New Zealand had boasted they had no nationality problem, the report continued:

> We have been, not Australian nationals in the British Commonwealth of Nations, but citizens of the Empire, claiming and enjoying British nationality exclusively. In South Africa, Canada, and the Irish Free State, however, the question of dual nationality arises and is sure to arise here too later on if precautions are not taken … Britain's view is that if a Dominion no longer wishes its nationals to remain British subjects, they can not continue to enjoy the privileges of British nationality. These privileges include passport facilities, protection in foreign countries and diplomatic representation through British embassies.[24]

Some individuals with European backgrounds showed they were willing to proclaim publicly a sense of British Australian identity and sought membership of the League. Former Italian soldiers who applied for League membership for example gained acceptance provided they were naturalised British subjects.[25]

The League remained vigilant with regard to affiliated groups of ex-soldiers within South Australian membership ranks. Desmond O'Connor in *No Need to Be Afraid* (1996), describes the activities of Giuseppe Amerio who tried to convert the Adelaide Italian community to the fascist cause. As Secretary to South Australia's honorary consular agent for Italy, and Fascist Party trustee for South Australia, Amerio could exert influence upon the outcome of applications to bring family members to Australia from Italy. When Italy joined the war against the allies in June 1940, police officers arrested known South Australian Fascists of both Italian and British nationality.[26] Following the arrest of two League members, former members of the Italian Army, for 'subversive activities' the League requested a return of the men's League badges.[27] A third Italian was asked to return his badge after admitting he had been a member of a Fascist organisation between the years 1927 and 1939. He had joined the Fascists to facilitate permission for his wife and daughter to leave Italy, because he wanted them to join him and his son in Australia. Having a number of brothers in the Italian forces he had no desire to fight for Australia against Italy. As a direct result of this case, in 1942 the State Board framed a resolution to the effect that any man who had been a member of the Fascist Party or any subversive society working against the interests of the British Empire could not hold League membership.[28] Persons of dual nationality, or suspected foreign allegiance, were not the only men subjected to scrutiny and discipline. During the war period League minutes disclose greater numbers of interviews took place examining men for conduct not becoming a gentleman in the Club, with some men being suspended or expelled as a result of drunkenness or misbehaviour.[29]

The second year of World War II saw a defining moment with the alteration of the RSSILA's name, a change that included returned Airmen trained at various locations throughout Australia, Canada, South Africa and England. The new name 'Returned Sailors,' Soldiers' and Airmen's Imperial League of Australia (South Australian Branch) Incorporated,' adopted in 1941, once again ignored League membership dimensions in relation to the gender of nurses and ex-servicewomen. Despite the blatant omission in relation to gender in the change of name, the League resolved to advise the Sisters Sub-Branch that they considered the Sisters part of the Army. In effect, the League told the Sisters they were soldiers![30]

With the nation at war, the League requested that Federal Office recommend to the Government the abandonment of the usual Anzac Day holiday. In March 1942, the League resolved to cancel the central Dawn Service in Adelaide, but supported League representation at any dawn ceremonies arranged by Sub-Branches.[31] Subsequently, in April 1942, the *Advertiser* reported:

> Several hundred citizens paid tribute at the National War memorial on Saturday to the memory of the men of Anzac who landed on the shores of Gallipoli 27 years ago. Though the march through the city was dispensed with, the simple service, held in brilliant sunshine, lost nothing in reverence and dignity. Among those present were members of the Second AIF and US forces.[32]

The *Advertiser* reported on Anzac Day services in 1943, services labelled 'Quiet, Solemn Commemoration':

> The commemoration centred largely round the service at the Cross of Sacrifice, Pennington Gardens. It was a simple one, concluding with the laying on the Cross of Sacrifice of hundreds of wreaths.[33]

The *Advertiser* noted that other States had record attendances at Anzac services.[34] Abandonment of the procession in 1942 and 1943 underlined the commemorative aspects of Anzac Day rituals. Sunday 25 April 1943 coincided with Easter Sunday. League Sub-Branches still sold Anzac badges throughout the Anzac Appeal, raising funds for the growing ranks of ex-servicemen and women, a number of Sub-Branches holding local marches from various assembly points to places of worship.[35] Despite war conditions, it was still important enough to conduct commemorative rituals and place wreaths around metaphorical communal headstones in recognition of burial sites overseas, burial sites that now included the graves of those killed in World War II. Effectively, no celebration of life and survival took place because ongoing battles still required a successful conclusion.

The League had endeavoured to resolve the problem in relation to indigenous ex-servicemen and those with a degree of caste in 1942, by asking Federal Office to take up the matter of full civic rights for 'returned soldier aborigines'. In August 1944, Mr H. J. Milera requested that the League take further action regarding citizenship rights for indigenous returned soldiers. In an attempt to rectify the situation, the League resolved to ask the Premier to grant a permit under the Licensing Act to every indigenous returned soldier.[36] The League lobbied for civic rights for indigenous ex-servicemen but, as we will see below, this problem remained for post war Boards to find a solution.

After 1945, Australian politicians solicited the electoral support of WWII returned ex-servicemen and women because the 'New Diggers' were a formidable group within the Australian community. The March 1947 edition of *Back*, the magazine of the RSL, contained advertisements from both sides of the political spectrum. Authorised by R. S. Richards, Trades Hall, Labour pledged:

> A FULL EMPLOYMENT POLICY
> LONG RANGE HOUSING PLAN
> PROGRESSIVE RURAL DEVELOPMENT
> REMEMBER Labor has Given you
> Better Pension Schemes
> Rehabilitation Training, and
> Stands for a Fair Deal for All[37]

Alternatively, the Playford Government set out six points on which they stood for election: tax reduction, real preference for ex-servicemen, assured employment, increased social services, primary production improvement and development. Authorised by A. S. Dunk, North Terrace, the advertisement carried the message *'TOM PLAYFORD HIMSELF IS A RETURNED SOLDIER AND HALF THE MEMBERS OF HIS CABINET ARE EX-DIGGERS'.*[38] In seeking the vote of veterans, essentially both advertisements gave examples of similar polices in relation to civilian ex-service men and women.

League minute books provide evidence that the main anxiety of the League after World War II concerned either housing or preferment in employment for ex-servicemen. Further items of worry were hospital and welfare, the comfort and treatment of veterans, and adequate pensions for war widows. All these problems were particularly pressing to ex-servicemen and women as they tried to settle down within the Australian community. Housing caused anxiety, because couples who had lived apart during war years, although anxious to get on with life and continue or begin families, first had to find suitable accommodation. Some ex-servicemen obtained housing loans. However, housing depended on building materials that were in scant supply. Building materials were restricted and private construction limited to executives in new industries, the bulk of home construction carried out by the Housing Trust and War Service Homes Departments. Some people chose to build 'back-enders', which supplied rudimentary accommodation, relying on the progress of time to enable eventual completion of their home. Lack of suitable housing could be one reason for the high membership figures as Sub-Branches kept a watchful eye, enabling the State Board of the League to dispute cases where naturalised persons received housing and accommodation while veterans remained on Housing Department waiting lists. The South Australian housing situation in 1947 prompted the Mount Barker Sub-Branch to ask that the League approach the Federal Government 'to defer immigration plans until such times as our own people are properly housed.'[39] In August 1947, *Back* reported on a failing within the immigration system saying:

> It is felt a census will reveal that in far too many cases the Government has been hoodwinked by nominators who, instead of keeping to the regulations and boarding those they sponsor, have been able, by means of the black market, to secure for them dwellings which should have been made available to Australians, preferably ex-servicemen and women.[40]

League minutes record thirteen civilians fined for building without a permit in December 1948.[41] League concerns relating to veterans' housing extended to include war widows' accommodation.

Although war widows were ineligible for League membership, the League nevertheless maintained a watch on the living conditions of war widows and legacy children. Widows in Melbourne organised a protest against the meagre war widow's pension whereas the South Australian League helped with the organisation of a button day for war widows to sell 'Monty' souvenirs. This effort to aid war widows took place in conjunction with Viscount Montgomery's visit to Adelaide in July 1947 to meet with returned men from the three services and the El Alamein Association.[42] In August 1947, *Back*, published an article, which favoured increasing the amount of war widows' pensions, arguing:

> This article is a challenge to any Australian, from the Prime Minister to the basic wage earner, and it concerns the foulest piece of legislation in existence today – that which gives war widows a pension sufficient only to live and bring up their families in poverty. Every Australian, and particularly every Federal politician, should hang his head in shame. Men gave their lives for their country. Their country repays their families with a pig-slop allowance. To put the matter bluntly, it stinks.[43]

In the face of Government neglect, the RSSAILA lobbied the Federal Government on behalf of the families of war dead.

Annual Reports and service magazines provide evidence that not only in Australia, but internationally, returned veterans from WWII preferred 'living memorials' in the form of libraries, memorial halls and hospitals serving the living, rather than the practice of listing the names of the serving and the dead on obelisks and pedestals so important to World War I veterans. In January 1948, *Back* introduced an article on 'Living Memorials' advising that a new spirit and a new idea had emerged among Anglo-Saxon peoples in relation to memorials. The article continued:

> The type of project suitable for consideration as living memorials will vary with the locale. They could range from Memorial Halls in the smaller towns to large-scale urban community centres designed to accommodate large groups of people and activities.[44]

Living memorials erected to memorialise the service of war dead and war serving provided practical benefits to the entire Australian community.

Although some returned men chose not to become members of the League, other returned men faced expulsion from League membership because of political affiliations. In April 1948, the State Branch resolved to request the next Federal Executive to ban communists from being members of the RSSAILA throughout Australia.[45] It would be fair to say at that particular period, (minutes circa 1948–49), the League considered communists 'un-

Australian'. The League defined a communist as a person who was a member of the Communist Party and, furthermore, the League ruled that 'the onus is on those laying the charge to prove that a man is a Communist.' Efforts made by the League to organise surveillance of Communist Sunday Rallies in the Botanic Park in October 1954 arose at the same time the League prepared to send Christmas parcels to Korea and Malaya.[46] The need to send parcels to Asian countries where members of the Australian Forces served during the Korean War and Malayan emergency, accounts for the League's vigilante interest and subsequent attempts to prohibit active communists as League members. The League's outspoken attitude against communists as a political party goes against the precepts of their non-party political stance, but parallels the attitude of the League against fascists during WWII. This attitude seems more in keeping with the League's patriotic objectives during time of war than its non-partisan political policy.

During the 1950s, the State Board of the League had access to the South Australian political hierarchy on a regular basis. New Australians, reported the *Advertiser* in 1950, saw the Anzac Day March as 'passing people of all classes, united in fighting for one flag', yet the League as a lobby group had entrée to the highest echelons of power within South Australia. The same edition of the *Advertiser* also reported the Premier Tom Playford, 'who has not missed an Adelaide Anzac march', marching with the 27th Battalion.[47] Photographed marching with the members of his old unit publicised the Premier's service qualifications and identified his Australian patriotism. League minute books record details of Parliamentary luncheons between 1951 and 1956. The luncheons provided a forum for League State Board members to meet with the Premier. 'Parliamentary luncheons' took place approximately once a month during 1951, 1952 and 1953; therefore, during this period the practice of the Premier meeting League representatives for consultation on a regular basis underlines the electoral implications cognisant with the ex-service community.[48] Although the League as a lobby group had a political advantage accessing politicians at Parliamentary luncheons, Brinkworth and Goolwa Sub-Branches protested in writing in 1953 against election advertisements in the magazine *Back*. Subsequently the State Board resolved to exclude party political advertisements from that magazine.[49]

In 1953, the League received information regarding the possibility of a visit to South Australia by a contingent of former Turkish enemies and made plans to welcome the delegation. The Federal Government financed the delegation's visit, with one Turk going to each State. Fêting the former enemy, the League made arrangements enabling the Turk's presence on the official Saluting Base during the Anzac march past of veterans. The Board left entertainment arrangements in the hands of the Secretary and President. Consequently, Mr Eastick, as State President went to the Woodside Camp and Migrant Centre with the Turkish delegate. Other gestures of friendship included a reception held by the Governor and Premier, and a presentation of a flag. The enthusiastic reception afforded to this former enemy was noticeably different from feelings evident against Germans and Japanese. However if one projects into the 1980s for a comparison, by 1980 under the heading 'Hospital Visits' minutes record 'It was resolved that the League policy today is one of goodwill and friendship towards these people [ex-enemy] and that after 35 years they should be regarded as any other ex-service persons.'[50]

Returning to the 1950s, the unresolved questions in relation to the full citizenship rights of indigenous ex-servicemen from World War II arose again in 1953. After a new act passed in 1954 regarding the serving of liquor, the board received the information: 'Aboriginal ex-servicemen can apply and get an exemption from the Act, and all Aboriginals coming to the Club will be privately interviewed and their exemptions sighted.' Questions relating to 'quarter' and 'half castes' remained a subject of investigation. Later in 1954, the Board received a list of ten Aboriginals granted permits received from the Aborigines Department. The State Board resolved to approach the Premier 'for the right to serve Aborigines at the RSL Club, on Anzac Day only, providing they are members of the League.' The President undertook to make a personal approach to the Premier.[51] Consequently, the Premier prepared to submit an amendment to the Act but was unable to grant concession to the League to serve indigenous ex-servicemen liquor on Anzac Day. Subject to discussion with the President of the Aborigines Advancement League in South Australia, (WWI returned soldier, Dr Duguid), and the Protector of Aborigines, the matter of amendments remained in abeyance.[52] Later the Board received the information that Aborigines and 'Half Castes' granted citizenship rights were still subject to the Licensing Act in South Australia. The Board left the matter aside for discussion with the Premier. At this stage the Board received the information that the effect of Section 2 of the Licensing Act 1934 was that 'only members of the Fighting Forces of World War I and prior Wars can obtain liquor', World War II members only being supplied at the expense of, and in the presence of a World War I member. Subsequently, the Premier advised the League it was unnecessary to alter the Act to allow rights to WWII members because the League could give the right to World War II men under its own rules and regulations. The Board also received advice in 1954 from the Premier that:

> Any man who desires may have full citizenship rights, which entails the whole of the

> rights of any white man, but by that step he debars himself and his family from having native rights again.[53]

Despite the League's attempts to obtain equal rights for all Australian ex-servicemen and women, State legislation forced indigenous ex-servicemen to choose between citizenship and 'native rights'. However, the League could determine its own policies with regard to non-indigenous ex-servicemen and women.

As we have seen above, after adopting the 1941 name change that included airmen, the League had found it necessary to advise the Sisters' Sub-Branch that that sub-branch was considered part of the Army, a move suggesting some insensitivity on the part of the RSSILA. However, when the RSL Victorian Branch asked women not to attend the Melbourne Dawn Service in 1953, the South Australian League resolved 'such proposal be vigorously opposed in this State.' In 1955, when a female member of the British Imperial Sub-Branch sought information regarding her right to drink in the RSL Club bar, State Board minutes record that the Returned Sisters and Returned Servicewomen members of the League had never exercised the right to drink in the RSL Club bar.[54] It is worth noting that in Australia at this time, conventionally women did not frequent hotel front bars. Australian culture customarily delineated women's presence to the 'lounge bar', therefore the League observed cultural standards regarding hotel bars and women that the Australian community generally accepted at that time.

In 1956, *Sentry-Go*, news-magazine of the S.A. R.S.L. (Incorporating 'Back') began publication. The Editorial asked 'How do you like it?' and expressed the view that 'Sentry-Go' was a good name for it put the whole meaning of the RSL pledge 'The Price of Liberty is Eternal Vigilance' neatly and compactly The editorial continued:

> The League, too, has its measured beat – the whole province of ex-servicemen's affairs over which it maintains a sentry's constant vigilance ...
>
> Above all our readers do not want their magazine to stagnate, but demand constant improvements and progress.[55]

Although *Sentry-Go's* mission was to avoid stagnation, the replacement of *Back*, a magazine published monthly from 1947 until 1956, with a bi monthly news-magazine indicated the League had already entered a period of reduced activity. Subsequently, the Annual Report and Balance Sheet of the RSSAILA SA Branch, for the year ended 31 December 1960, announced the final issue of *Sentry-Go* in January 1961, because of inadequate support.[56] The League's period of decline had become entrenched.

Mount Barker Soldier's Memorial, South Australia

Aware of the decline in its community standing, League management and administrative decisions adopted different approaches as fund raising began in aid of the ageing veteran community. In January 1963, the League turned its attention to the provision of 'Darby and Joan' Cottages in suburbs and rural areas, for older married couples of the veteran community. Increasing age was changing the accommodation requirements of veterans. The League also expressed concern with what it perceived as an 'image' problem with a younger generation. Acutely aware of the 'image problem', the League organised 'The Girl in a Million Quest' in aid of the Darby and Joan Cottages Scheme.[57] The 1964 Annual Report advised League members of the 'Churchill Doorknock' Appeal, an appeal used to collect funds for travelling fellowships that enabled young Australians to study overseas. The *Advertiser* coverage of 1964 Anzac Day activities announced that the Lord Mayor would crown the S.A. Girl of the Year and announce as the 'Star of the year, the quest entrant who raises the most money.'[58] In 1965, the *Advertiser* described the opening of the Darby and Joan Cottages on the Esplanade at Semaphore and reported:

> The Leader of the Opposition, (Sir Thomas Playford), said yesterday that he could think of no more fitting memorial to servicemen lost at Gallipoli and on other battlefields than the provision of homes for elderly ex-service people.[59]

The following year the Annual Report contained photographs of the Anzac Jubilee, and reported that the South Australian Garden of Remembrance, which provided burial sites for WWII ex-servicemen and women, was taking shape within Centennial Park Cemetery.[60] Previous Premier, Tom Playford, had become Sir Thomas Playford, Leader of the Opposition. The League's political advantage within the echelons of the parliamentary power base had begun to wane, along with natural attrition and the diminishing numbers of the ex-service community.

As discussed in 'The One Day', the 1960s and 1970s brought a sustained period of criticism and apathy from both within and without the League. This period roughly coincided with the development of the Vietnam 'Crisis' and extended into the Vietnam War and the immediate post Vietnam War period, a period when generational change confronted the RSL. We have seen in earlier chapters that the bodies of ex-servicemen and women who had volunteered and served as part of the British Empire remained buried overseas. In 1965, the League opted for the status quo, voting against the return to Australia of the bodies of men killed overseas. However, the families of some Australian soldiers killed during the Vietnam War wanted the men's bodies returned to Australia for burial. In 'The Digger's Grave', published in *Nation* in February 1966, Ken Inglis wrote that public donations enabled families to fly the bodies of some soldiers home. On 21 January 1966, the day after Robert Menzies announced his resignation as Prime Minister, the Liberal Government announced a change in policy. Inglis records the revised policy as '[b]odies of servicemen who were killed or died abroad might now be returned at public expense for burial, if it was practicable and if the next of kin requested it.'[61] The same year, the RSSAILA officially became the Returned Services League of Australia and the South Australian Branch experienced a sudden, marked decline in League membership. The Annual Report noted all who took pride in the vigilant endeavours and public prestige of the branch must be concerned at a fall of 3,600 in membership over the year. Acknowledging the rising death rate of ex-servicemen, the branch recorded the loss of over 800 members annually, but stated potential membership was thousands above the then present membership of 28,000.[62]

In 1981, sixty-two years after the resignation of Mrs Seager as a Vice President of the RSSILA, South Australian Branch, Mrs Ainsworth, a Returned Sister, became a Vice President of the State Board.[63] Ainsworth's appointment heralded a period of renewal in League directional dimensions and introduced subtle changes to the Board's decisions. Mrs Wilma Egnar, a migrant, had restored the 'Digger figure' of the Mt Barker soldiers' memorial, after its damage by vandals. Restoration of the monument suggests a desire on the part of a migrant to be part of Australian and Anzac culture. Subsequently, Mrs Ainsworth used the State Board as a forum to record League appreciation to Mrs Egnar. Further extending the influence of Anzac culture, minutes record an invitation to Mrs Ainsworth to address school children at Nuriootpa. On a different occasion, she, together with another returned sister, Mrs Dodson, went to Hackham Junior Primary School to talk to students about Anzac Day.[64] This provides evidence that returned sisters participated in the education of South Australian children in relation to Anzac Day, a process begun by the League's Education Department Sub-Branch and teachers who were members of the ex-service community.

The period of renewal and revival during the 1980s also saw the culmination of the long delayed identification of Anzac Highway as a 'living memorial'. In 1957, the League had begun negotiations with three local councils and the Highways Department for the erection of a plinth, arch, or some other suitable marker that would signify the memorial status of Anzac Highway. In 1984, the Glenelg Council refused to sanction the design that the League and Arts in Public Places Council favoured, because Glenelg Councillors found that particular design unacceptable, possibly a reaction to anti-war sentiments within the local community. After 30 years of negotiations, in 1988, with interest in Anzac Day increasing within the Australia community, the erection of the symbols designed to identify Anzac Highway took place on the median strip at both Keswick and Morphettville. Glenelg Council took a further 13 years until 4 March 2001, to approve an inclusive memorial dedicated to all military conflicts involving Australian troops and support services, at the Glenelg end of Anzac Highway. General Peter Cosgove unveiled the memorial, situated at the entrance to high-rise buildings on what was once a public car park. The memorial, identified as 'A Chorus of Stones', consisted of a collection of local granite, bluestone boulders and an audio commentary using the voices of South Australians who had served Australia, to outline the symbolism inherent in the 'installation'.[65] The fact that all three local governmental bodies eventually identified Anzac Highway as a memorial proved the League was a persistent lobby group and that it was capable of achieving desirable outcomes not only for the RSL membership, but also for all returned veterans.

Decisions taken by the League that improved its public image resulted in a period of renewal after the decline evidenced during and immediately after the Vietnam War. 'Turning points' also surfaced with League acceptance of the eligibility of various categories of units requesting permission to join the ranks of Diggers and nurses marching on Anzac Day, a dimension considered in detail in the next chapter.

CHAPTER 5

WIDENING THE RANKS

As illustrated in Chapter 1, 'Honouring the Debt', in October 1915, the South Australian Anzac Combined Committee arranged a street procession, and raised funds for wounded soldiers. John Moses, in a 2002 journal article, argued that the Brisbane Anzac Day Commemoration Committee, which organised the national observance of Anzac Day on the anniversary of the Gallipoli Landing in 1916, wanted the 'Day' observed as 'Australia's All Souls' Day'. That year the Returned Soldiers' Association held a memorial parade on Sunday 30 April.[1] In 1917, the South Australian Branch of the Returned Sailors' & Soldiers' Imperial League of Australia, (hereinafter League), obtained permission from the State War Council for a Button Day and procession on 25 April and arranged for the printing of 5,000 copies of hymns for distribution on Sunday 29 April.[2] Subsequently, the State War Council granted the League authority to raise funds for a Building Fund Appeal, through the period of 15 to 30 April 1918. There were three parades in 1918, a procession on Saturday 20 April, a memorial parade on 25 April, and a 'street pageant' on Friday 26 April in connection with the button day appeal for the League's residential club.[3] In 1919, the League applied to the Adelaide City Council for permission to hold a procession of returned men on 'Gallipoli Day' 25 April. The *Register* described the 1920 procession, which took just 5 minutes to pass, as 'poor'.[4] Subsequently in 1921, as Chapter 3, 'The One Day' demonstrated, the League accepted responsibility for the organisation of Anzac Day in South Australia. The League uses Anzac Day to commemorate war dead and to raise funds for the relief of distressed ex-service men and women and their families. Logically, fund raising in aid of those disadvantaged by war is not an activity that glorifies war; it actually highlights the misery caused by war. In 1946, the London and Adelaide victory marches celebrating the end of WWII did not take place on Anzac Day, but on 9 and 10 June respectively. The Adelaide Victory Day pageant did not follow the same route as the line of route on Anzac Day. The pageant, which symbolised the South Australian war effort, began in the South Parklands and dispersed at Victoria Drive, Frome Road and the Parade Ground.[5] Therefore, I would argue that the annual Anzac Day march held in Adelaide is commemorative, not triumphalist: it does not celebrate victory nor glorify war. After the 'Old Diggers' had passed the 'torch' metaphorically to the 'New Diggers', the number of veterans taking part in the Anzac Day march reached its zenith in Adelaide in April 1946, the first Anzac Day march after the end of World War II.

1946–1955

In 1946, before the now traditional annual procession, the State Board appointed a sub-committee responsible for solving problems related to the Anzac Day march. Once the eligibility of units was established, 'Orders of the Day' were compiled giving due regard to official procedural preference. The sub-committee solved the problem of suitable march music when it utilised the services of a company, Nomis Amplifiers, to relay live band music over the line of route, and requested well-known tunes from selected bands. The League provided buses for disabled veterans entitled to take part in the procession but unable to march. Clarence Park Sub-Branch protested against the League decision that confined the eligibility of marchers to those veterans who had been on active service, which meant that men and women who served only in bases were not eligible to march. Subsequently, the League advised them that the conditions were the same as in previous years.[6] However, the *Advertiser* on 25 April 1946 described members of the Australian Women's Army Service, who had 'served overseas or in areas north of Katherine' as eligible to take part in the march.[7] Attempts to deal with problems regarding the provision of music, together with the needs of aged and disabled veterans participating in the Anzac march, occur repeatedly throughout League minute books.

Minute books and 'Orders of the Day' provide evidence that post World War II, the ranks of the Anzac Day procession widened metaphorically. Not only did the Anzac Day march include the recently returned 'New Diggers', from the Second World War, but also persons from varied cultural backgrounds marched in the parade of returned veterans from overseas theatres of war. The *Advertiser* on 26 April 1946 reported:

> The number marching was a record for Anzac Day. Over 19,000 sailors, soldiers, airmen and members of the women's services, representing between 50 and 60 units with overseas service, took part.
>
> Nearly 130 returned sisters and other servicewomen – also a record number – were in the vanguard of the parade.[8]

Along the line of route, a crowd of 170,000 watched the parade as veterans marched along King William, Rundle and Charles Streets. The 'Church

Parade' saluted the State Memorial, and the South African Soldiers Memorial on North Terrace, memorials listing the names of war dead from the Great War and Boer War. The marchers wheeled into King William Road, giving 'eyes right' as they passed the official saluting base at Victoria Drive, then continued to Pennington Gardens. This line of route was the same as pre-war, despite a move to shorten the route in 1936. Significantly, a crowd of 35,000 remained for the concluding memorial service at the Cross of Sacrifice.[9] The number of units that subsequently gained permission to participate in Anzac Day marches grew because of Australian immigration policies.

'Orders of the Day' demonstrate that in 1946 British Imperials, Canadians and New Zealanders marched in Adelaide on Anzac Day. The New Zealand delegation proved so successful that thereafter an interchange of visits took place between Australia and New Zealand each year during April. January 1947 saw the appointment of a committee commissioned to deal with Anzac Day. New Zealanders received preference, listed above British Imperial and Canadian units in Adelaide in the 1947 'Orders of the Day, as reciprocally Australians received preference in New Zealand', a symbolic acknowledgment of the significance of ANZAC.[10] *Back*, magazine of the RSL, advised readers:

> The purpose of the interchange of delegates is to commemorate the spirit of Anzac by having both Australians and New Zealanders in both countries on the day of Anzac observance. Part of the contingent which will come to Australia will stay in Adelaide, and will be entertained by the South Australian branch of the League.[11]

Assuming the British Imperials and Canadians would have observed Remembrance Sunday had they been in their own countries, their willingness to march in an Anzac Day procession implies acceptance of Anzac culture and a desire to participate in a ritual associated with Allied ex-servicemen and women.

Other Allies who had no British connections also applied to join the ranks of ex-servicemen and women marching on Anzac Day. Greek ex-servicemen used the legal services of Messrs Nelligan, Angas, Parsons & Mitchell, for that firm advised the League of the formation of a Greek ex-service association and applied for League incorporation.[12] Subsequently, among the *Advertiser's* photographs illustrating the 1947 Anzac Day march was a Greek Ex-Servicemen in a 'fustanella' or Greek kilt carrying a Greek flag.[13] By 1948, the number of sub-branches defined by nationality had increased, for the State Board approved the formation of a Greek Sub-Branch along the same lines as the British Imperial Service Sub-Branch.[14]

The units of eligible marchers grew as other groups sought permission from the League to take part in Anzac Day processions. The RSL Federal Executive Meeting held on December 1950 decided that returned servicemen from active service in Korea and Malaya were acceptable as members once their Army service ended.[15] In 1951, the League decided to allow the participation of as many Australian Women's Army Service women as eligible and willing to march, but deemed the Citizen Military Forces' (hereinafter CMF), case not feasible.[16] In 1951, the *Advertiser* reported that ex-servicemen from the United Kingdom known as the 'Old Contemptibles' and men from the United States armed forces joined the march.[17] The 'Old Contemptibles' were British regular soldiers from the Great War who fought at Mons and Ypres.[18] The Rats of Tobruk requested the inclusion of a separate unit of the Polish Carpathian Brigade in May 1952. The Anzac Committee subsequently decided that the unit should march with 'Allied Forces'.[19] Despite League vigilance and control over the eligibility of marchers, page 3 of the *Advertiser* 27 April 1953 contained a photograph with the caption 'Mystery Woman of March'. Apparently, a young woman dressed in blue had marched in front of the interstate units. None of the RSL officials knew her identity.[20] As ex-service personnel from both World Wars included persons from other Allied nations and interstate units, it seems understandable that migrants and interstate visitors wishing to become part of South Australian cultural life would seize upon an opportunity to remember their own war dead in overseas burial sites. Anzac rites provided migrants from Allied nations and interstate ex-service men and women with an opportunity to participate in the commemorative rituals of the South Australian Anzac procession and memorial services.

Attempts to deal with problems associated with the participation of Legatees and children within the ranks of Anzac Day marchers occur repeatedly throughout League Minutes. The problems created by the presence of children as march participants demanded attention when complaints surfaced from the Navy that the Legacy Boys at the front of the procession slowed the smooth progression of the march. The League made arrangements designed to overcome the problem by suggesting that older Legacy boys leave early before the main procession. Provision was made for younger boys unable to 'keep the step', to form up near the Saluting Base to form a Guard of Honour for His Excellency the Governor.[21] Further, the League imposed an age limit on legatees participating in the march. The League resolved to curtail the inclusion of children marching with parents and endeavoured to discourage the practice 'in every possible way.'[22] Legacy girls received a mention for the first time in 1954 when the Legacy club requested that the girls march the entire route. November of that year saw a provisional recommendation made for a trial in

1955 for girls able to 'keep up the step'.[23] The problem of Legatees and children participating in the Anzac march remained unsolved.

In addition to units from other nations joining the marching ranks, groups outside the three services that had served in battle zones, and whose contribution helped the war effort, wanted to join the procession. The Air Force Association wrote to the League regarding ex-merchant seamen with overseas service participating in the march, a suggestion the State Board duly submitted to the Anzac Day Committee, (hereinafter AD Committee).[24] A decade after the end of World War II, the 1955 'Orders of the Day' list nine units from other nations marching within the ranks of veterans, a Serbian unit being the latest group of ex-service personnel to join the marching ranks.[25] The following table illustrates the change in extent of other nationals who participated during the decade ended 1955:[26]

Orders of the Day	1946	1955
Old Contemptibles		✓
British Imperials	✓	✓
Canadians	✓	✓
French		✓
American		✓
Greek		✓
Polish		✓
Serbian		✓
New Zealand	✓	✓

In the decade between 1946 and 1955 French, American, Greek, Polish, and Serbian units widened the ranks marching with Australian ex-servicemen and women in Adelaide on Anzac Day.

1956–1961

The period between 1956 and 1961 was a stage of consolidation and review. The League used broadcast media as an educative tool and encouraged publicity of every possible description. *Sentry-Go* advised readers of new ideas for the 1957 Anzac march and explained:

> A special message for children and newcomers to the State will precede the Anzac march this year.
>
> It will be broadcast from National stations and amplified through the public address system along the march route in the city on April 25.[27]

After each Anzac Day, the AD Committee endeavoured to improve march organisation by holding meetings that gave the rank and file an opportunity to express any grievances. At an Anzac Day 'grouch' meeting, in 1957, complaints arose concerning the system of recorded march music. Central Command bandmaster, WO1 Colin Thomas advised the meeting that the music played on Anzac Day 1957 was the 'wrong music' advising that had the music used been:

> 'Take Me Back to Blighty', 'Mademoiselle From Armentiers', 'Roll Out the Barrel', or 'The Quartermaster's Store', it wouldn't have mattered if the tempo had been 101 paces to the minute or 151 … In Charles street, as the World I columns had swung into the street, old wartime marching tunes of this kind had come over the amplifier.
>
> 'These old chaps threw their chests out and sang their heads off', he said, 'and it wouldn't have mattered if the tempo had been 200 paces to the minute.' [28]

Thomas believed tempo mattered less than the provision of familiar old wartime marching tunes. Problems concerned with music continued during the following decade, although the introduction of a new recording of marching music temporarily provided a solution to the problem.

Changes over the line of route caused consternation and controversy at Sub-Branch level and within the AD Committee itself in the lead up to the next Anzac Day march. *Sentry-Go* reported the options as either straight down King William Street, or the retention of the existing route. *Sentry-Go's* editor covered the debate writing that:

> Mr R. Somerville, an early speaker in the debate, opposed the 'straight down King William street' motion because, he said, the 10,000 marchers normally able to pay their respects to the dead as they passed the National War memorial would now be denied this opportunity.[29]

Mr C. Armbruster argued at Sub-Branch Conference that the meaning of Anzac Day was lost in by-passing the memorial. Mr E. Leckie favoured the straight down King William Street option for he believed that those attending the Dawn Service showed more respect than those who half-heartedly observed 'eyes right' at the North Terrace memorial.[30] Mr Armbruster's premise that the meaning of Anzac Day was lost when marchers did not march past the State Memorial was partially correct for some symbolism attached to the significance of the march was indeed lost.

The December 1957 edition of *Sentry-Go* reported on the 'furore' caused in limiting the options to either, straight down King William Street, or the status quo. Messrs R. S. Somerville and T. G. Clark resigned from the Anzac Day Committee believing the Sub-Branch Conference had passed a vote of no confidence in that Committee. According to *Sentry-Go*, Mr Pritchard, the State Secretary, had argued that the route down King William Street was the most fitting or logical route. Further, Pritchard said the Dawn Service was the main Anzac Day service and that marchers could pay sincere and effective respects at the Cross of Sacrifice, a memorial Mr Pritchard incorrectly described as 'the oldest war memorial in the State' for he either forgot, or ignored, the obelisk erected by the Wattle Day League in 1915.[31] With the close of all debate, *Sentry-Go* announced the shortened route, which was straight down King William Street. Saluting points included one at the junction of King William Road and North Terrace, which acknowledged both the Boer and State Memorials and another that recognised His Excellency the Governor at the saluting base. The City of Adelaide Regiment had an extra saluting point at the Town Hall, where it saluted the City of Adelaide Flag. A new music recording standardised all tunes at 110 paces to the minute. The report advised that the most important feature of the 1958 Anzac celebration was the added emphasis that the AD Committee placed on attendance at the Dawn Service, held at the State Memorial.[32] In retrospect, the added emphasis on the Dawn Service at the State Memorial lessened the 'meaningful purpose' of attending the concluding service of the march at the Cross of Sacrifice.

The shorter marching distance not only lightened the burden of the ageing ex-servicemen and women, but also removed a layer of symbolic significance from the Anzac procession. With only implied 'respects' made from the corner of North Terrace and King William Street, rather than an actual salute made to the State Memorial and the names of war dead it contained, the implied 'respects', did not pass on intact to younger generations the commemorative purpose of the Anzac procession. However, in the event, the May edition of *Sentry-Go* reported that the numbers of marchers (11,075) had been the best in five years and that thousands watched the march, adding that few attended the usual post march 'grouch' meeting.[33] It had taken fifteen years from the time the League took over control of the Anzac procession in 1921 for a move to acknowledge the age of Great War Diggers and the need for a shortened route. War, controversy and the desire to conform to the traditional rites of Anzac mourning rituals, stopped any permanent shortening of the route for a further twenty-two years before the AD Committee bowed to the inevitable passage of time. The shortened route lessened the symbolic memorial purpose of the Anzac Day procession, which contributed to subsequent misinterpretation of the imagery of the Anzac Day procession.

A 'turning point' in relation to the Anzac Day procession and use of publication and educational media by the League occurred with the advent of tele-

'Hannaford Cartoon', drawn to represent the steps around the base of the State Memorial on North Terrace, the cartoon read.

> Fifty years on,
> Lest We Forget,
> They Died to Preserve peace
> Vietnam Crisis.[53]

The media reflected anti-war concerns within the community and coupled Anzac Day with the Vietnam crisis. On 29 April 1965, the Menzies Government committed the first Regular Force to Vietnam. That year also saw the formation of the Save our Sons movement.[54]

1966–1972 – Vietnam War – Australian conscripts in Vietnam

During the Vietnam War, Australian television portrayed the anti-war response of various sections of the Australian population. In South Australia, students John Schumann, a future Democrat candidate, Lynn Arnold, a future Labor premier, and Jon Chittleborough, a future museum director, marched against the war. Arnold spent time in Adelaide jail because of his actions as part of the protest movement.[55] Controversies and criticism stirred up by the Vietnam War affected the RSL and veterans to a degree, in the same way community controversy affected soldiers returning from Vietnam. In 1967, the League's Annual Report acknowledged that apathy knocked on the door, from both within and without the RSL.[56] Undoubtedly a fact engendering some apathy was the increasing age of veterans, evidenced by Boer War veterans and WWI sisters now taking part in the annual procession in Army Landrovers, while limbless and disabled members filled a number of buses. The apathy from inside and outside the League resulted from veterans feeling the depreciation of their standing within the Australian community. Literally forced to defend their own beliefs and the symbols upholding those beliefs, the League inhibited its response and attempted to maintain the status quo, yet struggled to combat desecration at memorials.

Changes in crowd control also affected the Anzac march. Thinning lines of spectators, allowed the League and City Council to use honour lines where possible instead of crowd barricades.[57] The old guard changed metaphorically with the resignation of Colonel Waite as Chief Marshal.[58] Alterations to the layout of Victoria Square caused more work for the Assembly Sub Committee in the lead up to the 1967 march. A redesigned Victoria Square necessitated consultation and new assembly plans in co-operation with Police, the City

Council and Metropolitan Tramways Trust. Noting a recurring halt each year at approximately that same site along the route of march, the Despatch Marshal concluded in the 1967 Assembly Sub-Committee report, that the Town Hall saluting point caused problems within the march, for the action of 'eyes right' carried out by the City of Adelaide Regiment caused halts to units following behind them.[59] 'Orders of the Day' in 1967 recorded the entry of Vietnam Veterans into the marching ranks.[60] As we have seen in 'Honouring the Debt', Vietnam Veterans did not receive a euphoric welcome home during the 1960s and 1970s.

The Committee for Vietnam Protest was active on Anzac Day 1968. On 24 April, the *Advertiser* reported that Anti-Vietnam students from the University of Adelaide had been criticised by Mr Eastick, chairman of the Anzac Day Committee and by Professor G. C. Harcourt, Professor of Economics at Adelaide University, the acting chairman of the Campaign for Peace in Vietnam, because the Committee for Vietnam Protest intended to hold 'silent vigils' at the Anzac Day services. According to the *Advertiser*, Harcourt said it was 'rather like spitting in Church', while Eastick described the student's plans as 'hypocrisy'.[61] The *Advertiser* on 26 April reported that the Committee for Vietnam Protest laid a wreath at the State Memorial after the Dawn Service, '[i]n memory of the fallen in the Vietnam War', and noted that the thirty members of the Committee for Vietnam Protest were absent from the remembrance service at the Cross of Sacrifice.[62] It would seem that the actions of the Committee for Vietnam Protest had little impact within League ranks, as the Annual Report did not refer to the protest. Nevertheless, the protests did register with the Vietnam Veterans. In his 1985, honours degree thesis, 'A forgotten Sacrifice: South Australian National Servicemen returning from the Vietnam War', Andrew Rice records that the men he interviewed found Adelaide receptions were less eventful than the Sydney reception where onlookers threw red paint during a 7RAR (Royal Australian Regiment) march, but overall it appeared to them 'that their sacrifice was unrecognised.' The majority of the men Rice interviewed had 'dismissed the protests because "it was a time that's what it was, a time. Protesting was something to do".'[63]

Problems related to the Vietnam War, the Anzac procession and memorials escalated. January 1969 League minutes record that 'considerable publicity' followed when the State Memorial was splashed with pink paint. In April, League Secretary, K. W. Hoffman, reported on the possibility of further demonstrations at the Cross of Sacrifice and State Memorial. Preparing for that eventuality, members of the 2/48th Battalion and Rats of Tobruk Association, which expected more visiting 'Wild Flower Rats of Tobruk' from

WA, made plans to mount a vigil throughout the night until the Dawn Service. The League sought the co-operation of the police in this endeavour and devised plans for a double guard at both the State Memorial and the Cross of Sacrifice from 23 April.[64] Despite co-operation in relation to the memorials, the Police commissioner advised that he did not favour police cadets taking part in the march as disc bearers. The Commissioner felt it preferable for school cadets to carry the discs of any units needing assistance, deeming police uniform inappropriate in the Anzac march. He preferred seeing khaki uniforms rather than police uniforms.[65] In a bid to weather the continued criticism and apathy, in the 1969 Annual Report, the League asked members to 'enlist a mate' in 1970.[66] The League maintained its vigilance and considered the future.

Australian troops began withdrawing from Vietnam on 22 April 1970 when John Gorton was Prime Minister.[67] Despite the controversy stirred up by the Vietnam War, other units applied for participation within the Anzac Day procession. Dunkirk veterans and the Royal Australian Regiment, both applied to the AD Committee seeking permission to march as a unit on Anzac Day 1970.[68] In an endeavour to further shorten the route for WWI veterans, the League sought the opinion of members, this time suggesting North Terrace as an assembly point. Subsequently, the special sub-committee that investigated a shortened route for WWI veterans recommended no change to current march arrangements. However, the sub-committee did suggest shortening the end of the march, rather than the beginning. The following month, the State Board received the information 'unit clubs refused to accept any change at this stage.'[69] It would appear that although the State Board was advocating change to accommodate the increasing age and disability of ex-servicemen and women, membership at grass-roots level was unwilling to compromise or abandon established Anzac Day rituals.

A hiatus occurred in 1971, when the Dawn Service took place on Sunday 25 April, but the official Anzac march on the Monday public holiday did not. The *Advertiser* on 27 April 1971 reported that Mr Phillip Smith made a one-man protest against the abandonment of the march. Smith moved off punctually at 9.45 a.m. 'leading a company of men I left behind'. Smith said 'I felt also it was vital to march because those Moratorium people were meeting at Elder Park. ... Cancelling the march meant they were stronger than the Anzacs'. A Korean War Veteran joined him at Currie Street but they did not reach the Cross of Sacrifice. About eighty supporters of the Vietnam Moratorium Campaign co-ordinating committee rallied in Elder Park against the war and conscription.[70] During the Vietnam War, some anti-war protestors projected an image of the Anzac Day procession, or 'church parade', as a victory march and a glorification of war. As we have seen, the South Australian WWII Victory pageant did not take place on Anzac Day and Mr Smith, 'with his legs heavily bandaged because of war injuries', was remembering the men he 'left behind'.[71] There was also a common perception in Australia that the RSL membership consisted of conservative men from another era. Age may have wearied some of the remaining Diggers, and a number may well have been conservative, but there were others with enough energy and foresight to work for the continued observance of Anzac Day.

However, at that stage, the State Board endorsed the action of State President, Sir Thomas Eastick, who had abandoned the march because of inclement weather.[72] The unfavourable weather also thwarted tactics involving Legacy children. Earlier, Legacy notices posted to war widows sought the widows' co-operation in enabling greater participation of Legacy children in the march.[73] One can attribute the necessity for this approach to either apathy and or criticism, but the chances are the Vietnam War was also a cause. Perhaps, war widows dissuaded their children from marching with the Legacy unit. It is plausible that having already lost husbands, war widows may have endorsed the 'Save Our Sons' movement formed in 1965, as well as the moratorium street protests against Australia's involvement in the Vietnam War. Conceivably Legacy children were themselves members of the radical student movement and therefore unwilling to join the Anzac march.

Anti-war rallies did have an effect on the participation of young people in the Anzac Day march for the following year. The Cadet Brigade advised the availability of less than 100 cadets instead of the usual 400, but was unable to provide an explanation for the reduced number.[74] National press statements relating to a 'Vietnam Day of Tribute' required alteration to suit the South Australian 'special status' situation in 1972, because the RAAF received permission for a contingent of serving air force personnel to take up the position heading the march in recognition of its fiftieth anniversary. Serving army personnel, recently arrived back from South Vietnam, led the 2nd AIF units as a special tribute.[75] In his thesis, Andrew Rice records the feelings of neglect felt by the Vietnam Veterans he interviewed. He also records that '[f]or many years Anzac Day was the only time they felt their sacrifice was even half acknowledged'.[76]

Even though the Whitlam Government recalled the remaining 179 Australian troops from Vietnam and abolished conscription in December 1972, there remained a need for vigilance in relation to Anzac Day.[77] Criticism forced the Federal body of the RSL to consider the future fate of Anzac Day. In South

Australia, age and disability, especially in relation to the condition of WWI marchers pressed the League into endorsing proposed changes to the march after Australian Vietnam Veterans returned to Australia.

1973–1979

Despite dismal weather in 1973, those able to do so completed the march to the Cross of Sacrifice. Unhappily, others found the banner carrying army cadets and the pace of the broadcast music too fast, leaving the Annual Report to lament that 'age and stiffening joints caused dozens to drop out.'[78] In an Appendix to Minutes dated 20 August 1973, the report of an Extra-Ordinary Meeting of National Congress in relation to Anzac Day, expressed the opinion of the National Executive that it very strenuously opposed the exclusion of Anzac Day from the national scene.[79] In an endeavour to maintain the relevance of Anzac Day, the League investigated changes in relation to suitable marching music and considered using live bands but delayed their actual implementation because of an impending royal visit.[80] On the sixtieth anniversary of the Landing, sixty Gallipoli veterans paraded near the approaches to the 'Stone of Remembrance' forming an honour guard for Princess Anne who, together with Captain Mark Phillips, attended the service at the Cross of Sacrifice, before travelling to the Willomurra Quarter Horse stud at Kersbrook. The 'unfortunate condition' of members of the 1/10 Battalion, after marching from Victoria Square in 1975, elicited the comment: 'these members realised they could not march this distance.'[81] Age had indeed wearied WWI veterans. The next day the *Advertiser* reported the closure of the Australian Embassy in Saigon. The League's Annual Report disclosed the highest attendance for the decade.[82] In 1975, the closure of the Australian Embassy in Saigon did not stop the presence of royalty at Anzac Day functions from boosting attendance figures.

Despite problems related to age, music and increased costs, as always, there was some objection to any change in Anzac Day rituals from the participants. Despite financial difficulties, letters received from 10th Battalion Assoc, the 27th SA Scottish Regiment and Partially Blinded Sub-Branches all wanted the 'Anzac Day march retained in its present form.'[83] Other service organisations offered help, but approaches to possible sponsors willing to contribute towards or share expenses proved futile. The Air Force Association was willing to consider some contribution, while the Deputy Premier, Mr Corcoran, an ex-serviceman himself, requested the League make a specific submission for Government consideration. On the other hand, the City of Adelaide expressed concerns against ratepayers bearing any costs for Anzac Day expenses. The League had remarks made by the President published in the daily press, with the specific intention of 'acclimatising' people to the fact that 'sooner or later something would have to happen to the form of the Anzac observance', and placed the matter on the Sub-Branch Conference agenda. Despite examination of the problem, the 1977 Annual Report advised readers that financial assistance was unavailable to the League for Anzac Day. Subsequently, the League resolved to trace the history of the League's original acceptance of Anzac Day expenses. Sub-Branches expressed a willingness to support the appeal for Anzac Day costs.[84] The question of live bands versus the current charge for amplification remained a matter for final decision.

Significantly, notwithstanding all the supposed apathy and criticism, increasing numbers of units applied to participate within the ranks of the Anzac Day march or requested special status. The British Commonwealth Occupation forces and British Ex-Service-Women's Association requested and gained inclusion in the march in 1976 and 1977.[85] The 27th Battalion approached the State Board wanting special consideration for the 1977 Anzac Day in celebration of its centenary. Consequently, the 27th Battalion was in the vanguard of the 1977 procession.[86] The City of Adelaide Squadron gained approval to march as a unit and received the right of freedom of the City of Adelaide. Another organisation that made application for inclusion to march as a unit was the 58th Searchlight Battery. A further request for inclusion came from the SA Women's Ex-Land Army in 1978.[87] SA Ex-Land Army women would not have been on active service; as the RSL relaxed eligibility conditions for participation in the annual procession, more groups applied.

1980–1986

By the 1980s, community attitudes towards Anzac Day had ameliorated, but problems persisted. The British Legion gained approval to march at the rear of the British Imperials, while the surviving 'Dambusters' marched as a 'special group.'[88] Attendance at the Cross of Sacrifice remained a problem: the symbolism of the remembrance service required further reinforcement because Australian culture had become increasingly secular. The RSL Assembly Sub-Committee added a rider to the 1980 'Orders of the Day':

> The Commemorative service at the Cross of Sacrifice is the meaningful purpose associated with the whole March arrangement. An appeal is made for marchers to remain for this service.[89]

The following year, Prince Charles was a 'drawcard' at the Adelaide Dawn Service, when he placed a wreath on the State Memorial before flying to New

South Wales. Attendance at the Dawn Service proved to be the largest for many years.[90]

Despite the report of a good attendance at the Cross of Sacrifice commemoration service, the 1981 Annual Report commented again on the Anzac Day Committee's disappointment that many participants of the march chose not to remain for the service that the Committee viewed as an integral part of the 'Day's' arrangements.[91] The Assembly Sub-Committee report continued to appeal for marchers to remain for the commemorative service at the Cross of Sacrifice.[92] Lack of spirituality in a post-Christian society had eroded the memorial's symbolism.

As we have seen in 'Diggers and Slackers', the scales of gender balance moved ever so gently when Mrs Ainsworth, became a Vice-President of the League's State Board in 1981. One of Ainsworth's first actions was to organise an invitation to a WWI Sister to review the Anzac march from the official Saluting Base.[93] The same year, the *Advertiser*, reported that 200 women attempted to join the Canberra Anzac march in protest against women raped in war.[94] Women's groups in Adelaide attempted to draw attention to women's suffering during war yet seemed unaware that women had erected the Cross of Sacrifice, or that the symbolism of that memorial represented women's sacrifice during war, albeit the loss of loved ones and family members. Anzac Eve 1982, the *Advertiser* reported that members of the International Women's Day Collective together with Women against Rape in War had withdrawn support for a 'women's march'. Anyone who marched would do so illegally.[95] As we have seen in 'Sacred Ground', women had obtained permission from the Adelaide City Council to march on Anzac Day in 1922, and arrived at the Cross of Sacrifice before ex-servicemen and women. In 1982, the women originally scheduled a march from Victoria Square half an hour after the Anzac march commenced. The Adelaide City Council invoked the Public Assemblies Act, which prevented the women marching legally before midday. Apparently, the women's groups were ignorant of the extent and duration of the Anzac march, which did not conclude until after 11 a.m.

Had the women known about wreath laying procedures at the Cross of Sacrifice, they may have achieved one of their aims, which was to place wreaths on the memorials. The *Advertiser* reported that onlookers destroyed the wreath placed on the North Terrace memorial and that Police removed a second wreath placed by the women 'during the service of remembrance at the Cross of Sacrifice'.[96] Archived Orders of Service and the *Advertiser* march bulletins regularly provided information related to the placement of wreaths. The 1940 Order of March provided the information:

> Under no consideration will flowers be permitted to be placed on the Cross until after the Service, other than the official wreaths placed by His Excellency the Governor, the State President of the League, and other official representatives. Those of the public who cannot wait until the placing of the official wreaths may place their tributes in charge of the party of V.S.D's [sic] especially detailed – who will attend to the placing of them after the ceremony.[97]

Likewise, instructions for the 'Anzac Day March Assembly' published in the *Advertiser* 25 April 1981 provided the information under a sub-heading 'Placing of Wreaths' that there would be only one official wreath placed at the Cross of Sacrifice by the Governor. Those wishing to place wreaths on the cross were free to do so after the official party had left.[98] Any member of the public had the right to place wreaths on the memorial after the official ceremony. However, the women's groups did achieve media publicity that drew attention to the object of their protest, which was to remember women raped during war.

Through the medium of film, *Gallipoli* (1981) renewed and stimulated interest in Australian history as Australians realised that *Gallipoli* not only depicted the waste and sacrifice of young Australian lives, it also showed the experiences suffered and endured by some WWI ex-servicemen. The Director of *Gallipoli*, Peter Weir, described himself as feeling 'overwhelmed by an emotion' he could 'only partly understand', after a visit to Anzac Cove. Weir wrote 'It wasn't only pity at the waste of it all but also a sense of discovery – *it did happen, they did die, we do have a past.*'[99] In an introduction to David Williamson's screenplay, Bill Gammage, advisor to *Gallipoli* referred to the extras, who were men from Port Lincoln and Adelaide. Gammage wrote that their curiosity about the film revealed a 'massive ignorance about Gallipoli' and that most had not heard of the Light Horse, Lone Pine or the Nek.[100] Mr Morrissey, a State Board Vice-President, was alert to the possibilities provided by the film industry and expressed the hope that the outcome of the film *Gallipoli* might be of help to Anzac Day.[101]

It would appear *Gallipoli* did help with Anzac Day for more groups sought incorporation within the ranks of marching veterans, filling the gaps left by those units no longer capable of marching. New units appeared on the 'Orders of the Day'; the United Nations Forces plus Regular Army and Reserve Units, while the 50th Battalion Club ceased to exist. The South Australian Yankalilla 3/9 Light Horse Association received permission to participate in the 1982 march, but with the stipulation that permission was for 1982 only.[102] Correspondence received in 1984 put revival firmly on the agenda as multiculturalism permeated through the layers of Australian culture. A letter from the Associazione Nazionale Partigiani Italiani de Liberazione in Australia requested participation in the Anzac Day march. The State Board agreed in principle 'that those members of the Association who were eligible for League membership would be entitled to march.' Evidence submitted by the group proved their membership consisted of Italian ex-servicemen, who had enlisted after the downfall of Mussolini and his government and fought with the Allied Forces. Without giving any reason for the Serbian stance, League minutes record that Serbians were 'upset' because Italian partisans participated in the Anzac march.[103] According to Ralph Churches, who escaped from German imprisonment in Yugoslavia with the help of Slovene partisans in 1944, most WWII Serb ex-service men in Australia marching in the Anzac Day march are ex-Chetniks, Serb guerrillas who wished to restore Serb King Peter II to the throne in Jugoslavia. During WWII, the Chetniks also fought against the partisans. In *Europe* (2000), Norman Davies writes that the Royal Yugoslav Government fled to London and 'Hungarians, Bulgarians and Italians all took chunks of the carcass.'[104] When the League gave Italian ex-servicemen permission to participate in the Anzac march, it stirred tensions between European migrants that related to old nationalistic rivalries, but the Anzac march adapted to change and continued.

Women became more active in League organisational roles and gained a higher profile in the Anzac Day procession. In 1985, Mrs Ainsworth informed the State Board of the organisational skills displayed on Anzac Day by Miss Campbell of the Returned Sisters Sub-Branch. Subsequently, the Board decided to extend an invitation to Miss Campbell to act as a future Anzac Marshal.[105] Showing a greater acceptance of female participation, the State Board agreed to encourage a request from the Girl Guides Association asking for an opportunity for greater involvement at the Cross of Sacrifice. This stance demonstrates the change in League sensibilities regarding gender. Forty years earlier, the League considered that the only young people capable of Anzac Day participation were Legacy boys.[106] League decisions allowed more recognition of ex-servicewomen's contributions to the Anzac Day march.

The year of the State's sesquicentenary, 1986, units from America and Vietnam joined the ranks. The National Guard Band from Texas, which was also celebrating its anniversary, participated in the march, while a contingent of South Vietnamese took part at the rear of Group 9. The League's Annual Report recorded that for the first time in thirty years, 17 live bands, both brass and pipe, situated at intervals among the participating units, accompanied the Anzac Day march in Adelaide.[107] The use of live bands enabled even more community groups to participate in the Anzac procession. In December 1986, the Demobilised Sailors, Soldiers & Airmen's Association advised of their inability to participate in any further Anzac marches. Correspondence received from the Australian Army Training Team Vietnam, requested permission for a place of honour in the 1987 Anzac march in order to mark the Training Team's 25th anniversary.[108]

The anti-war mood had receded. In 1998, Jeff Turner of the *Advertiser* interviewed a number of Vietnam anti-war protestors, among them 'the songwriter' John Schumann, 'the charity chief' Lynn Arnold and director of the National Motor Museum, Birdwood, Jon Chittleborough. Schumann said of the men who fought in Vietnam '[t]hey had only been doing their job'. Lynn Arnold, alleged 'If the circumstances were the same today, I would have an obligation to say my piece.' Jon Chittleborough, believed:

> We were right and we were lucky. I still get choked, looking at the Vietnam vets marching on Anzac Day. The ones who survived were stuffed by the experience. While we were still fighting, I met army officers who believed the government had lied to them. They saw the war as a mistake.[109]

Both Schumann and Chittleborough recognised that akin to the Australian volunteers of previous conflicts, the Vietnam Vets were doing a job, a job that entailed sacrifice and suffering. Anzac Day continues to acknowledge sacrifice and service on behalf of the Australian nation.

There has been a downwards trend in the numbers of marchers participating in Anzac processions during the forty-year period, 1946 to 1986, but, as age and infirmity thinned and levelled ex-service units and caused ex-service men and women to leave the ranks on Anzac Day, new units filled the gap because of changing circumstances within Australia and overseas. Government immigration polices led to an increase in the numbers of multicultural units that participated within the annual Anzac procession. The League also adopted different criteria in relation to marchers' eligibility within procession ranks. The participation of children in the Anzac Day march presented a conundrum. On the surface, it appeared that in the interests of ensuring the continuation of the Anzac Day march the presence of children should be encouraged. On a deeper level, the League understood that to maintain the symbolic significance of a march in remembrance of war dead, the children marching should be confined to those whose ex-service father or mother was dead, or, alternatively, the children of veterans who were unable to march unaided. Pragmatically, after having virtually eliminated the presence of children from the marching ranks, the League increasingly looked to cadets as unit bearers, and the support of scouts and guides at the Cross of Sacrifice memorial service.

The 1960s period of criticism arose from conflicting passions internationally, and more particularly from opinions within the Australian nation associated with the Vietnam War. Nevertheless, Vietnam Veterans, both Australian and Vietnamese, increased the numbers of those marching on Anzac Day. The relatives of Vietnam Veterans joined those watching along the line of route and helped increase attendance figures for the Anzac Day march. Throughout waves of immigration, Asian conflicts and Australian peacekeeping initiatives, the State Board of the League, worked with and through the Anzac Day Committee to maintain the implied symbolic obligation in relation to the 1915 'Debt of Honour'. After the end of the Second World War, the League accepted the responsibility handed on to them by the ex-service men and women of the Great War, to uphold the concept that the main objective of the Anzac Day march was a memorial 'Church Parade', that concluded on the 'Sacred Ground' around the Cross of Sacrifice. The League's vigilance ensured that the Anzac Day march was not representative of a pageant, but portrayed instead an image of the ex-service community as a dimension of Australian national identity.[110] At the same time, as part of the remembrance connection, the League participated in the commemoration of Armistice Day each November until 1945. In November 1946, the League followed the British example and observed Remembrance Sunday, at which time the League used 'Poppy Day' as a fund raising opportunity and further supported the needs of disadvantaged Old and New Diggers and extended the influence of Anzac culture.

CHAPTER 6

HAREFIELD AND THE REMEMBRANCE CONNECTION

The funeral of the Unknown Australian Soldier took place on 11 November 1993 observed as Remembrance Day, a day with empire connotations. Observers at the funeral linked the identity of that Unknown Soldier with Anzac Day, the dominant day in Australia for the commemoration of war dead. In an article written after observing the funeral Ken Inglis wrote 'Remembrance Day has taken on the mood of Anzac Day' and credited John Lahey with interpreting the 'change of mood'.[1] In Australia, Anzac culture absorbed the rites of Armistice Day and Remembrance Day, subsuming the global and empire connotations of remembrance into a celebration of national identity.

The commemoration of war dead is a multicultural practice. As we have seen, in South Australia in 1915 Anzac Day emerged from grass roots concern about honorary debt repayment to the fallen and maimed from the Gallipoli Landing. Since the first anniversary of the Gallipoli landing, Britain also remembers war dead on Anzac Day. Some Australians who answered the Empire call to arms during the Great War have burial sites in Britain. The Union Jack displayed in Adelaide High School's 'War Memorial' foyer has special significance because of the Anzac Cemetery adjacent to the parish church of St Mary the Virgin in Harefield. The history of the Union Jack that once belonged to Harefield Village School highlights the South Australian connection with global remembrance rituals implicit in Anzac Day as described in 'Widening the Ranks', whereby Allied veterans join the Anzac March and commemorate fallen comrades.

The Imperial War Museum, London holds enlistment posters from around the Empire from places such as South Africa, Canada and Australia. The Australian poster reads 'South Australians, Fall in! We want *you* at the front, Come and Help, Enlist at Once'. The poster projects patriotic fervour symbolised by both a Union Jack and a 'bushman' dressed in AIF uniform calling 'coo-ee'.[2] In England an Australian from New South Wales, Mr Charles Billyard-Leake, who together with his wife Letitia resided in Britain, offered his property, Harefield Park to the Australian Ministry of Defence for use as a convalescence hospital to house the inevitable casualties from Gallipoli and the battlefields of Europe during World War I.[3] Some Australians hospitalised at Harefield did not survive their injuries, while others succumbed to influenza.

Sir Francis Newdigate Newdegate, a former Governor of both Tasmania and Western Australia, made provision for the burial of the Australians who died while in the Australian Military hospital at Harefield. Newdegate, a Member of Parliament, donated a parcel of land next to the Harefield church of St Mary's as a cemetery for the burial of Australian war dead.[4] Upon the death of the first Australian soldier, the headmaster of the village school lent that school's Union Jack to drape the coffin of the dead Australian when the funeral cortège carried the soldier from the hospital to the Australian Military cemetery. Thereafter that same Union Jack draped the coffins of the succeeding dead from the 1st Australian Auxiliary Hospital, Harefield.[5] In Britain, the people of Harefield cared and provided for Australian injured and ensured that Australian war dead received appropriate burial services.

Recognising that the symbolism imbued in the Harefield School's Union Jack would resound and strike a chord with grieving Australians, the Village headmaster forged a link that grew with succeeding generations. With the end of the Great War, the headmaster, Mr Earnest F. Jeffery, offered the Union Jack to Lieut.-Colonel C. Yeatman of the Australian Army Medical Corps, the last commanding officer of the 1st Australian Auxiliary Hospital, in exchange for a replacement Union Jack from an Australian school. On his return to Adelaide, Lieut.-Colonel Yeatman gave the flag to the South Australian Schools Patriotic Fund, previously known as the Children's Patriotic Fund, which eventually arranged for an exchange of flags between Harefield and Adelaide High School. The Fund also supplied Harefield School with an Australian flag.[6] The connection between Harefield and Adelaide High School began with an exchange of the British Union Jack.

South Australians received information relating to the Anzac Cemetery at Harefield from Government and League sources. In 1920, a booklet was prepared under instructions from the Australian Minister of State for Defence, Senator G. F. Pearce, which was entitled 'Where the Australians Rest'. A description of Harefield provided the information:

> The 1st Australian Auxiliary Hospital at Harefield, 22 miles north-west from London, stands on high ground, 2 miles from Denham Railway Station. Half-a-mile down the village roadway, nestling in the green valley, is Harefield Cemetery, where 200 Australian soldiers are buried. Noble trees guard the graves. Here there are 48 stone

> and marble scrolls, in memory of Australians. Six are to men who served and suffered on the stern heights of Gallipoli. These uniform stone memorials were erected "as a token of respect" by the dead soldiers' comrades in hospital.[7]

The *Diggers' Gazette*, in 1921, published a letter received from Mrs Venning of Rickmansworth, because it was of interest to 'comrades and relatives'. The letter refuted reports that the Anzac cemetery was overgrown and unsightly. Venning wrote that in contrast to the local Harefield cemetery, which was indeed overgrown and unsightly, the Anzac cemetery was well cared for with mown grass. On Anzac Day, School children decorated every Anzac grave with flowers.[8] The same year Sir Francis Newdegate and Charles Billyard-Leake erected an obelisk with a symbolic Rising Sun carved in bas-relief. The inscription on the memorial read:

To the
Glory of God Who
Giveth us the victory
And in memory of Brave
Australian soldiers
Who after taking
Part in the Great
War now Rest in
Harefield Churchyard[9]

Although the central obelisk thanked God for victory, the memorial was in remembrance of Australian soldiers who had served the Empire, and was the centre of Anzac Day ceremonies.

League minutes recorded during the interwar period disclose the continued link between Adelaide and Harefield. It seems reasonable to suggest that knowledge of the Harefield connection was of benefit to Adelaide High students because in 1936, students from Adelaide High School won medals from the League as prizes in the Anzac Essay competition.[10] Minutes also reveal that Mr W. J. Adey communicated with the South Australian League in 1937, reporting on his visit to Harefield. Adey advised that the lettering of some headstones at Harefield Anzac cemetery needed attention.[11] The League referred the matter on to Federal Headquarters. In 1939, another two Adelaide High School students received medals in the Anzac Essay competition. On that occasion, Mr Greenham, formerly of the Agent-Generals Office in London, addressed the students of Adelaide High informing them of the Anzac ceremonies sponsored in England by Harefield School.[12] The League and Adelaide High School maintained the Empire link with Harefield School and the Anzac cemetery during the period between WWI and WWII.

As a student of Adelaide High School in 1946, Mr William Pearce, Honorary Archivist, attended school assemblies where the school displayed the Harefield Union Jack. Pearce provided evidence that the connection with the British school was maintained, not only on Anzac Day, but with 'pen friend' correspondence between the pupils of the two schools and broadcasts to Australia of the annual ceremony carried out in the Anzac Cemetery at Harefield on Anzac Day.[13] In 1946, the *Advertiser* reported:

> An Anzac Day service of special interest to South Australians, from the Village of Harefield, Middlesex, England was broadcast from Station 5CL at 4.45 a.m. yesterday ... The special service has been held annually since 1922 at the parish church of Harefield, where an Australian General Hospital was situated in the First World War. ... The broadcast commentator said that with the exchange of flags after the 1914–18 war, an exchange of letters began between the children of Harefield school and Adelaide High School.[14]

The bond between the two schools extended to the provision of individual food parcels to all the teachers and children of Harefield School when food rationing existed in Britain during and after the Second World War.[15] Adelaide High School students were not the only group that sent food parcels to Britain after WWII. The RSL in Australia organised a roster of State Branches to provide the Chelsea Pensioner's home with a Christmas cake each December. League minutes record provision of the annual gift for at least three decades.[16]

Australian War Memorial files provide evidence that the link between Australia and the Anzac cemetery in Harefield grew at a federal level. The personal files of Gavin Long held in the Australian War Memorial contain minutes of the Australian Battlefields Memorial Committee recording a proposal by the Rev K. T. Toole-Mackson of Harefield Parish Church, which suggested the establishment of an Australian memorial chapel within St Mary's Church itself. Brigadier Brown, Secretary-General, Imperial War Graves Commission and Secretary & Executive Member of the Australian Battlefields Memorials Committee, supported the suggestion because in addition to the 11 o'clock Anzac Day memorial service, a church memorial service took place in the early morning timed to coincide with 11 o'clock Australian services.[17] In 1950, the *Advertiser* reported:

> In driving snow, 140 children from the Harefield, Middlesex, village school marched half a mile to the Australian war cemetery in the parish churchyard today and placed bunches of gay coloured flowers on the graves of 110 Australian buried there during World War I.

> The Children were carrying out a 29-year-old ceremony.
> Later in the day the Bishop of London (Dr Wand) dedicated a 16th century chapel in this 13th century church to the World War I, Australian soldiers, who were nursed at Harefield Park Hospital.[18]

The Harefield Parish Church honoured the Anzacs by the dedication of the Anzac-Breakspear Chapel.[19] The link between Australia and Harefield extended to New South Wales in 1950 when Mrs Robert Walton of Sydney presented a further Australian flag to the Harefield School in memory of her nephew, Australian test cricketer and Airman, Ross Gregory. According to the *Buckinghamshire Advertiser*, Gregory had received his RAF training at Ruislip and 'was shot down in Burma in 1942'. Flight-Lieut G. T. Dick attended the ceremony as a representative of the Royal Australian Air Force. A number of Australians visiting Britain, together with Major Von Bibra, OBE, agent general for Tasmania also attended the service.[20] The RSL National Executive continued to support the Australian Chapel of Remembrance within Harefield parish church, forwarding a donation to Harefield in 1960. State Branches proportionally contributed to the RSL donation of five hundred pounds.[21] Officials and school children continued to observe the link between Australia, Adelaide and the Anzac cemetery in Harefield after WWII.

Adelaide High is but one of a number of schools, colleges and universities in Australia within which are honour boards listing the names of scholars who left Australia to fight during the Great War and World War II. During 1977, Adelaide High School transferred the honour boards originally in the old Adelaide Girls High School hall in Grote Street, together with important historical artefacts such as the Harefield Union Jack, to the present campus on West Terrace. League State Board minutes of 18 November 1981 recorded the tabling of a letter from Adelaide High School requesting the replacement of the Harefield Union Jack.[22] Despite the adoption of an Australian flag as a national symbol, Adelaide High School wanted to replace the Union Jack previously given to the school in unique circumstances. The South Australian League did not recognise any incongruity in the appeal for a 'Jack' as the Board approved the request in May 1982. The League duly presented a new Union Jack to Adelaide High 'to be hung in a place of honour in the school'.[23]

By 1986, some Harefield villagers had left Britain and maintained the link from Australia. On 26 April 1986 the *Advertiser* reported:

> The unfurling of a crumpled and fading Union Jack in Adelaide yesterday highlighted a little-known link between a small English village and Australian diggers …
> As a mark of respect for the village, a number of its former residents, now living in Australia, were allocated a special place between the guest dais and the saluting base

> on King William Street for the Anzac Day march. Representing the village that befriended ailing Australian servicemen the group gathered at Adelaide High School after the procession to honour the Union Jack and its memories.[24]

Subsequently, the League library and Adelaide High School received video recordings of the Anzac ceremony, which depicted village children placing both flowers and Australian flags among the headstones.[25] Through the auspices of Revd Andrew Gandon, Vicar of Harefield Parish Church, Mr O. P. Q. Whitman of Harefield, provided me with the information that:

> Apart from the Service on Anzac Day, we also hold a 2 minutes silence in the Australian Cemetery at the 11th hour of the 11th month every year. Both these events are regularly attended by Australians.[26]

In both Australia and Britain, educational, religious and civic institutions maintain the Harefield Anzac Day connection.

Anzac Day observances in memory of Australian and New Zealand war dead in the United Kingdom differ from the memorial services held there on Armistice Day. On Armistice Day, the British are not only remembering Empire fallen, but also celebrating a victory, the Armistice signifying Britain and the Allies' triumph on World War I battlefields. The Empire remembrance connection, originally unambiguous, now shrouded by time, lies at the heart of Armistice Day observances. The Australian War memorial, erected to preserve the memory of Australian war dead, opened on Armistice Day 1941.[27] Armistice Day remembered war dead who had fought for the Empire under the Union Jack and recognised that the sacrifice of their lives had ultimately achieved victory.

The first anniversary of the Great War Armistice saw the installation of Armistice Day, which originated because of instructions from King George V to authorities throughout the British Empire. In South Australia, the Chief Secretary's Office, Adelaide, disseminated the King's commands by circular number 570. The King desired the cessation of work for two minutes to enable people to concentrate in reverent silence on those who gave their lives to achieve a 'glorious victory'.[28] The second anniversary of the Armistice provided the stage setting for the funeral service of the Unknown Warrior, buried in Westminster Abbey, the body exhumed from a French battlefield deemed representative of all those warriors of the British Empire whose bodies lay in unnamed graves, unknown burial sites or beneath the sea. In Australia, the Governor-General received a cablegram from the Secretary of State for the Colonies, dated London, 2 November, 1920 stating:

> It has been decided that on Thursday November 11th, being the second anniversary

of armistice, cenotaph in Whitehall shall be unveiled by His Majesty the King and that as part of the ceremony on that day there shall be buried in Westminster Abbey an unknown British warrior whose body shall be taken from amongst those buried in France. Every precaution will be taken to prevent his identity being known. Coffin will be brought to cenotaph where it will be met by the King attended by representatives of the whole Empire. There will be short service at cenotaph consisting of singing of hymn 'Oh God our help in ages past' and the Lord's prayer. This service will be so timed that unveiling of cenotaph takes place at 11 a.m. exactly after which there will be two minutes silence followed by 'Last Post'. Wreaths will then be laid by His Majesty, the Prime Minister, and representatives of the Empire. Funeral procession then will proceed to Abbey where funeral service will take place, body being buried in a grave in the nave of the Abbey. It is proposed just as last year there should be during the two minutes silence complete suspension of all normal business, work and locomotion throughout United Kingdom, that thoughts of all may be concentrated on reverent remembrance of the glorious dead.[29]

The same day, in Paris, the French buried an unknown soldier at the Arc de Triomphe.[30] In his essay 'War and Death, Grief and Mourning in Modern Britain' (1981), David Cannadine wrote that in London it was estimated that by the end of the week one million people had visited the Cenotaph and the graveside in Westminster Abbey, with at least 100,000 wreaths laid either at Whitehall or in the Abbey.[31] In Britain, the bereaved sought solace from grief by performing funeral rites at the symbolic communal headstone of Great War dead, the Cenotaph, and at the burial site of the Unknown Warrior in Westminster Abbey.

The British Unknown warrior buried in Westminster Abbey was seen as a representation of all those who served the Empire and ultimately achieved victory. The official voice of the South Australian League, the *Diggers' Gazette*, reported the Empire stood in silent reverence as a token of humility and then continued:

Whence came this unknown warrior – from the whirl of the Empire's capital, from the snowy lands of the Canadian North, from the illimitable veldts of Africa, from the neighbouring New Zealand plains, or from our own Sunny Land – the world will never know. But that immortal soldier who now rests silent amongst other glorious dead represents those millions of loyal soldiers and citizens of the Empire who sprang to her aid when the Mother Country called them.[32]

On 11 November 1920, South Australians, as part of the British Empire, observed Armistice Day in response to King George V's instructions for reverent remembrance of war dead and an achievement of 'glorious victory'.

During the interwar period in Australia changes made to Armistice Day rituals attempted to maintain and enhance the tradition begun in 1919. In 1927,

Union Jack in Adelaide High School memorial foyer

Memorial to honour the men and women of South Australia who gave their lives in France during both World Wars.
North Terrace, Adelaide

The ANZAC Cemetery Memorial, Harefield, England, and (right) the globe on the village green symbolising the link between Harefield and Australia.

the Prime Minister's Department requested leave for veterans to attend Armistice Day Services.[33] This short period of leave was necessary because State Governments did not legislate for public holiday status on Armistice Day as they had for Anzac Day. With the completion of the South Australian State Memorial on North Terrace in 1931, Armistice Day services shifted from the Adelaide Town Hall to the State Memorial in an endeavour to replicate the United Kingdom service held at the London Cenotaph. During interwar years, three services took place on Armistice Day in Adelaide; an 11 am service, a 3 pm service, and an evening torchlight procession. The League abandoned the evening torchlight procession in 1933.[34] Remembrance observances underwent further adjustments in Adelaide. During 1935, the League eliminated the 3 pm service from Armistice Day proceedings. As early as 1938, the South Australian League defended Armistice Day services held at the State Memorial from criticism, claiming that the intent of the memorial service was not a deliberate, studied humiliation of the German nation.[35] Although the three remembrance services held in Adelaide on Armistice Day ultimately reduced to the memorial service held at the State Memorial, those changes endeavoured to reproduce the service held at the London Cenotaph, a memorial that symbolically represented all Empire war dead from the Great War.

By the end of the 1930s, the RSL no longer imported poppy facsimiles from France, as discussed in 'Honouring the Debt', for the RSL called tenders for Australasian produced poppy facsimiles. The number of poppies sold in the six Australian states and Federal capital rose between 1930 and 1937 from 200,641 to 306,151. Sales of poppies in South Australia rose from 17,088 in 1930 to 48,896 in 1937.[36] From my reading of League minutes, it appears that in South Australia there was less sub-branch support for the Poppy Day Appeal than the Anzac Appeal, because sub-branches had less control over the distribution of the appeal proceeds as Poppy Day sales incurred a royalty, which the State Branch then forwarded to the Federal RSL. State Board minutes record correspondence with the Federal RSL between 1931 and 1934 relating to an alleged liability regarding poppy royalty payments. At the same time, the League Board endeavoured to reduce the price of poppies, together with a proportional reduction of the poppy royalty. In April 1934, minutes record that the League had paid the amount owing to Headquarters for the poppy royalty in full. During May, the League again requested adjustments to a disputed amount of poppy royalty.[37] The League conducted prolonged negotiations with the RSL to clarify the disputed situation in relation to the federal levy placed upon the sale of poppies.

Changes to Armistice Day observances occurred overseas when Britain was again at war with Germany during the Second World War. In Canberra, the observance of Armistice Day took place on Tuesday 11 November 1941 with the opening of the Australian War Memorial by Governor-General Lord Gowrie. The Prime Minister, Mr Curtin, authorised an appeal to the public to co-operate in paying the tribute of two minute's silence at 11 o'clock. The Prime Minister's Department allowed Returned Soldier officers time off to attend Armistice Day ceremonies on Wednesday 11 November 1942.[38] In Britain, King George VI gave instructions that Armistice Day observances should take place locally, with poppy collections on 11 November itself and dedication services on a Sunday. The King nominated Sunday 7 November 1943 and Sunday 5 November 1944 as the days of dedication and remembrance in Britain. However, the *Argus* advised Australians in 1943 and 1944, that Prime Minister John Curtin had decided to adopt the same practice as in previous years.[39] During World War II, Curtin continued the observance of Armistice Day on 11 November in Australia, in spite of instructions from King George VI relegating the observance of Empire war dead to a Sunday.

With the end of the Second World War, Remembrance Sunday officially superseded Armistice Day in both Britain and Australia, an initiative authorised by King George VI. Although Armistice Day 1918 was also essentially a spontaneous victory celebration as the pent up emotions of the Great War years were released with the silencing of the guns, Remembrance Sunday 1945 retained the connotations of remembrance rather than any recognition of victory. As argued in 'Widening the Ranks', the celebration of victory at the end of WWII took place on neither Anzac Day nor Armistice Day, but in June 1946.[40] In *The Silence of Memory*, Adrian Gregory provides the information that 11 November 1945 fell on a Sunday enabling authorities to observe Remembrance Sunday on the actual date of the 1918 Armistice. The remembrance rituals observed on that Sunday in 1945, eased the general populace into an acceptance of Remembrance Sunday in Britain. In Australia, the Prime Minister received procedural advice from His Majesty's Government in the United Kingdom and passed that advice on to Australian Premiers and Commonwealth Departments.

A circular dated 9 Aug 1946 informed Australian Premiers that the Commonwealth Government approved 'of the procedure suggested by His Majesty's Government in the United Kingdom'. The circular advised that 'National remembrance, Thanksgiving and Dedication should in future be concentrated on a Sunday'. Unless either 11 November or 12 November was a Sunday, Remembrance Sunday should be before 11 November and known as 'Remembrance Sunday'. The British Government's proposal included the two minutes' silence at 11 am at the Cenotaph as part of Remembrance Sunday. The circular also advised that before presenting the proposal to 'Dominion Governments' the British Government had consulted interested parties in the United Kingdom, namely Church and British Legion representatives 'with regard to fixing in the future a Day of Remembrance to commemorate those who fell both in the late war and the war of 1914–18.' The interested parties in the United Kingdom had been unable 'to suggest any one day specifically connected with the late war which would be regarded as generally suitable for this purpose'. For this reason and because of the association with 11 November, the consulted parties felt it undesirable 'to propose a change to any other season of the year'.[41] The Australian Government circulated instructions for the observance of Remembrance Sunday in Australia because of decisions made in the United Kingdom by His Majesty's Government after consultation with Church representatives and the British Legion. Despite Curtin's encouragement for the continued observance of Armistice Day during WWII, the Australian Government followed British directives and Australians observed the formal commemorative observance honouring British war dead from both WWI and WWII, on 10 November 1946, as Remembrance Sunday.[42]

In conjunction with the observance of Remembrance Sunday, the RSL in Australia maintained the practice of selling poppy facsimiles to raise money for the Poppy Day Fund and held Poppy Day on Friday 8 November 1946. The League decreed Poppy Day collections covered both 'old' and 'new' diggers. Amounts raised from the sale of poppies provided immediate relief and succour to needy members of the ex-service community, including ex-Imperials and New Zealanders who received equal treatment with Australian ex-servicemen and women. The Poppy Day Fund also disseminated local help to widows. Such help took the form of wood for winter. Urgent and necessitous cases received clothes, and the League in South Australia donated amounts to local charities likely to help ex-service personnel, especially during the Christmas season. As mentioned above, South Australian sales of poppies returned a royalty to the federal RSL. With the passing of time, the League called tenders for the production of locally produced poppies for Armistice Day.[43] By 1947, volunteer workers headed by Mr Cyril Baxter of Henley Beach had produced over half a million poppies in a five-year period.[44] Poppy Day took place on 7 November 1947. State Board Minutes record that the League approved a Poppy Day Trust Deed in 1948, which allowed the inclusion of benefits to personnel of the Merchant Navy, who by virtue of their service, were eligible for membership of the RSL.[45]

The divergence of South Australia's observation of Remembrance Sunday from that of the United Kingdom began in 1950 when the League expressed the desire to revert to the normal practice of observing Armistice Day at the eleventh hour, of the eleventh day, of the eleventh month. Superseding Remembrance Sunday, Remembrance Day celebrations in South Australia returned to the anniversary of the Great War Armistice on 11 November 1950.[46] On 28 November 1950, the State Board received a report concerning Remembrance Day advising that the Premier would ask for League co-operation and request councils and corporations to commemorate Remembrance Day.[47] Subsequently, the League resolved to notify the South Australian Premier, Sir Thomas Playford, that they believed the 11 o'clock Remembrance Day ceremony needed classification as a civic responsibility.[48] The League did not take up responsibility for Remembrance Day as it had for Anzac Day.

In South Australia, by 1951, it was the responsibility of local government to organise the civic observance of Remembrance Day. The National Australian Archives hold evidence that, nationally, Australia had reverted to Remembrance Day observances on 11 November by 1952. League minutes revealed the Premier had made a press statement that 'made it clear that the responsibility of these functions rests with the local government.'[49] In 1952, the Naval Board circulated a memorandum concerning leave to attend Remembrance Day ceremonies, which passed on the following advice received from the Prime Minister's Department:

> I desire to inform you that the Prime Minister has directed that ex-service personnel in the Commonwealth Service, the efficiency of whose work will not be affected or whose absence will not be detrimental to the public interest, shall be allowed time off on the morning of Remembrance Day (Tuesday, 11th November, 1952) for such period as is necessary to attend Remembrance Day Ceremonies, and that, in addition, Commonwealth Officers, other than ex-service personnel, whose services can be spared under the conditions set out above, may also be granted time off to enable them to attend Remembrance Day Ceremonies.
>
> I am to add that the arrangements set out in the preceding paragraph will apply similarly in future years when Remembrance Day (11th November) occurs on a normal working day.
>
> The official Commonwealth Remembrance Day Ceremony will be held at the Australian War Memorial, Canberra, on Tuesday 11th November, 1952 commencing at 10.30 a.m. and terminating shortly before 11.15 a.m.
>
> A period of two minutes silence commencing at 11 a.m. should be observed as far as possible by Commonwealth officers who are required to remain on duty on Remembrance Day.[50]

Remembrance Day in Australia had reverted to the date of the original Armistice Day, 11 November, with the Prime Minister allowing ex-service personnel time off to attend the morning Remembrance Service.

In South Australia, the messages of Anzac Day and Remembrance Day were converging. In October in 1954, *Back* proclaimed the particular message of Remembrance Day was a reminder that 'THERE IS A DEBT WHICH CAN NEVER BE REPAID'. *Back* went on to assert that despite three subsequent Armistice Days – Europe VE, Pacific VJ and Korea, the dates of which the majority could not recall – almost everyone knew the date of the First World War Armistice. To *Back* 'the thing that really matters is THAT WE SHALL SHOW THAT WE HAVE NOT FORGOTTEN THEM'.[51] The reference to 'a debt' in the magazine article echoes the debt of honour associated with the first patriotic button days held in South Australia in 1915 that heralded the emergence of Anzac culture, before the inception of Armistice Day.

The remembrance connection in relation to those killed during times of war extends beyond Britain and the old empire. In South Australia, after World War II, migrants from various national groups contacted either the RSL and its antecedent bodies, or the Adelaide City Council, requesting permission to place wreaths on the State Memorial. In the last chapter, we saw that as cultural groups, 'New Australians' had already become part of Anzac culture and marched in the Anzac Day procession. Cultural groups unable to join the ranks marching on Anzac Day, either because of insufficient numbers to muster the strength of a unit, or because they had not served with Allied forces, sought permission to use the State Memorial for their own memorial services. The Serbian Cultural Club requested approval to lay a wreath on the State Memorial on 28 June 1952, as did the Legation of Philippines on 6 October 1952.[52] Edwardstown Sub-Branch protested against the use of the memorial by Ukrainians for a service commemorating a famine. However, after discussion with the Town Clerk, the State Board received assurances the service was primarily for commemoration, the famine was of secondary concern.[53] Records in the National Archives of Australia reveal the Consul of the Netherlands observed the Netherlands 'National Day of Remembrance in honour of all those who fell in the second world war either in the Armed Forces or the Underground Movement', on Friday 4th May, 1956.[54] However, later that year, the League objected when Hungarians wanted to march to the State Memorial in memory of those killed in 'street riots'.[55] Evidence exists that multicultural groups continued to seek permission to observe rituals in connection with their own national history.

Despite objecting to remembrance services related to Hungarian 'street riots', the League did endeavour to facilitate the participation of migrants in remembrance rituals. League minutes record the State Board's decision to open a Field of Remembrance in association with Remembrance Day.[56] The

1954 Field of Remembrance featured both the cross of sacrifice and the poppy emblem. Although the poppy was an international symbol of remembrance, the League made efforts to explain its significance to 'New Australians'. *Back* reported on the field of white crosses near the State Memorial where members of the public could place a poppy cross as a personal tribute to 'a dear one'.[57] The first edition of *Sentry-Go* in 1956, reported that the RSL Hospital Committee, which was responsible for the organisation of the Field of Remembrance, had decided to make the white 'poppy crosses' a permanent feature of Remembrance Day.[58] In December 1959, *Sentry-Go* reported:

> Attendants of the field reported that many German migrants had asked for crosses to plant in memory of friends or relatives who died on war service.
>
> One German woman, came with her twin four-year-old daughters to plant a cross for her ex-service husband, who died in Australia since the family's arrival here.
>
> Another German migrant said he had been held in a concentration camp in World War II. He, too, planted a cross in memory of departed comrades.
>
> So great was the interest in the field this year that 600 crosses went in within half an hour of Lady George opening it.[59]

The League's decision to develop the 'field' adjacent to the State Memorial further enabled the inclusion of German migrants within Remembrance Day rituals.

In the decade between 1962 and 1972, Australia's involvement in the Vietnam War forced subtle changes to Remembrance Day observances, just as it had affected changes to Anzac Day. In a memo dated 1 April 1966, a report to the Commonwealth Railways suggested alterations to what had become the traditional practice of stopping passenger-carrying trains for the Remembrance Day two-minute silence. Taking note of the date of the memo, may lead one to question the motives behind the memo's initiation, but it is unlikely that the author of the memo, N. F. Buaby, the Chief Traffic Manager of the Commonwealth Railways, Port Augusta, intended it as an April fool's joke! The Chief Traffic Manager compared the 'silence' observed on passenger trains on Remembrance Day and Anzac Day. The same passenger carrying trains did not stop for the silence on Anzac Day as they did on Remembrance Day and therefore the letter called for 'concentrating upon a real recognition of Anzac Day, which is by far the nearer to the hearts and minds of most of the people'.[60] There was no proof in the file to provide any evidence of the claim in relation to Anzac Day, but subsequently, the Commonwealth Railways put arrangements in place for passengers to observe the 'silence' while trains continued moving.[61] The Commonwealth Railways were not the only institution to make changes regarding Remembrance Day. Other institutions joined in the retreat and reduced support for Remembrance Day. The Army abandoned the provision of an honour guard at the North Terrace memorial. In 1970, the Police Department notified the League that in future, the provision of buglers for Remembrance Day observances would result in a charge for such services, plus any travelling time.[62] Although the above changes by the various Commonwealth and State Government institutions do not indicate a complete withdrawal of support for the civic Remembrance Day observance, they do indicate an awareness of anti-Vietnam War protests within the community and a desire to 'sit on the fence' during periods of controversy.

Irrespective of community protest during the Vietnam War and continued anti-war feeling throughout the 1970s, multicultural community groups continued to commemorate war dead. In South Australia, the National Aborigines Day League sought, and subsequently received permission for, a memorial service at the State Memorial in 1961.[63] In 1974, the League showed concern about some multicultural groups' use of the State Memorial for the League forwarded a letter to the Adelaide Town Hall protesting about the intentions of the Cyprian Society, which wanted to conduct a protest march as well as placing a wreath at the memorial.[64] At the State Conference of the Naval Association of Australia in 1975, a motion was carried expressing concern about the many and varied groups obtaining permission from the Adelaide City Council to hold services at the State Memorial. The Council subsequently compiled a schedule, dated 19 September 1975, which listed organisations that conducted services at the memorial during 1973 and 1974.

Services held at National War Memorial, North Terrace

Organisation	*1973*	*1974*
RSL Women Indoor Bowls Assoc	12 March	
Greek Orthodox community	25 March	25 March
Royal Consulate of Greece	25 March	31 March
RSL		25 April
Air Force Association		28 April
Australian American Association		4 May
Baltic Council	17 June	16 June
Czechoslovakian Society		20 August
39's Association	1 September	7 September
Maltese Council	9 September	8 September
Naval Association		4 October
Old Comrade	6 October	
Greek Consul		3 October
RSL	4 November	11 November

19.9.75[65]

An examination of the dates requested for use of the memorial provides evidence that apart from the League's requests for use of the memorial on Anzac Day and Remembrance Day, other groups used the memorial at various times of the year, for their own cultural purposes. Some of the commemorative rites and rituals may form part of the 'cult of the Fallen Soldier', but the Baltic Council used the memorial in June to commemorate the massacres, and mass deportation to Siberian labour camps, of peoples from the Baltic States, perpetrated by the Russian Government in 1941.[66]

Community memory concerning the original reasons for the two distinctive commemorative days of Anzac Day and Remembrance Day appears to have waned after the Vietnam War, for in 1975, the Archbishop of Adelaide sought to discuss the future of Remembrance Day with the South Australian League with a view to consolidating Remembrance and Anzac Day celebrations. With the future of Anzac and Remembrance Days remaining an issue in 1976, the ABC produced an Anzac Requiem at the Adelaide Town Hall in November. The actions of the ABC evidenced some confusion about the significance of each observance, it being more appropriate to have an Anzac Requiem on Anzac Day. The South Australian League sought to encourage participation in commemoration observances by Australian youth by providing free tickets to the ABC Anzac Requiem in November 1976. Meanwhile, at a State Board meeting held later in November, the League decided to ignore the placing of wreaths by protesting students during the Remembrance Day ceremony at the State Memorial, feeling that any protest by the League against student activities would only prolong adverse publicity.[67] Under siege, the League worked to maintain the significance of both Anzac Day and Remembrance Day.

In Adelaide, the League refused some requests for permission to place wreaths on the State Memorial by members of the South Australian community because of political implications, a move that appears consistent with the RSL being non-party political. Enquires made by the League into an incident in 1978 when Czechoslovakians used the memorial for a political anniversary, revealed the City Council had given its approval.[68] The League's Secretary reported his opposition to a request from the IRA to place a wreath on the State Memorial in June 1981, because of its political nature. On 17 August 1981, the League President reported on a 'situation' on 6 August 1981, when the SA Hiroshima Committee had conducted a vigil and 'draped' figures on the memorial. The President had contacted the Lord Mayor, who also expressed displeasure at the vigil. The acting Town Clerk did not grant permission, but the Police received advice not to take any action. Consequently, the State

Board sent a strong letter to the Lord Mayor, which expressed the Board's complete disgust. The bombing of Hiroshima does not have any party-political implications, but the WWII memorial contains the names of some service personnel killed by Japanese forces. The actions of the SA Hiroshima Committee did have a direct impact on South Australians still suffering from the effects of Japanese actions during WWII. League minutes of August 1981 record that the Town Clerk advised Polish veterans that they needed the RSL's agreement for them to place a wreath at their likely protest meeting. Alternatively, the Korean and South East Asian Forces Association sought and gained League approval to place a wreath on the memorial 27 June 1982. Despite different national groups having to seek permission to use the memorial for commemoration services, the Greek community objected to the suggested erection of an 'Ethnic monument' in June 1982, and continued to utilise the State Memorial, suggesting that multicultural groups preferred to utilise that memorial for their own cultural remembrance rituals.[69]

In South Australia, the League sought to continue the observance of both Anzac Day and Remembrance Day with good publicity. Minutes record a decision against any special publicity for Victory Europe or Victory Pacific Day; the State Board decided any promotional publicity should centre on Anzac Day and Remembrance Day. During the same year, the League received a letter from Peter Young, Director of the Australian War Graves, advising that the Remembrance Day Service would continue at the Australian War Memorial.[70] League minutes record a request from the British Legion for an Australian representative at the Legion's Festival of Remembrance in 1986 to honour the 70th Anniversary of the Battle of the Somme. Rather than send an official representative to England, the South Australian Board passed on a request from the National Secretary for any veteran proposing to be in London at the time, who might be willing to attend the UK Festival to represent Australia.[71]

During 1986, the National Office of the RSL looked at the possibility of designating Anzac Day as Australia's national day of remembrance. When passed on to the Prime Minister, the request received the reply that the Commonwealth Government did not have the Constitutional power to declare national days. Each State and Territory would have to make such a change individually. As outlined earlier in chapter 3, 'The One Day', different State Acts control the manner in which each Australian state celebrates Anzac Day. The success of any attempt to designate Anzac Day as Australia's national day of remembrance requires changes made to each individual State and Territory Act governing the observance of Anzac Day. In reality, commemoration services on Anzac Day and Remembrance Day feature common rituals but League minutes disclose that a smaller amount of administrative effort is necessary on the part of the League in the organisation of Remembrance Day, even though the RSL actively promotes the Poppy Day Appeal. A study of relevant orders of service shows that the secular commemoration services held on both Anzac Day and Remembrance Day in Australia, are similar in that 'Last Post', the 'Silence', the 'Ode' and 'Reveille' are common attributes.[72] Although religious and veterans' institutions had suggested the consolidation of Remembrance and Anzac Days, the two days remained as separate commemorative days for the commemoration of war dead.

Supplying evidence of a revival of interest in remembrance services, the Rats of Tobruk and the Greek Association both sought permission to hold a commemorative service at the State Memorial on the same day in 1986. The Greek Association agreed to hold an early service, afterwards removing their wreaths to allow the Rats of Tobruk to hold a second service. Subsequently, the Adelaide City Council requested the State Board to determine that no two services could take place the same day in future, except by mutual timing agreement.[73] As outlined above, because the League was non-party political, it prescribed the parameters of remembrance activities based upon the political intentions of ethnic bodies using memorials erected for the commemoration of Australian war dead, but, apart from the aspect of censorship related to political intent, the League encouraged multicultural participation in remembrance services.

Although veterans and Government institutions observe Anzac Day internationally as part of remembrance rituals related to the commemoration of war dead, Anzac Day has developed an association with Australian national identity. Adelaide High School wanted the Harefield Union Jack replaced in the 1980s, because the 'Jack' was associated with Australian war dead buried in Britain. The request for a replacement flag provides evidence in the form of material history that South Australians wanted to remember Australian lives sacrificed overseas in the preservation of Empire ties and Australian democracy. Australia had progressively weakened formal ties with Britain, and adopted new national symbols in the form of an Australian flag and anthem, but school children in both Harefield and Adelaide remembered the Australianness of the soldiers and nurse buried in Harefield Anzac cemetery. South Australia still maintains a connection on Anzac Day with the burial sites of Australians and New Zealanders buried in Britain suggesting that successive Australian Governments have wanted to underline Australia's and New Zealand's participation in two world wars by continuing rituals begun in

1916 that commemorate the Gallipoli Landing, even though that military operation ended in defeat.

In South Australia, the League endorsed the use of the State Memorial by multicultural groups for remembrance ceremonies, provided the reason for the ceremonies was not of an overt political nature. The League also encouraged migrant participation in the Field of Remembrance, which began in 1954 in conjunction with Remembrance Day. Despite community protest during the Vietnam War, multicultural groups continued to apply to the Adelaide City Council for permission to use the State Memorial. The continued desire of various multicultural groups to use the official South Australian memorial suggests that although community concern over Federal Government, Vietnam War, conscription polices reduced numbers at Remembrance Day ceremonies, migrants still wished to remember the dead from European wars. The French community in South Australia still hold commemorative services at the State Memorial on Bastille Day and join Remembrance Day services. League and Adelaide City Council approval given to multicultural groups for use of the State Memorial suggests acceptance on the part of both the League and Council that various multicultural groups form part of the Australian community.

CHAPTER 7

GOD SAVE AUSTRALIA

From the beginnings of commemorative services, especially on Anzac Day and Armistice Day, singing the national anthem, 'God Save the King', was a patriotic gesture of loyalty to King and Empire that at the same time called upon a primarily Christian God to bless the endeavours, and maintain the safety of Australian men and women fighting overseas.[1] Originally Anzac Day commemoration services followed Judeo-Christian funereal rituals practised not only within Australia and New Zealand, but overseas in Europe, particularly Britain, Belgium and France, as well as in Canada and the United States of America. The spiritual beginnings of Anzac Day emerged from the special services held in churches throughout Australia and in South Australia at the South African Soldiers' Memorial. In July 1915, women organised Violet Day as a patriotic commemorative service based upon the rites of the Christian and Jewish religions. The Violet Day commemoration service took place around the purple and white draped soldiers' memorial decorated with large wreaths of fern and violets. The Military Commandant thought the Violet Day service premature, believing that a better policy lay in the deferral of any such memorial service. That service, consisted of hymn singing, as well as the national anthem, 'God Save the King', at both the beginning and end of the service, together with the symbolic bugle call of 'Last Post'. The funereal tone of the gathering, which numbered many thousands, was set by the Police Band playing the 'Dead March' from *Saul*, continuing with 'Lead, Kindly Light' and 'Strike hard, and strike again'.[2]

The following year, the Brisbane Anzac Day Commemoration Committee attempted to influence first anniversary celebrations of Anzac Day throughout the Australian States.[3] Item (2) of the published 'fuller statement' asked '[t]hat all the religious bodies be requested to observe the day by such religious services as each such body shall decide'. Subsequently, in South Australia the *Advertiser* 'Religious Notices' for 25 April 1916 referred to services at St Peter's Cathedral, the Methodist Church Parkside and a United Commemoration Service at the Adelaide Town Hall. Services at St Peter's Cathedral offered Holy Communion during the morning of 25 April, with Rev G. H. Jose, MA,

Deputy Senior Chaplain AMF, preaching at the evening service, which a detachment of the Military Forces attended. The advertisement specifically stated 'No cards have been issued for this service, THE SEATS ARE FREE', providing the information that the South Australian Soldiers' Fund was the beneficiary of the collection. Subsequently, the Anzac Souvenir issued under the authority of the Premier (Hon Crawford Vaughan, MP), reported the complete occupation of the seating accommodation.[4] The Council of Churches arranged a United Commemoration Service at the Adelaide Town Hall, with reserved seats available for returned soldiers and the relatives of the fallen, naming Chaplain Colonel McPhee as preacher. Patriotic funds received monies left after expenses. Pirie Street and Parkside Methodist churches advertised evening services, Pirie Street's collection in aid of wounded soldiers. Pirie Street church provided a programme of suitable Requiem music that included Handel's 'Dead March' from *Saul* and Chopin's 'Funeral March', together with the anthem 'What are These'.[5]

Later in the week, on Sunday 30 April, the League's antecedent organisation, the Returned Soldiers' Association, organised a civic service, a memorial parade on the Parade Ground, King William Road, inviting relatives of fallen comrades to the service.[6] The *Register* reported that every detail of the ceremony inspired a hallowed and lasting memory of Australian feats at Gallipoli, and the price that individual Australians paid for their bravery. During the service of memorial and intercessions, a crowd consisting of soldiers, returned soldiers and civilians, prayed for 'courage and victory to us and our Allies'. They asked for protection for those in danger, help for the wounded, recovery for the sick, and rest and peace for the dying, with comfort for the mourners. The prayer finished with '[a]nd in Thine own good time grant us all abiding peace. For Jesus Christ's sake. Amen'. After Chaplain Capt G. H. Jose, MA, read the lesson from Hebrews XI, 34, Chaplain Colonel J. C. McPhee gave the sermon, advising his audience that '[n]ot one of their heroic dead had fallen in vain'.[7]

Australian 'Diggers' marched in London in 1919, the first Anzac Day after the end of hostilities. Later Sir George Pearce wrote in the *Advertiser* that English authorities did not see eye to eye with this observance at first, believing that Australians should be content to take part in the Victory march. But Australian Prime Minister 'Billy' Hughes insisted on the observance of Anzac Day in London. Pearce found Hughes's insistence on the observance of Anzac Day a more appropriate recognition of Australian war service, than an Empire victory march.[8] In Australia, members of the Methodist Church praised God for the blessings of peace. A resolution recorded in a Methodist Church Minute book of the Alberton Circuit in 1919 expressed to Almighty God the meeting's sincere gratitude for the signing of peace and the successful termination of the war.[9]

With ex-servicemen and women back in Australia, attention shifted to 'honouring the debt' previously acknowledged as owed to veterans. One means of repayment was to raise funds for the AIF Cemetery Committee, for the care of soldiers' graves at Light Oval Cemetery, West Terrace, Adelaide. To further this aim, the League held memorial services on Anzac Sunday, supplementing the 'collections' on 'Memorial Sunday' from various church donations throughout South Australia. The *Diggers' Gazette* of March 1921 advised its readers of the decision to hold a memorial service at Elder Park on Anzac Sunday in connection with the appeal for £5,000 needed for the maintenance of soldiers' graves at Light Oval Cemetery. The magazine further advised that the League would approach various Church Councils with a request to reserve the proceeds of one collection on Memorial Sunday for the appeal.[10] At the RSL Anzac service held at Elder Park on 24 April 1922, with an attendance of approximately 5,000 people, the service included an additional tribute in memory of 'departed heroes'. The exploits of the aviator Sir Ross Smith, an ex-serviceman, received special attention following Smith's death in 'another great flying adventure'. The *Advertiser* reported that Smith's Great War comrades dressed in uniforms 'had the second button of their tunics draped in black', while others dressed in civilian clothes had 'a piece of black ribbon at the back of their badges'. The *Advertiser* also remarked on the sincerity shown by both members of the clergy and the public and the memorial service.[11]

Christianity remained central to the cause of national social service, as advocated by clergymen who linked religious rituals with patriotism at religious and civic services commemorating war dead on Anzac Day. At St Peter's Anglican Cathedral in Adelaide in 1922, a huge congregation attended the Anzac landing anniversary service in the evening. Prayers followed hymn singing and a 'confession of faith', the service concluding when the congregation stood and sang 'God Save the King'. The sermon, preached by the warden of St Barnabas College, the Rev John Forster, BA, acknowledged 'the great deeds of the untried Australian soldiers at the landing'. To Forster, Anzac Day made his congregation proud and 'Everyone who loved Australia realised what it meant'. A civic or quasi-religious service took place at Wattle Grove under the auspices of the patriotic Wattle Day League and Australian Natives Association. The congregation at Wattle Grove in 1922 consisted of a large number of parents, together with friends.[12] Meanwhile, at the Synagogue, spiritual leaders of the Jewish faith recognised the symbolic significance of Anzac Day within the Australian community, joining in the desire to commemorate war dead by conducting memorial services for those of their congregation who had joined the AIF and remained overseas in Imperial war graves. Rabbi I. A. Bernstein read the Memorial Service for the dead, especially for the young men of his congregation who had paid the 'supreme sacrifice'. Stressing the importance of Anzac Day, Bernstein, urged members of the Jewish faith to show sympathy by attending public services, one of which was the unveiling ceremony for the Women's Memorial.[13] With the completion of the Women's Memorial erected with the specific intentions of providing a space within which the bereaved of all religious persuasions could mourn 'the men who fell in the Great War', this venue for memorial services underwent a transition. The League undertook responsibility for civic non-denominational services held at the conclusion of the annual Anzac Day procession.

At the League's Ninth State Council Meeting, the first meeting held at the new Club premises in Angas Street in September 1922, the Council confirmed the action of the Rev T. P. Wood, who had obtained the support of the Anglican Synod regarding Anzac Day observances. The Council further resolved that Wood endeavour to bring the celebration of the 'Day' before the Conferences of different South Australian Christian denominations.[14] Church Services took place during Anzac week: clergymen of the Christian faith, of both Roman Catholic and Protestant denominations, recognised the significance of Anzac Day within the Australian community. St Peter's Cathedral held Anzac landing anniversary services, whereas at St Francis Xavier's Cathedral requiem mass was conducted. In Adelaide suburban areas, services took place at suburbs such as Unley, Hindmarsh and Brighton. The League sought the help of all religious bodies by asking for donations of freewill offerings during Memorial Sunday.

Following the tradition of the Combined Church Service held at the Town Hall on the first anniversary of the landing, Protestant Churches held joint, as well as separate services. A united Anzac memorial service took place at the Baptist Church, Flinders Street, in 1923, representing Baptist, Congregational and Presbyterian denominations. Rev F. G. Benskin, linked sacrifice on overseas battlefields to Christ's death on the cross at Calvary.[15] In 1926, during the absence of the Rabbi Hirsh in Melbourne, the President of the Hebrew Congregation, Mr W. J. Solomon, acknowledged those of the Adelaide Jewish congregation who had paid the ultimate price. At the Synagogue during the Saturday morning service, Solomon offered special memorial prayers in connection with Anzac Day. Notwithstanding that the Jewish community numbered barely 600 in South Australia, the honour roll listed no fewer than 72 Jewish names, representing both soldiers and nurses who served with the AIF:

Talbot House Chapel, Toc H, Poperinge, Belgium

Headstone, the Unknown Australian Soldier,
Adelaide Cemetery, Villers-Bretonneux, France

eight of those listed paid the supreme sacrifice.[16] At Wattle Grove, the group of Soldiers' Mothers referred to variously as a 'Band', or 'Association', met at a service where the Rev E. A. Davies praised women for the sacrifice of their menfolk.[17] At St Andrew's Presbyterian Church, Unley the same year, the Rev W. Floyd Shannon, explained the Defence Department of the Commonwealth requested the annual Anzac memorial service. To Shannon 'Christ was the only remedy for the ills of humanity'.[18] The Commonwealth used Anzac Services to promote a core culture imbibed with sacrifice and patriotism.

With the beginning of the commemorative civic Dawn Service at Unley in 1931, early morning focus shifted to the suburbs with that service soon extending to the then outer suburban areas of Rosewater, Semaphore, Brighton and Burnside. Country areas followed suit. The *Advertiser* reported that 'mystically at dawn', more than 1,000 people attended the picturesque service held at the 'Garden of Honour', Unley, advising readers that as the first rays of the sun climbed over the hills, a more inspiring sight could not be imagined, than that of hundreds of people standing with bowed heads.[19] Either the mystique of the picturesque outdoor service, or the symbolism of commemoration services emulating the conditions of the first landings at dawn on 25 April 1915, appealed to a wide section of the community, for Dawn Services extended throughout the South Australian community. After the dedication of the National War Memorial (hereinafter State Memorial) on North Terrace in 1931, the League received correspondence from the Secretary of the 10th Battalion AIF Club and Goodwood and SW Districts Sub-Branch, suggesting the organisation of a Dawn Service at the State Memorial, a suggestion passed on to the League's Anzac Day Commemoration Committee.[20]

Overseas, memorial services conducted on the anniversary of Anzac Day, took place in various towns and cities of Britain and Europe, Anzac Day being but one facet of the 'cult of the Fallen Soldier'. Commemoration rituals occurred in London, in Belfast and at the Arc de Triomphe in Paris. Following the London Anzac Day service in 1935, Mr Abe Shannon of Eudunda, placed a wreath of Australian flowers on the Cenotaph, on behalf of the 10th Battalion in Adelaide. The flowers survived the journey from Australia to Britain packed in ice.[21] Broadcasting Dawn Services put Anzac Day commemoration services within reach of greater numbers of Australians. The *Advertiser* radio stations 5AD Adelaide and 5PI Crystal Brook, broadcast the 6 a.m. Dawn Service from the flood-lit memorial arch at the Unley Soldiers' Memorial Gardens of Honour in 1935. Over 1,000 people heard the St Augustine's Church of England choir singing 'O Valiant Hearts', accompanied by the

Salvation Army Band. Meanwhile, two or three hundred people attended the Dawn Service at the State Memorial.[22] The next year, 1936, Dawn Services took place at the Rosewater memorial and at Semaphore. In 1936, Toc H, a movement begun in Belgium by the Australian born Rev Philip 'Tubby' Clayton, held morning services at the Adelaide Cross of Sacrifice on Anzac Day. Toc H, which believes in breaking down barriers and the practical expression of Christian ideals, provided refuge and comforts for men going to and from battlefield front lines overseas.[23] By 1937, the *Advertiser* advised the Dawn Service at the State Memorial was 'the central service of the State', but that similar services took place 'throughout the suburbs and country districts'.[24] The popularity of the Dawn Service was becoming entrenched.

Towards the end of the interwar period, sermons linked national defence with Christian duty and called for moral rearmament. Making a plea for spiritual revival in a 1939 manifesto, a representative group of Adelaide citizens called for 'Moral Rearmament' on Anzac Day. The Rev Principal Kiek of Parkin College provided the *Advertiser* with an accompanying article to the manifesto. Kiek wrote that the manifesto's importance grew when one considered that the signatories were 'laymen of reputation and influence'. The signatories included men of almost every occupation, many holding differing religious and political views. 'Christian laymen' believed in 'moral rearmament' linked to the spiritualism of Anzac Day services.[25]

In 1939, as on the first anniversary, St Peter's Cathedral marked Anzac Day with two special services. The Rev A. E. Kain celebrated Holy Communion at 7 a.m. while at 10 a.m. the Rev Norman Crawford celebrated a requiem Eucharist. With Rev H. P. Finnis at the organ, the Cathedral Choir sang music by Dr Basil Harwood.[26] Members of the League and Members of Parliament attended Requiem Mass at Adelaide's St Francis Xavier's Roman Catholic Cathedral on Anzac Days, which combined religious rites with civic rituals at the completion of the service. The Premier, Mr Playford, participated in the Requiem Mass at St Francis Xavier's Cathedral before marching with his old comrades and placing a wreath on the Cross of Sacrifice on behalf of the Government.[27] Under the direction of Mr Harold Wylde, the organist, the Cathedral Choir sang Sir Richard Terry's Requiem Mass. Wylde played 'Dead March' from Handel's oratorio *Saul* and Corporal-Bugler K. Look of the 27th Battalion sounded 'Last Post'. Taking the text 'I am the resurrection and the Life' from St John 11.25, the preacher, the Rev Father J. P. O'Doherty, paid particular tribute to the dead lying in alien shores, dead whose souls were with God, and whose memory lived with their loved ones. O'Doherty publicly recognised the failure by politicians and financiers to repay the 'Debt of

Honour' still owed veterans and their dependants, but in doing so looked to a younger generation of militia to uphold 'Anzac' ideals and traditions.[28]

The League held a significant memorial service after the Dawn Service at the State Memorial, North Terrace, designed to provide a tangible link between the missing in overseas battlefields with mourners in South Australia. The focus of the service was a memorial tree from Villers-Bretonneux, France. Before organising the memorial service, the State Secretary of the League conferred with the City Gardener regarding the most suitable spot for replanting of the tree in Adelaide, choosing the State Memorial from three possible sites, the other two being the Cross of Sacrifice and the AIF cemetery. Quarantine authorities gave permission for the use of French soil when replanting the memorial tree, soil taken from the spot where the King and Queen of England met the President of France the year before.[29] At that time, King George VI had unveiled a memorial at Villers-Bretonneux. The memorial, a 'Battle Exploit Memorial', is the Australian National War Memorial for the missing in France, being part of a chain of 'UK and Dominion Memorials' extending from Nieuport in the north to La Ferte-Sous-Jouarre, east of Paris. Sir Edwin Lutyens, designer of the Adelaide cenotaph, designed the entrance to, and the memorial at Villers-Bretonneux cemetery.[30] At the unveiling of the gum tree from France, replanted in the gardens near war grave crosses at the rear of the memorial, the French wife of an Australia soldier placed a wreath of flowers in the French tri-colour. Rev A. L. Bulbeck addressed the gathering after hymns and a prayer for the fallen. Bulbeck drew attention to the significance of the student's figure in the North Terrace memorial, pointing out that the figure commemorated youth. 'Youth, he said, must carry on work left unfinished'.[31]

Civic and religious services held during the period of the Second World War ensured the dissemination of Anzac culture locally, nationally and overseas. In the early months of 1940, the League focussed attention on the Sunday memorial service and the desirability of revising the service format, asking Rev Perry for recommendations to pass onto a meeting of representative clergymen.[32] The popularity of the civic memorial Dawn Service grew exponentially throughout South Australia as representatives of City Councils and RSL Sub-Branches appointed representatives to lay wreaths on Anzac Day at local memorial sites. Suburban Dawn Services, described in 1940 as 'customary,' took place at Unley, Norwood, Kensington, Brighton, Edwardstown and Woodville. Listing services in the Port District separately, the *Advertiser* reported several hundred people attended the service at the memorial at the end of the Semaphore jetty. Naval ratings and civilians attended a service at Birkenhead Reserve, where Councillor G. M. Mackay placed a wreath on behalf of the Port Adelaide Council and the President of the Semaphore and Port Adelaide RSL Sub-Branch. Marching from their clubrooms on Grand Junction Road, Rosewater, members of the Alberton and Rosewater Sub-Branch of the RSL, followed the Salvation Army band to the memorial situated in Rosewater reserve. Adjutant Smedley, of the Salvation Army conducted the service with Councillors H. Martin and T. Symonds in attendance on behalf of the Port Adelaide Council. Suburban Dawn Services enjoyed local 'grass roots' sub-branch support.[33]

The Second World War gave a younger generation of Australian servicemen an opportunity to pay respect at burial sites out of reach of the average Australian. With serving men of the Second AIF overseas, troops attended remembrance dawn services at the Jerusalem and Gaza war cemeteries, in memory of the fallen of the First AIF who had served in those cities twenty-five years earlier. At Beersheba War Cemetery, a morning service remembered the many Light Horsemen buried there, while two hundred and fifty members of the Second AIF, together with a band, marched through Tel Aviv to the memorial pillar at Hayarkon River.[34] Back home in Australia, the exploits of earlier generations of Australian soldiers provided an exemplary example of the 'Anzac spirit' for a younger generation of combatants during 1941. Reporting St Francis Xavier's Cathedral as 'thronged' for Solemn Requiem Mass, the *Advertiser* noted Roman Catholic returned soldiers paraded in charge of Captain O. Pratt, together with Army nurses, Girl Guides, Boy Scouts, VADs and VSDs. The Governor and Commonwealth Government sent representatives, while 'the Premier (Mr Playford), the Speaker of the House of Assembly (Sir Robert Nicholl), the Lord Mayor and Lady Mayoress (Mr and Mrs Barrett)' attended with Mr Justice Richards.[35]

Customary services held at dawn becoming the norm, some veterans choosing to attend earlier services 'fell out,' from the morning Anzac Day procession, rather than attend a further civic service at the Cross of Sacrifice. Notwithstanding the absence of some ex-service personnel, larger crowds attended the service at that venue during the war. Troops leaving the procession before reaching the Cross of Sacrifice presented problems to the State Board of the League in 1941. The board also addressed the question of providing suitable assembly space for ex-servicemen and women nearer to the memorial.[36] The *Advertiser* in 1941, reporting on the annual service during the war reported that the crowd attending the Cross of Sacrifice remembrance service was bigger and more reverent than in previous years.[37] Australians turned more overtly to religious spiritualism in times of crisis.[38]

Representative of all Australian States, the official opening of the Australian

War Memorial, took place in Canberra on 11 November 1941. Lest anyone doubt that the memorial honoured the 'Anzac tradition,' that aspect of Australia's legends featured in an opening speech. The Right Honourable Lord Gowrie, Governor-General and the Honourable Prime Minister John Curtin gave addresses to the assembled gathering. His Excellency the Governor-General prophesied that, with peace, many citizens would visit the Shrine from time to time. Some to revive memories of lost loved ones, others to conjure visions of 'a happier and saner world,' but all would declare 'never again, never again'.[39] Although officially 11 November 1941 was Armistice Day, to Curtin as Australian Prime Minister the symbolic War Memorial signified Anzac.[40]

In Adelaide, the League resolved to cancel the central Dawn Service in 1942, deciding instead to send representatives to dawn ceremonies arranged by sub-branches, but only on the assurance that any such ceremonies did not clash with the national effort.[41] Undaunted by League decisions, Toc H arranged a Dawn Service at the Cross of Sacrifice, at which Toc H Area Commissioner, Mr J. H. Burgess lit the Toc H Lamp while others placed wreaths and bunches of flowers, as well as a 'huge red double cross' at the foot of the cross. The organisation that originated in Belgium, continued working at grass roots levels within the South Australian community.[42] America having entered hostilities after the bombing of Pearl Harbour in December 1941, visiting troops, together with the Chief of the United States Army and Major-General Allen received invitations to the Sunday Service held in 1942.[43]

The Catholic Archbishop of Adelaide, (Most Rev Dr M. Beovich) presided over solemn Requiem Mass in 1942. In attendance was a congregation of troops home from abroad, returned soldiers from the Great War and uniformed civilians; nurses and women of the auxiliary services, and uniformed children from patriotic guide and scout groups. In preaching the sermon, the Rev Father W. Cantwell, 2nd AIF chaplain coupled the Anzac spirit with the need for 'prayer to God to remove the scourge of war and bring peace to the earth'.[44] Faith and Christian assurance linked to the original 'Anzacs' provided a sermon topic at St Peter's Cathedral in 1942. Taking as his subject 'God' and those 'gone before,' when conducting the Requiem Eucharist, the celebrant and preacher, Bishop of Adelaide (Right Rev B. P. Robin) took the sermon text from St Paul's second letter to the Corinthians, chapter 5, verse l:

> For we know that if our earthly house of *this* tabernacle were dissolved, we have a building of God, an house not made with hands, eternal in the heavens.[45]

According to the *Advertiser*, Robin preached about faith and 'a home not of earth'.[46] The promise of a home not of this earth no doubt bought solace to those whose loved ones lay under the sea, and under the foreign soil of overseas burial sites. God and the nation became part of the rhetoric at civic memorial services during the Second World War, with the original 'Anzacs' used as an example of bravery and sacrifice in the service of the nation.

Anzac Day 1943 fell on Easter Sunday. The RSL debated the merits of holding Anzac services on Easter day, with the Primate of the Anglican Church and the Apostolic Delegate, eventually coming to the decision Anzac Day would be held on Sunday 25th April. The RSL left the State Branches to make their own arrangements regarding Anzac Day observances. Abandoning all AIF unit reunions and cancelling the March, the League held a 3 p.m. commemoration service at the Cross of Sacrifice. Rev H. G. Hackworthy gave the address, after which the SA Caledonia Pipe Band played 'Scottish Lament'.[47] The *Advertiser* reported that in delivering the address Hackworthy preached:

> Anzacs, Tobruk Rats, and their fellows do not belong to differing generations; they are of the immortals ... From Gaba Tepe to Fisherman's Hut each grain of sand in Anzac Cove is sacred ... Anzac lives in the glorious deeds of those who are of the new generation of Australia. They call to us from the battle fronts of the world, not to an act of empty memory, but to a life of dedication and devotion to the ideals for which they count the world well lost.[48]

Memorial services took place in most suburbs, with large afternoon gatherings in connection with RSL Sub-Branches. The confluence of Easter Sunday and Anzac Day underlined the nexus between Christian service and self-sacrifice for the benefit of the nation.

As mentioned above, Easter Sunday and Anzac Day occurred on one and the same day in 1943 although not synonymous in intent, the first being a celebration of Christ's resurrection and the second having a component that commemorated war dead and the survival of returned veterans. Nevertheless, the State Board nominated League representatives to attend Adelaide Cathedral and suburban church services on Anzac Day. The State Secretary, Mr F. E. Reynolds, and Mrs Reynolds, attended North Adelaide Baptist Church. Requesting that representatives go to a service at Maughan Church on 25 April, the League promulgated the church's invitation to all Metropolitan Sub-Branches.[49] A Scripture lesson read in Greek by a Minister of the Greek Orthodox Church (Dr C. Palsovannis), followed by an English translation was a highlight of the Maughan Church evening Anzac Day service. Although organising a civic service on Anzac Day, the League made every endeavour to organise for its representation at Christian denominational services on Easter Sunday.[50]

Victory was the subject of 1945 services, and although complete victory remained an aspiration, global plans were a topic of discussion in America. Padre A. L. Bulbeck conducted the service at the Cross of Sacrifice that prayed for God's blessing on the San Francisco Conference, a Conference on International Organization, convened by the United Nations.[51] Bulbeck continued with a prayer of remembrance for those who paid the supreme sacrifice and their relatives, for servicemen and prisoners-of-war everywhere, not forgetting to acknowledge the 'measure of victory achieved in the present war'.[52] After the Dawn Service at the North Terrace State Memorial in 1945, the *Advertiser* reported on a number of significant wreaths laid at the base of the memorial. One of the wreaths remembered those who died in the Boxer Rebellion, while ex-AIF veteran, Gordon Rigney, placed another wreath on behalf of returned soldiers from Point McLeay Mission. Six ex-Japanese prisoners-of-war were responsible for a third wreath placed 'in loving memory of our cobbers who fell at Malaya and Singapore, and to our mates who have died in Japanese prisoner-of-war camps'.[53] Australians began to recognise a new dimension within Anzac culture, the attributes of mateship forged in the battleground of Gallipoli, tempered in Japanese prisoner-of-war camps throughout Asia. Another account rendered, added to the 'Debt of Honour.'

Writing in the *Advertiser* on Anzac Day, 1945 Mr E. R. Greer described a previous commemoration service held on Malta. A description indicative of the spread of Anzac culture throughout Europe, the Middle East, Asia, the Pacific, Canada and America. Greer reminded returned sailors, soldiers and airmen of the simple but moving commemoration services held 'in the Western Desert, Libya, Palestine, Malta, North Africa, Sicily, Italy, Great Britain, Burma, the Pacific Islands, America, Canada and on many strips of foreign soil.' Greer also noted the occurrence in 1945 of services in Germany and other countries that previously suffered under Nazi tyranny.[54] The Second World War completed the globalisation of Anzac culture and confirmed it as part of the 'cult of the Fallen Soldier', for during World War II, Anzac Day services extended to war cemeteries in Middle Eastern and Asian countries.

South Australians commemorated Anzac Day as usual during the Korean War. The League made every effort to accommodate the views of various Heads of Churches in relation to service sheets and hymns used for extant civic services. Questions raised in 1951, relating to services suitable for all denominations received the answer that the only services acceptable to all religions, were those of a non-denominational nature, conducted by laymen.[55] To this end, the Rev Perry and Archdeacon Bulbeck received instructions to submit a list of laymen available for non-denominational service duties.[56]

Anzac Day civic services had reverted to the RSL Anzac Memorial Sunday service, the Dawn Service and the now traditional service at the Cross of Sacrifice that concludes the annual Anzac Day procession. *Sentry-Go* stated in 1958 that the Anzac Day Committee placed added emphasis on the Dawn Service, which was officially the service at which to honour war dead because Marchers no longer passed the State Memorial during the Anzac March.[57] The same year Mount Gambier Sub-Branch suggested the investigation of possible modifications to the combined service in 1958, while Port Adelaide Ministers changed the Anzac Service, resulting in a resolution from the State Board that the Secretary personally approach the Mayor of Port Adelaide and initiate discussions with him regarding the actions of the ministers.[58]

As attitudes and service sheets changed so did the repertoire of commemorative music. The League had deemed 'The Song of Australia' unsuitable for the opening of the State Memorial in 1931, but in 1956 one verse of 'The Song of Australia' featured at the unveiling and dedication of the memorial for the dead of WWII on Sunday 11 November, 1956. The Unley Salvation Army Citadel Band provided music for two hymns 'God of our Fathers, known of old', and 'Lead Kindly Light'. The National Anthem, which was 'God Save the Queen,' subsequent to the coronation of Queen Elizabeth in 1952, followed on the Order of Service. In February 1959, St Peter's Church, Glenelg was the venue for the annual remembrance service to commemorate nurses who died in both World Wars. A feature of the service was a prayer, composed by Miss M. Dryburg, in Palembang, when she was a prisoner-of-war. Choirmaster, Mr Trembath, offered copies of 'The Captives Prayer,' to other choirmasters wishing to use the suite for similar services.[59] Women, as prisoners-of-war, forced a greater recognition in Australia of the contribution of ex-servicewomen. In Canberra, dedication of the Hall of Memory at the Australian War Memorial took place on 24 May 1959. The Governor-General's address at the dedication of the spiritual centre of the Australian War Memorial made mention of the 'great bronze figure of an Australian serviceman' installed in the Hall of Memory, which at that time was bereft of any exhumed relics from overseas burial sites.[60]

In South Australia, the RSL Anzac Sunday memorial service featured as an Anzac commemorative service until the 1960s, when it ceased in order to encourage larger attendances at local sub-branch services. Earlier in 1956, the League Minutes had recorded that the attendance at the Anzac Sunday service was poor, resulting in a decision in 1959 to combine with the 10th Battalion's 1960 service at the Parade Ground.[61] A resolution in 1961 sealed the fate of the Anzac Sunday Service, which was discontinued, with steps taken to impress upon suburban sub-branches that the service was given up in their interest, therefore their full co-operation was expected to ensure local Anzac Services grew bigger and better.[62] Both the Dawn Service at the State Memorial and concluding March service at the Cross of Sacrifice still occurred in Adelaide in the year 2006. Although the passage of time forced the closure of some sub-branches in suburban and rural areas, in the same year Dawn Services still occurred in areas where sub-branches still operated.

John Luttrell, in a journal article entitled 'Cardinal Gilroy's Anzac Day problem,' (1999), described how, influenced by the Second Vatican Council, in 1962 Australian Cardinal Norman Gilroy designed a religious service acceptable for all faiths.[63] The same year, Mr Eastick, a Past President of the South Australian League, discussed with Bishop Gleeson the question of Roman Catholic participation in 1964 civic memorial services. Reporting to the State Board, Eastick advised that he considered Roman Catholic clergymen's full co-operation attainable given the provision of slight changes. Subsequently the Board confirmed the suggestion of two immediate changes, with others to follow in 1965.[64] League minutes record the tabling and approval of proofs for redesigned service sheets in 1965.[65] Maitland Sub-Branch communicated its concern regarding the form of service later the same year, an act that resulted in the deferral of any further consideration of change until the finalisation of deliberations with churches.[66] Subsequently, the League's 1965 Annual Report extended grateful thanks to all denominations for participating in the deeply religious Anzac commemorative observance program.[67] In 1966, League minutes recorded a Roman Catholic Padre's officiation at the Dawn Service, and a Baptist Padre at the Cross of Sacrifice.[68] Negotiations took place with the Council of Churches during 1967 and 1968 regarding suggested alterations to the Anzac hymn sheet that the Services Committee had the task of reorganising.[69] Although gaining the support of the Roman Catholic Church, to participate in conducting Anzac services, in 1969 the League faced new problems, with the refusal of Strathalbyn Ministers to participate in Anzac Memorial Services because the League supported the Vietnam War.[70] Padre Whereat undertook enquiries into the Strathalbyn situation and after forwarding a letter to the local Anglican Priest, assumed the matter satisfactorily concluded. Typical of the period of apathy and criticism noted in previous chapters, the Vietnam War caused problems regarding civic religious services.[71] The style of the hymn sheet became the subject of debate again in 1972, when the League referred the matter to the Anzac Day Padres, authorising them to place any change before the Heads of Churches.[72] The League worked hard to gain the approval and acceptance of various denominations to ensure spiritual significance in accordance with Christian principles when addressing the symbolism of civic Anzac Day commemoration services.

The Whitlam era during the 1970s introduced a period of rapid political change wherein part of the agenda of that Labor Government was breaking ties with Britain, and the British monarchy, as well as strengthening the sense of Australian identity within the Australian nation. The election of a Federal Labor Government in 1972, under the leadership of Gough Whitlam, an ex-serviceman who served overseas during World War II, triggered a time of division between the Federal Government and the RSL concerning memorial services and the national anthem. Whitlam, described by a Staff Reporter of the *Sydney Morning Herald* in December 1973, as attempting to introduce a 'New Nationalism' promoted 'Advance Australia Fair' as a rival Australian national anthem to 'God Save the Queen.'[73] The first warning of an impending 'battle' appeared in South Australian League records as an 'Appendix' to League minutes dated 20 August 1973. Reporting on an extraordinary meeting of RSL National Congress, Eric Smith, the State President, advised the State Board that the RSL National Executive accepted that the national anthem was the appropriate anthem for ceremonial occasions. However, the report added, 'The Song of Australia' met a different fate. The 'Song of Australia' Committee had previously sought the League's support in an attempt to instigate 'the song' as the 'National Song,' a request the League agreed to without any delay. Nevertheless, subsequent events proved the League's support ineffectual against the desires of more populous States.[74] With Tasmania abstaining, all other States voted against 'Song of Australia,' being unfamiliar with it, favouring instead 'Advance Australia Fair.' The final determination regarding the use of the anthem was the ultimate responsibility of the RSL National Congress. Evidently, the RSL National Executive decided on 'Advance Australia,' having little knowledge of the 'Song of Australia' composed and written in 1859 by two migrants to South Australia, Berlin-born intellectual Carl Linger and English-born poet, Caroline Carleton.[75]

Primarily, civic memorial services continued to include the 'Queen' as the national anthem. Reporting on Anzac memorial services, the *Herald* advised that bands played 'God Save the Queen' in six states, even though 'Advance Australia' was successful in achieving a vote of 51.4% in a government-run poll of 60,000 people. However, the article drew attention to the omission of 'God Save the Queen' from the poll. The article continued, pointing out that one of the requisites of a successful Anthem was the ability to deeply move the spirit, as well as having fundamental and universal acceptance, and portray the prevailing *Zeitgeist*, by striking a chord in people's hearts. Though some recognised 'God Save the Queen' as 'out-dated jingoism', the commentary posed the question – was an anthem reminding Australians that Captain Cook sailed from 'Albion' using 'true British courage' to a country 'girt by sea' any better? In conclusion, the report declared the 'attempt to dictate a new and dubious replacement is becoming a farce. God Save Us All!'[76]

As the choice relating to both anthems remained the prerogative of those persons organising ceremonies, confusion reigned supreme.[77] Nevertheless, the League maintained the conservative 'status quo' for in November, the Secretary Mr Hoffman advised of the pleased reaction to the playing and singing of 'God Save the Queen' at the Remembrance Day service.[78] Eventually making a definite decision, the Prime Minister acted, curbing the Army's ability to continue playing the 'Queen'. Whitlam instructed the Minister for Defence, who likewise instructed the Army, 'that *God Save the Queen* must not be played again, except in special circumstances.' The *Bulletin* reported in April 1975, that the order stunned and angered the army because it meant the withdrawal of permission for any service band to play the 'Queen' at Anzac Day functions. The prevention did not apply to police bands and pipe bands.[79] Controversy continued, but with the Army gagged regarding its ability to render the old anthem, the new anthem gained a stronger grip along the path to 'New Nationalism'. Later, a roundup of Anzac Day ceremonies in State Capitals the same year judged the result 'a fair advance for the anthem *Advance Australia Fair*'. Brisbane played only 'Advance Australia Fair'. In Sydney, 'God Save the Queen' featured twice, once for the arrival of Lieutenant Governor Mr Justice Street, the second time for his departure, after 'Advance Australia Fair'. Melbourne, Adelaide and Hobart exclusively selected 'God Save the Queen'. In Canberra, a military band played 'Advance Australia Fair' as the national anthem at the Australian War Memorial, whereas 'God Save the Queen' accompanied the departure of Sir John Kerr, as he left the memorial.[80] In another step towards 'New Nationalism', League minutes of April 1984 record musical arrangements on Anzac Day; for the Vice Regal Salute, eight bars of the first verse of 'Advance Australia Fair', with hymn 'God Save the Queen', no 707, from the Anglican Hymn book, used to conclude each memorial service.[81] Surrendering to the inevitable, two years later in 1986, the League agreed to reproduce from the Yellow Pages telephone directory, the words of the national anthem 'Advance Australia Fair ' for circulation to subbranches.[82]

Having to resort to the Yellow Pages for reproduction of a national anthem highlights the inadequate institutional procedures adopted to promote community acceptance of the new anthem as an important symbol of Australian identity. It also emphasises lack of total support for a Government's assumption that the Labor Party's slogan 'Its Time' applied to all facets of the nation. Holding a partial plebiscite that completely omitted the old anthem, rather than a constitutional referendum that offered a choice of both old and new, resulted in a large proportion of Australians having no say at all in the decision to change the national anthem. Including both 'Advance Australia Fair' and 'God Save the Queen', on RSL orders of service, achieved two objectives. 'Advance Australia' confirmed the patriotic nature of the RSL in recognising the changing symbolism of Australian identity. The 'Queen' gave older veterans a chance to preserve the traditional rituals of Anzac culture by singing the anthem symbolic of their Empire service. Whitlam concentrated on symbolism, changing symbols such as the national anthem and the Australian 'crest.' In trying to change the direction of Australian consciousness in terms of identity, from Britain to Australia, Whitlam did not recognise the significance and possibilities inherent in 'Anzac' as a dimension of Australian culture. Australians debated the significance of Anzac Day in terms of 'spirit', 'myth' or 'legend', or whether it deserved celebration as the metaphorical birth of the nation.[83]

Historian Hank Nelson chronicled the efforts of another Labor Prime Minister, Paul Keating, who at a 1992 Anzac Day service commemorating World War II attempted to use 'Kokoda' as a force for directional change. Nelson's journal article 'Gallipoli, Kokoda and the making of national identity' (1997), described the ceremony, as 'formal, international and Christian'.[84] Ultimately, in a civic memorial service on Remembrance Day, Keating transformed Australian spiritual direction in terms of identity, at the burial, not of an 'unknown warrior', but of the 'Unknown Australian Soldier' at the Australian War Memorial in November 1993. At the time of the Keating Government, the Australian nation appropriated Remembrance Day and an indigenous God into Anzac culture.

The funeral of the Australian Unknown Soldier moved Australia further along the path to the concept of 'New Nationalism' because it harnessed the latent force of Anzac culture as a dimension of Anglo-Celtic core culture within Australia.[85] A task force consisting of a tri-service bearer party, which was provided by the Australian Defence Force, went with funeral director, Rob Allison, who was a WWII veteran, Brendon Kelson, the Australian War Memorial's Director, and Dr Richard Reid, co-ordinator of the project, to France to supervise the exhumation of remains from burial sites of unknown soldiers of Australian origin. On exhumation, the chosen body still had items of Australasian military clothing and equipment. In the tradition of the 'cult of the Fallen Soldier', British, Commonwealth and French officials ensured that the body was treated with respect and due ceremony until officially handed over to Australian representatives. The skeletal remains, selected from four graves opened in Adelaide Cemetery, France on All Souls Day 1993, still included pieces of AIF uniform, gas mask and brass boot fastenings. The headstone when replaced over the empty burial site linked the site with Canberra, described in a video produced by the Funeral Directors' Association as the 'Soul of the Nation'.[86]

The casket, draped in the Australian flag and 'dressed' with a bayonet, and Digger's slouch hat, lay in state in France and was the centre of ceremonies attended variously by the Duke of Kent, his lapel complete with the symbolic red poppy of Flanders fields, Officers from all Commonwealth countries, the Prefect of the Somme and Mayor of Bullecort, before its eventual transfer to a Qantas 747 Jumbo named 'Spirit of Remembrance'. On arrival at Sydney airport a Guard of Honour of Australian servicemen and women, together with French sailors from a French frigate berthed at Woolloomooloo, paid their respects as the casket underwent transfer from the Jumbo Jet to a Hercules C130 aircraft that ferried it to Canberra. During a period of 'lying in state' for three days in Kings Hall, (7–11 November), 4,000 people laid flowers around the casket before a ceremonial state funeral.[87]

The Australian Funeral Directors' Association took great pains to ensure that the symbolism and spirituality of a 1920s style military funeral was faithfully re-enacted in Canberra. Simon Berry of Charles Berry & Sons Pty Ltd, Norwood South Australia, as President of the Australian Funeral Directors' Association, was responsible for funeral arrangements for the Unknown Australian Soldier. Underlining the important significance of the occasion to all Australians, as the burial took place in Canberra, some South Australians watched the funeral ritual screened at Adelaide University's Bonython Hall. Multicultural Australia took up a position on the world stage, displaying the ceremonial, symbolic importance attached to Australian sovereignty by the return of the Unknown Soldier to the land that had sent him overseas.[88]

As the funeral cortège made its way from King's Hall to the forecourt of the Australian War Memorial, the actions of representatives from ex-service organisations lined up along Anzac Avenue, showed respect, as well as an awareness of the symbolic importance of the funeral. Leaving Kings Hall at 9.26 a.m., accompanied by a guard dressed in various heritage uniforms from the Boer War to Vietnam, the cortège proceeded in slow march up Anzac Avenue. Simon Berry, leading the procession, heard the unforgettable beat of one drum, the sound of feet shuffling to attention, the words 'Lest we Forget'.

Prime Minister Paul Keating was one of eight pallbearers. The Mayors of Villers-Bretonneux and Ypres attended in acknowledgement of the Allies' 'Debt of Gratitude'. In Adelaide, at Bonython Hall, people moved to the State Memorial on North Terrace to take part in the South Australian Remembrance Day ceremony, as the funeral party of politicians and officials moved up the stairs to the Hall of Memory, in Canberra. Berry, supervising proceedings in the Hall of Memory, observed the actions of World War I Digger, Robert Coomb, who had fifty seconds to perform the task of applying soil from Pozières to the coffin: Coomb winked at Paul Keating, held out a quivering hand, sprinkled the soil in the form of a cross and said 'Welcome home mate'.[89] The sprinkled soil fell onto the casket where, whether intended or not, the juxtaposition of the bayonet laying across the casket's name plate formed the image of the cross that symbolises Christian sacrifice.[90] From the day of the funeral until workmen sealed the grave with a red granite slab three or four days later, some 24,000 people laid flowers in the Hall of Memory, which Berry described as a 'believable and sacrosanct place of peace'. The literal symbolism of the funeral proceedings was 'very powerful stuff indeed'. A narrator concludes the video recording the *Return of the 'Unknown Soldier' November 1993*, produced and directed by Peter Tobin, with:

> This Young Australian soldier
> Had lost all
> He had lost his identity
> But in losing both
> Had now gained national immortality.[91]

Paradoxically, the Unknown Australian Soldier, having lost his identity, symbolically provided all Australians with a metaphorical conversion, transforming the focus of civic memorial ceremonies from London, the heart of the British Empire, to the symbolic centre representative of Australian identity, the nation's capital, Canberra. As Prime Minister, Paul Keating said in delivering the eulogy:

> This Australia and the Australia he knew are like foreign countries. The tide of events since he died has been so dramatic, so vast and all-consuming, a world has been created beyond the reach of his imagination.[92]

The Funeral Service 'Order of Ceremony' for the Unknown Australian Soldier provides eminently obvious, evidence of the omission of any reference to Christ or a Christian God in the civic service sheet. Although Psalm 23 of the Old Testament features as a hymn in the 'order', Jesus Christ of the New Testament no longer enjoys the same encompassing, tangible link to Australian identity evident in sermons delivered during the two world wars or interwar years. The Prayer of Remembrance called upon 'Eternal God/ Creator and sustainer of all things', 'God of all time', 'God of eternity', 'God of each person', and 'God of every generation'. Arch Deacon Bruce Horton, Army Chaplain, offered the Prayer of Committal to 'Creator God', 'God of eternity', 'Almighty God', and 'God of the living, God of the dead'.[93] The prayer of dedication encompassed a 'God of yesterday, today and forever', calling upon that God to:

> Grant us the willingness to live by this ideal.
> May Australia advance in fairness and in the service of humanity.
> Spirit of this ancient land
> Bless, preserve and keep us,
> now and always. AMEN.[94]

After singing an amended version of 'Advance Australia Fair' with all reference to 'Albion' and 'Captain Cook' deleted, a prayer for Australia called upon 'God of the Southern Cross', 'God of the outback, God of the cities', finally praying:

> To the 'Eternal God'
> the God of the Dreamtime,
> the God of the present,
> the God of the future,
> the Great Spirit of this ancient land,
> be glory and praise for ever.[95]

As recorded by Ken Inglis in 'The Funeral of the Unknown Australian Soldier', (1993) [t]he 'Prayer for Australia' invokes among other Gods 'the God of the Dreamtime'.[96] What had begun as a 1920s style funeral with pomp and ceremony ultimately reflected a multicultural sense of Australian identity.

The dimension of spirituality in religious and civic memorial services connected to Anzac culture reflects the decline of Christian symbolism and involvement in memorial services and an indelible change in Australian identity. In changing the focus from a Christian God and singing a national anthem that called upon God to save an overseas monarch, Australia's national anthem now omits any reference to God, calling upon all Australians to utilise nature's gifts for the advance of the Australian nation. The Keating

Government used Anzac culture not only to appropriate Remembrance Day but also to incorporate an indigenous 'God of the Dreamtime' into civic memorial services completely changing the original concept of Anzac memorial services that linked a Christian God to sacrificial service for preservation of the nation.[97]

CHAPTER 8

AUSTRALIAN BRITONS

Earlier chapters draw on archival, institutional and media resources to illustrate changes in the observance of Anzac Day and Armistice Day within South Australia. Much documentary evidence exists within Australian culture that links a sense of Australian consciousness with the 'Anzacs' and Anzac Day. Memory, and therefore commemoration, is 'intertwined with the basic identities of individuals, groups, and cultures'.[1] I want the South Australian story of Anzac Day to provide a composite picture and for this reason include some examples of named South Australians' individual memories in relation to their civilian experience and military service during time of war, especially any subsequent evidence of commemoration. Documenting war experience is in itself a form of commemoration because in doing so the author must necessarily remember the service of those who died. The WWI section of this chapter deals specifically with South Australian authors William Denny (1872–1946), Charles Duguid, (1884–1986) and Adelaide-born Stella Bowen (1893–1947), together with correspondence written by Caroline Cooper (1871–1961). The remaining section of the chapter studies works by and about WWII Australian ex-servicemen and women. During the 1980s and 1990s, ex-POWs were prolific writers of memoirs related to their experiences during WWII. Those memoirs provide examples of Anzac Day and Armistice Day remembrance services undertaken while in captivity. South Australians Edwin Broomhead (1910–1985), and Ralph Churches, (born 1917) were both prisoners of the German Army. Broomhead published his recollections, *Barbed Wire in the Sunset*, in 1944, while Churches waited until 1996, before writing *A Hundred Miles as the Crow Flies*.[2] I draw upon the diary of South Australian Don McLaren, born at Islington South Australia on 25 December 1922, as an example of memory concerning the 1942 Selarang Barracks Square incident in Singapore, linked to Lieut-Colonel Galleghan and Anzac Day.[3] The experiences of Vivian Bullwinkel, (1915–2000) provide evidence that the observance of Anzac Day also provided a sense of Australian consciousness for Bullwinkel and fellow captives while prisoners-of-war.[4] Recorded examples of Anzac Day services conducted in prisoner-of-war camps (hereinafter POW camps) provide evidence that South Australian POWs had inculcated the rituals of Anzac culture. Anzac Day services provided South Australian POWs with a sense of national identity in the midst of dehumanising experiences.

It is reasonable to accept that a concept of dual identity, which was that of Australian Britons/British Australians, did exist in Australia at the time of the Gallipoli Landing and the Great War. As discussed in chapter 1, 'Honouring the Debt', the Australian Wattle Day League endeavoured to nurture the seeds of Australian identity along with the wattle trees planted in memory of Australian war dead at Wattle Grove in Adelaide's parklands during the Great War. One of the objects of the Federal Wattle Day League called upon 'all the people' to proclaim themselves as Australian and 'Australian Britons'.[5] My first example of Australian consciousness in relation to individual Australian British identity during WWI, a time when there was no Australian citizenship, comes from *The Diggers*, written by British subject, South Australian William Denny, who was awarded the Military Cross for his actions in France where he was severely wounded at Ypres.

We have already read Denny's arguments in 1922 for observing Anzac Day as a public holiday in Chapter 3, 'The One Day'. Denny's designation in 1919 when he wrote *The Diggers* was that of Capt. W. J. Denny, M.C., M.P., Ex-Attorney-General for South Australia. He recorded his observations of the Great War 'from an Australian point of view'.[6] Denny found some experiences he underwent in England 'astonishing', in particular the deference paid to those in a position of wealth despite their obvious lack of personal attainments or qualities. Bemoaning the fact that 'the peoples' suffered and died for the aggrandisement of Kaisers, Czars and Emperors, Denny believed Australian democracy, united with other democracies, had a duty to prevent any reoccurrence of the 'catastrophies' rulers of the earth had inflicted upon their subjects.[7] Although acknowledging Australians as British, South Australian born, Denny portrayed a consciousness particularly Australian, actively labelling some aspects of English culture detrimental. Referring to the Gallipoli landing Denny wrote:

> It is not in my province, nor is this the place to speak in detail of the famous landing of April 25th, 1915. The unparalleled feat of achieving what was, even after the event, described as the impossible, has been told by many of the finest pens of all nations. The event is enshrined in every Australian heart; it is the topic of many tongues; it is the subject of much discussion; it is the regret of every Australian soldier who was not privileged to take part in it. There have been many famous exploits by the Australian troops in other parts of the far-flung battle line in France, in Flanders, in Palestine, and in Egypt; but none – though equally heroic – will ever compare to it in the memory and imagination of the Australian people.[8]

As we have seen, Denny as a Member of Parliament used his power and influence to enshrine Anzac Day as a public holiday within South Australia.

Charles Duguid, born and educated in Scotland, established himself in private medical practice in Adelaide in May 1914, and subsequently joined the AIF. In 1916, Duguid was in army camp as a Medical Officer. Duguid, OBE, MA, MB, ChB, FRCS (Glas.) FRACS, recorded his wartime experiences in *Doctor and the Aborigines* (1972). Signifying his identification as Australian, Duguid uses the personal pronoun 'we' when referring to Australia.[9] 'Willie', Duguid's brother, was already in Egypt, having joined the Australian 8th Light Horse Regiment. Together with Light Horse reinforcements and Lieutenant Kelly of the 3rd Light Horse, the Doctor sailed for Egypt in February 1917 aboard Transport A6. Describing himself as 'thinking of Rene and of home', coupling 'home' with his wife in Adelaide, Duguid reported to AIF Headquarters, Cairo. From there, he travelled by train to the Australian Stationary Hospital at El Arish, via Kantara East. Here Duguid found old school friends from Scotland and was delighted to hear that most of the soldiers spoke with Ayrshire and Glasgow accents.[10] Although Australia was home, Duguid also identified with the accent associated with his native land; Duguid was multicultural.

Displaying his humanitarian instincts and philosophy, Duguid's autobiography highlights the interaction of various nationalities serving under the umbrella of the British Empire. After the first battle for Gaza, Duguid treated the injured, whom he described as mostly Welshmen and East Anglians. He also referred to other groups of men from the then British Empire.[11] Although serving with the AIF Duguid had obvious empathy with men from Scotland and specifically mentioned the many Scots among the wounded infantrymen from the disastrous Gaza action – 'Highland Light Infantry, Scottish Rifles, Royal Scots Fusiliers, and King's Own Scottish Borderers'.[12] Duguid records his increasing anxiety for his brother and his grief when he finally received confirmation of Willie's death.[13] Exhibiting a Scottish Australian consciousness in relation to identity, Duguid's perception of his Australianness in relation to nationality extended beyond Australia to include the land of his birth in recognition of his Scottish heritage and culture. Duguid's concept of his individual identity was the dual identity of an Australian Briton. Duguid remembered and commemorated the men he met while on active service by including their stories in his memories. In particular, he commemorated his brother's death and recognised the impact on death on overseas battlefields upon those remaining on the home front.

We have already seen Duguid's position as President of the Aborigines

Advancement League in South Australia in Chapter 5, 'Diggers and Slackers'. On his return to Australia, Presbyterian Dr Duguid worked to alleviate the misery of indigenous Australians. Sir Mark Oliphant, former Governor of South Australia, wrote the 'foreword' of Duguid's book *Doctor and the Aborigines*. Although Oliphant referred to Duguid as a Scot, he significantly recorded the magnitude of the Doctor's humanitarian work as an Australian among indigenous Australians.[14]

In 1931, on the anniversary of the outbreak of war Duguid delivered the Violet Day Memorial Address, which he entitled 'Pro Deo, Pro Rege, Pro Patria'. During the address, he referred to the sites of former army camps at Morphettville and Mitcham. He remembered the soldiers' send-off at the Cheer-Up Hut and the trench comfort parcels sent to the men, together with the gifts the Red Cross sent to the wounded. Duguid also honoured the nurses referring to them as 'that noble army in grey and scarlet' going on to mention the 'near and dear who did not return' and added a litany of other Allied nations who participated in the sacrifice; France, Belgium, Italy, Serbia, Roumania, Russia, Japan and the United States of America. However, to Duguid 'love of friends is not enough' for he had deep compassion. He asked his audience to honour and salute 'the fallen brave of every nation'.[15] When delivering the 1931 Violet Day Memorial Address Dr Charles Duguid took care to make an inclusive Memorial Address. Notwithstanding, the interchange ability of Australian Briton or Australian Scots identity evident in the life history of Dr Duguid and the obvious patriotism demonstrated by Captain Denny in relation to Australian identity, the two men were both British subjects. Despite Duguid, being an Australian Scot of the Protestant Presbyterian faith and Denny, Australian born and educated in the Catholic faith, both men exhibited a sense of Australian consciousness together with a desire to commemorate those who served the British Empire during the Great War.

South Australian women living overseas at the time of the Great War, also provide evidence of Australian British identity, while recording their individual feelings during that period. Caroline Ethel Cooper was born on Christmas Day 1871 at North Adelaide and lived in Germany between 1914 and 1918. Cooper's letters, written to her younger sister, South Australian, Emmie Bevan Carr, on a week-by-week basis, describe wartime conditions in Leipzig. In a letter dated 22 November 1914 Cooper wrote:

> I think we as a race are rather apt to think we have certain divine prerogatives, but in having an over good conceit of ourselves we have certainly got a dangerous rival now in Germany, which is sitting with a halo round its head and an absolute monopoly of right in both hands ... But our little circle here has honestly tried to look at things dur-

> ing the last four months from various standpoints – we have English, German, Hungarian Polish and Turkish for our nationalities – that is mixed enough to help one to be a little broadminded. And it staggered me rather to find Frl. Sander riding a patriotic high horse, and yet not able to grasp that if my letters were written from an opposite standpoint I had an equal right to that standpoint.[16]

In the introduction to *Behind the Lines*, Editor Decie Denholm introduces the probability that Cooper acted as a British spy. Deholm concludes that Cooper remained British, even though she had divided personal loyalties and felt nothing justified war.[17] Adelaide born Cooper mentions the Australians at Gallipolli but continually refers to herself as an Englishwoman and an enemy of the Germans.

Artist Stella Bowen, who was living in London during the same period and spent her time meeting with other writers and artists, described herself as 'a half-baked young colonial.' Even so, Bowen felt proud when Ezra Pound's wife, Dorothy, 'pronounced that "the little Australian was quite charming!"'[18] Bowen writing about her group of friends says: 'we remained in a state of rather confused pacifism.' Bowen admitted she 'suffered the usual torments and uncertainties of young people who don't go with the crowd', but felt nothing justified the constant killing and wounding of soldiers.[19] Both Cooper and Bowen exhibited interchange ability between concepts of Australian and English, or British identity when writing about their lived experiences during the Great War.

At the time of the Second World War Stella Bowen was one of only three women appointed official artist by the Australian War Memorial. In the Adelaide *Advertiser* in July 2002, Arts Editor Patrick McDonald described Stella Bowen as a 'passionate war artist' when reporting on the opening of the Art Gallery of SA first retrospective of her career 'Stella Bowen: Art, Love and War'.[20] In particular, Bowen's painting of the lost men of Bomber Crew commemorates the service and sacrifice of those young men, both Australian and South Australian who lost their lives defending Britain while on bombing raids over Europe during WWII.

The four authors discussed above did not include the observation of Anzac Day as part of their war experience. In comparison, Australian authors writing of World War II experiences did refer to Anzac Day. In May 2001, the Howard Government 'acknowledged the unique hardship and suffering endured by Australians in Japanese PoW camps.' All Australian service personnel and civilians interned by Japan during WWII, and their surviving widows/widowers, still living on 1 January 2001, were entitled to receive a one-off ex-gratia payment of $25,000.[21] Some thirty-six percent of Australian soldiers taken prisoner by the Japanese died in captivity. In comparison, only four percent of Australian soldiers held as prisoners of Germany and Italy died while incarcerated.[22] In October 2001, Phillip Satchell of ABC radio interviewed Mr Bill Schmitt, Hon Secretary of the Ex-POW Association of South Australia. During the interview, Schmitt pointed out that any experience of imprisonment under the Japanese was quite different from that of imprisonment under the Germans because Japan was not a signatory to the Geneva Convention.[23]

One obvious result of Japan's failure to sign the Geneva Convention was a decision to execute any recaptured prisoner who escaped from Japanese custody. During the interview with Satchell, Schmitt alluded to the results of one particular break-out, which resulted in the execution of two Australian and two British soldiers recaptured after a failed escape attempt, which provided a deterrent to any intending escapees. At the time of the execution in 1942, Japanese soldiers had crowded a large number of prisoners into the Barrack Square at Selarang, and had to that stage unsuccessfully demanded that the prisoners sign a paper confirming that they would not escape.[24] The execution of Corporal Breavington (1904–1942) and Private Gale (1919–1942), both members of the AIF, together with two English 'Other Ranks' took place on 2 September 1942, during the prisoners' confinement in Selarang Barrack Square.[25] After the execution, Australian Dick Francis, (born 1912) a sergeant in General Headquarters, wrote down the story of the execution of the four POWs. Subsequently hidden in Singapore, the retrieval of the document took place after Japan's surrender to Allied Forces.[26] An Indian Officer and a Sikh firing party that had earlier fought as part of the British Army carried out the execution for the Japanese. That execution forced a subsequent decision from prisoners-of-war that ended the Selarang Barracks Square incident. Ultimately the decision saved the lives of other prisoners-of-war in the square where men had already died from dysentery in the cramped unhygienic conditions.[27]

As a consequence of the execution, the Australian Commander, Lieut-Colonel Galleghan, recognised the foolishness of escape attempts and the Japanese document was signed under duress by the prisoners.[28] Finally, as requested by their captors, the men confined in Selarang Square lined up and signed a non-escape form.[29] Don McLaren, recorded in his diary 3 September 1942 '[i]f I live to be a million, I will try and accept a Jap, but I will never ever accept a Sikh.'[30] Writing of the men's capitulation in signing the non-escape form McLaren recorded:

> Let's be honest, we had no alternative. What good would a great heap of dead bodies be to anyone. The bastards set up this bloody table and the queue was enormous. The

> wording, as I mentioned before, read '*I, the undersigned*', so you put your name in that blank space.
>
> Well it was a complete farce. My name is Don McLaren, and I signed 'Donald Duck', no bull shit. The Japs must have had some idea that not every sixth or seventh man was either 'Ned Kelly' or 'Mickey Mouse'.[31]

McLaren's diary entry, written with the inclusion of indicative Australian profanities and colloquialisms, contains an element of subversive, frustrated, anger and makes distinctions in relation to the nationality of his foreign captors and the traitorous Sikhs. When publishing his diary Don McLaren took care to commemorate the men 'left behind' by listing their names on the back page of the diary.[32]

Members of the Second AIF, who grew up in Australia after the Gallipoli landing in 1915, expected to observe Anzac Day rituals whatever the circumstances. Another example of an Australian ex-prisoner-of-war referring to Lieut.-Colonel Galleghan and Australian rituals observed during captivity occurs in the writings of Guy Baker (born 1918). In *More Lives than a Cat*, published in 1998, Baker records that Galleghan took charge of all Australian troops and eventually became second in command to Lieut.-Colonel E. B. Holmes, who commanded all British and Australian troops in Malaya. Baker records that Galleghan held parades and troop reviews on special occasions like Anzac Day and Australia Day.[33] Recalling a march that left early one Sunday morning to avoid the hot rays of the sun at noon, Baker writes of his amazement and exhibits his sense of Australian identity by recording the lack of important Anzac Day rituals. The unusual omission focused this march in his memory because of the failure of Australian troops to observe customary Sunday and Anzac Day services.[34]

Likewise, South Australians captured in the Middle East also made distinctions between the nationalities of fellow prisoners and their captors, the Axis powers, between members of the British Empire and men of the German front line, German Nazis and Italian 'Fascisti'.[35] Edwin Broomhead MA, BD, MPhil, completed recording his experiences as a POW in *Barbed Wire in the Sunset* in 1944. A Methodist Minister born in Adelaide, Broomhead's memoirs read like a travel diary when describing some aspects of the natural environment. He included details of his experiences as a medical orderly working with wounded Germans, Italians, Britons and Indian Hindus in Derna, his forced labour under the 'Nazi' bully and 'cad' at Tripoli, and religious services held in German and Italian POW concentration camps.[36] Realising that the 'Jerries' were not 'getting their own way' when injured German soldiers from Tobruk were brought into the wards, Broomhead described himself and fellow medical orderlies as 'less jubilant' when injured British soldiers arrived at the camp. Describing the reactions of 'our own' wounded men Broomhead wrote:

> But for them, our presence was a godsend. To hear British voices!
>
> Consider what that means to men who are not only wounded and in pain, but who are also suffering from the mental distress and apprehension of capture. They have been hurt, some grievously, and they have been taken prisoners, separated from friends and from all possible connection with home, with the grim incertitude of the concentration camp ahead! For two or three days maybe, they have been surrounded by enemy personnel, have heard only strange uncomprehensible tongues. Then the first great gates close behind them – hospital gates, but they are the gates of a prison. But, from under the trees in the dark courtyard, come figures in familiar uniform, come sounds of English speech, come friendly voices. Voices that hospital experiences and fellowship in distress make very tender.
>
> Tough old Ken Day, digger from the last war, approaches. 'Ow are you doing, cobber? All right, eh?'
>
> Gordon Rooney, the churchman, fusses up like a kindly old secretary-bird, 'Hullo, mate. Wait just a minute and we'll have you inside with us.'
>
> British voices, British friends. And, in a few minutes, they are carried in and put to bed in the British ward.
>
> So many men spoke in those days of the uplift of spirit they felt on hearing and meeting us there, that it would seem that our capture was the work of Providence.[37]

Although a prisoner, Broomhead counted his British compatriots in captivity as a blessing from God.

Broomhead, recorded feelings of euphoria at finding himself in British company during his period of imprisonment as a medical orderly, yet while subsequently working as a labourer, he began to make distinctions amongst his fellow prisoners in relation to nationality, exhibiting a preference for a mixture of men from Britain and Australia. Leaving the hospital situation, Broomhead described the depression caused by working to a state of exhaustion while in German captivity, under brutal Nazi Kommandants. The prisoners had no time for rest or relaxation, for they were continually exhorted to '"Heraus! 'Raus!" – "Move" or "Keep going!"' Afraid of breakdown and collapse Broomhead prayed 'How long, O Lord?' Describing the groups of working prisoners as 'slave gangs' Broomhead records:

> The spirit in which the men endured those hardships was worthy of everything that is best in British tradition. There were at first more than four hundred of us; the Indians were soon removed, leaving Australians, British and a few Sudanese … [F]inally, our numbers settled down to roughly three hundred – about 120 Australians and about 180 British. We who had started as a mixed collection of strangers, an odd group here, an individual there, with strain and quarrel not infrequent, became welded into a com-

munity to whom the trite phrase 'one big family' really could apply.

We grew in that pit of common hardship, to be extraordinarily attached to one another; sterling friendships have been formed for life; the invidious distinction between 'Aussie' and 'Tommy' was completely forgotten. I have worked in the gangs with both British and Australian lads, and I know that a mixture of English and Australians is one of the finest in the world. And like most of us from the Tripoli days, I have a very deep affection for the lads of 'the lost three hundred'.[38]

It is evident that deprivation and hardship led to mutual interdependence between British and Australian compatriots who shared a common British cultural heritage.

A new German Kommandant granted permission for the prisoners to conduct Christian and civil rituals enabling the maintenance of British cultural traditions. Men in the sick room wrote hymns on odd sheets of paper while the healthy were away working. Using the hymn sheets during the rituals of Divine Service Broomhead records that in the words of the old proverb 'in for a penny in for a pound', he encouraged the 'boys' to stand and sing the national anthem. The sound of the prisoners singing 'God Save the King' in the evening twilight at Tripoli elicited an astounding reaction. Broomhead records:

The German interpreter who was at the service sprang to attention. That was perhaps understandable enough, as we were doing the same. But the indisputable fact is that in the German canteen outside the prison walls, where the Kommandant and all the guards were relaxing after their evening meal, they too sprang to attention and remained so during the singing of our National Hymn.[39]

Subsequently required to discontinue the rendition of the national anthem of the British Empire, the prisoners sang an Empire song, 'Land of Hope and Glory' instead.[40] On 11 November 1941, the prisoners obtained permission 'to observe the holy silence at 11 a.m.'.[41] As POWs, Australians and Britons observed traditional Armistice Day rites while in the German prison camp, but as we shall see, only the 'Anzacs' marched on Anzac Day.

Transferred from Middle Eastern to European camps, Australian and New Zealand prisoners demonstrated Anzac Day rituals to their Empire compatriots and 'Fascisti' captors.[42] Although originally captured by German soldiers, Broomhead's subsequent transfer from Tripoli on 6 January 1942 took him along the coast and across the waters of the Mediterranean Sea to Sicily, from a German to an Italian POW camp, which appeared a rest camp, after his sojourn with the Germans.[43] Recording an instance when the prisoners illustrated to the 'Colonello' of the *Campo di Concentramento* that they were still soldiers Broomhead wrote:

> On Anzac Day, 1942 – the 25th April, sacred to the memory of the Australian and New Zealand Army Corps and our national blood-baptism at Gallipoli, 1915 – we, following in the footsteps of our fathers in our quiet way, observed the National Day. There were now about fifty Australian and about two hundred New Zealanders in camp.[44]

Continuing with his description of Anzac Day 1942 Broomhead detailed the parade held in the camp compound; the improvised saluting base, the organisation of a choir and the borrowed Italian bugle. Also borrowed by the commemorating 'Anzacs' parts of equipment and uniforms 'from all and sundry.' With English and South African prisoners around the sides, the Italians beyond the wire watched the parade. Navy and Air Force representatives stood on the saluting platforms together with Empire representatives, Indian, Canadian, South African and Imperial Armies, while in front of them all Captain Padre Mitchell took the salute. The surviving 'Anzacs' of Sidi Rezzeg, Greece, Crete, and Libya marched past the base where Mitchell received their salute.

Given the limitations imposed by their captivity the Australian and New Zealand prisoners organised a stirring commemorative service true to the rituals of Anzac Day. Describing that Anzac Day Broomhead wrote:

> It was the triumph of our little broken bands. Still soldiers! For ever and a day! Some had been prisoners for more than a year, all had passed through squalor and hardship to their present camp, but all marched that day with the flawless precision of Imperial troops. To those of us who stood and watched them march past, the sight was one for triumph and tears. Many parades would be held on that day in various parts of the Empire, to commemorate the glorious dead – not the least impressive was the parade of the captives in the prison-camp at Chiavari in Italy.[45]

Traditionally, the prisoners followed the parade with dedication, sang remembrance hymns, prayed and listened to Broomhead's short address. Binyon's 'Ode' followed the two minutes silence, after which came the bugle calls 'Last Post' and 'Reveille'.[46] Progressively developing throughout Australia, New Zealand and the British Empire since 1915, Anzac ritual had firmed to the extent where it provided incentive to the prisoners-of-war who found their sense of identity reinforced in the comfort of the established 'liturgy' of the Anzac service.

Unlike Australian POWs of the Japanese who, dependent upon when they received news of the Japanese surrender, remained captive until sometime around 15 August 1945, as a prisoner-of-war of the Axis powers Broomhead was more fortunate; his repatriation took place before the end of the war. Written after his release from an Italian POW camp, the book reveals

Broomhead denied his Australian background because he had always wanted to visit England. Broomhead recorded:

> All Australians were to return home via the Middle East; all Englishmen were to return to the Old Country by way of France, Spain and Portugal. And I was an Australian! But – to see England! Possibly even the King! To cross Europe – IF ONLY I WERE AN ENGLISHMAN! The little Italian colonel saw me. 'Ah, Pastore!' he said, 'You go to Egypt! You are Australian.' I gave him two packets of tea that had NOT been used before. 'No, Signore!' I said, 'I go to England!' And it was so! I crossed Europe to England for four ounces of tea![47]

Successfully bribing the Italian colonel, Broomhead pursued his ambitions as an Australian British subject, and visited the 'Old Country', hoping to see his King. Although he acknowledged his Australianness and carried out the rites and rituals of Anzac Day, Broomhead's sense of personal identity was a dual one, which also led him to acknowledge that his Australian identity encompassed a British element.

Broomhead was ordained in England by arrangement with the British Methodist Conference in 1943.[48] The Rev Edwin N. Broomhead, M.A. called his article published in *Back* in April 1947 'Common Folk'. The Methodist Minister believed 'there is no place for histrionics on Anzac Day' that the men commemorated on Anzac Day 'were not the sort of men to inspire the brazen voice of rhetoric'. Quoting the lines 'Take up the torch and wave it high-' the work of First World War poet, Colonel John McCrae, author of 'In Flanders Fields', Broomhead awaited the poet of the Second who would write a sequel. The clergyman saw 'Our Fathers' as having passed 'the torch' on from Gallipoli, France and Egypt to Cyrenaica and 'the reeking jungle islands', the air and the seven seas. Referring to the execution of the Carpenter at Calvary, the changed world and the millions of men 'fallen after their Redeemer' upholding Christian principles Broomhead wrote:

> They left us in a hurry, caught up in War's wild work, but when we overtake them, in the last great reunion of all – there will be abundant leisure for the renewal of all those broken friendships that have brought us together, on Anzac Day.[49]

Using his position as a clergyman and an ex-prisoner-of-war, Broomhead sought to explain mourning on Anzac Day for the men left in overseas burial sites by referring to the death and resurrection of Jesus Christ as part of the ritual of the South Australian Anzac Day at the Cross of Sacrifice.

In November the same year *Back* published another article written by Broomhead entitled 'Take a Minute Off for Reflection', this time on the observance of Remembrance Day, which was celebrated on 9 November. Projecting fifteen years into the future Broomhead predicted the completion of the 'settling down' process, the ownership of homes, and the possible 'stodginess' of veterans. Acknowledging by then ex-servicemen could 'slip out for an occasional evening with the boys,' Broomhead wrote:

> Fifteen years hence, you may not be as rich as you would have been had you stayed at home, for in every job various misbegots have wriggled into the best positions while you fought.
>
> Who cares? They are forever poor where you are the richer – in the friendship of the best of men.
>
> After all, you couldn't exchange places with them and retain your self-respect, could you?
>
> If it's a better world in fifteen years time, well and good. You will have lived to see the world for which you fought.[50]

To Broomhead, Australians lived in a 'wonderful country,' and it moved ahead 'in spite of Governmental encouragement'.[51] Despite foregoing the chance of advancement gained by those who profited while others were fighting overseas, the Methodist Clergyman relished the experiences gained in his war service for Australia and the British Empire, and counted himself richer because of the friendship of former ex-prisoners-of-war and ex-servicemen.

Ralph Churches signalled his identity for readers in the title of his memoirs *A Hundred Miles as the Crow Flies,* (1996) a crow being Australia's colloquial label for South Australians. Written for relations, especially his nephews, as an exercise to pass on the story of his escape in 1944 from German captivity, Churches described his readership as 'eclectic' given '[o]ne of our colleges bought 20 copies as an English text for Seniors. Not surprisingly, it has been translated into Slovene'.[52] Besides preserving the story of Churches' escape from German imprisonment, the *Crow Flies* supplied the information that No SX 5286 Private Ralph Frederick Churches of the AIF received 'the British Empire Medal (Military Division) in recognition of gallant and distinguished services in the field'.[53] On a deeper level *Crow Flies* further labels Churches a 'high achiever'.

Although the title of Churches' narrative indicated his achievements and Australian identity, Churches used the presence of British troops as a means of encouraging fellow escapees to persevere in their flight from the Germans when a number of his fellow escapees expressed disillusionment with the apparent lack of structure in the escape strategy.[54] Reaching comparative safety behind Allied lines, Churches ensured that Allied forces accepted their credibility as Allies by referring to the blanket identity of the group, rather than volunteering individual nationalities. The group of escapees included twelve Australians, nine New Zealanders and seventy troops from the United Kingdom.[55] Upon reaching Italy in September 1944 and returning to the 'real world' Churches designated the nationality of the group of successful escaped prisoners-of-war he had led out of captivity as some English, and 'we're all British'.[56] Although claiming himself as British, Churches records that he was soon identified as Australian by a British Colonel because of his forthright manner and use of Australian epithets when answering back during a debrief.[57] As an ex-POW Churches's sense of Australian consciousness exhibits a further dimension, a sense of Australian identity containing an 'ex-prisoner-of-war component' rather than recognition of any sense of another heritage or cultural dimensions.

Australian women also saw prisoner-of-war experiences in terms of Australian and British Empire connections. Betty Jeffrey shared her imprisonment under the Japanese with other Australian women and published a record of their experiences in *White Coolies* in March 1954. The title draws attention to the Sisters' degradation in terms of colour, as well as their reduced occupational status. Reprinted six times in 1954, the book underwent a further four reprints between 1955 – 1958, an indication of the interest of the Australian community in the experiences of women ex-POWs.[58] Jeffrey specifically mentions two South Australians, Jean Ashton, senior sister of the 13th A.G.H. and Vivian Bullwinkel. Bullwinkel was the sole survivor of a group of servicemen and twenty-two Australian Army Nursing Service sisters. Japanese soldiers bayoneted the servicemen near Muntok, then forced the nursing sisters to walk into the sea, where the Japanese machine-gunned the women from the beach. Although injured, Bullwinkel struggled ashore once the Japanese had left. Together with a wounded English serviceman she discovered a few days later on the beach, Bullwinkel gave herself up to a Japanese officer who later brought them to join Jeffrey's group in jail.[59] In writing the account of the massacre, Jeffrey recognised the relief of British prisoners of the Japanese finding themselves among compatriots in the midst of foreign captivity, in the same manner that Broomhead detailed the relief of British prisoners upon finding themselves amongst other Britons in the Middle East.

The prisoners maintained Christian rituals and British commemoration services. In December 1942, they held a combined English and Dutch service and the Australians sent gifts to Australian servicemen.[60] In *White Coolies* Jeffrey describes an Anzac Day service held on 25 April 1943 in Palembang. Jeffrey recorded that the Australians 'found this service very hard to take'.[61] Without the pomp and ceremony of the Anzac march, remembering loved ones during the Anzac Day service while in Japanese captivity, did not have the same uplifting effect on the Australian nurses as it had on the 'Anzacs' observing Anzac Day in Italy. Nevertheless the commemorative service in the Australian nurses' house underlined the importance of the service in establishing a sense of personal identity while suffering imprisonment amongst a mixed group of prisoners from other nations.

With news of the war's end, the nearer the group of Australian nurses came to freedom and home, the more Jeffrey deals with her release in terms of her Australianness. To Jeffrey, the sight of the rising sun badge on two young Australian paratroops did the Australian nurses more good than anything that they had experienced since the Allies arrived in the camp on 7 September 1945. Her Diary entry of 11 September 1945 records the questions asked of 'Bates, from Thornbury' and 'Gillam, from Perth' and highlights the nurses' British Australian heritage. Endeavouring to catch up on four years of news from Australia, the women's queries concern the Melbourne Cup and football final, the 8th Division prisoners and the Prime Minister of Australia and therefore betray their national consciousness.[62] Published in the 1950s, Jeffrey's diary of the Australian Army Nursing Sisters' captivity was the first account of the women's sufferings as prisoners-of-war. After directly living through the turning point in Australian-British relations commensurate with the fall of Singapore, Jeffrey's account of the Australian Army Nursing Sisters' imprisonment under the Japanese shows a changed perception in her consciousness regarding British Australian relations that is different from that of Edwin Broomhead, since Americans feature in parts of Jeffrey's diary. Written after the fall of Singapore, the Francis's document recording the execution of the two AIF servicemen and two English Other Ranks illustrated a similar perception of difference permeating the relationship between English and Australian Officers held captive by the Japanese in Selarang. Even though Broomhead was desperate to get to England, Australian memoirs produced during and immediately after the Second World War do not exhibit the same degree of interchange ability of Australian British or British Australian relations as illustrated in the memoirs of Australians who lived through the Great War. WWII memoirs that recount stories of individual remembrance exhibit a greater awareness of individual concepts of Australian identity and contain written descriptions of Anzac Days while incarcerated.

Norman G. Manners' 1999 biography, *Bullwinkel*, provides further insight into Vivian Bullwinkel's story. Manners compiled the biography at a point when Bullwinkel's community service had received acknowledgment, in particular by the Red Cross, which awarded her the Florence Nightingale Medal.[63] Accepting the medal Bullwinkel said:

> In having the Florence Nightingale Medal awarded to me I feel it has been awarded not to myself personally but as a tribute to our friends we left behind in other lands.
>
> Our Matrons, Matron Paschke and Matron Drummond, by their ability and level headedness in a time of crisis, were responsible for the calm behaviour of the nurses at the time of the sinking of the *Vyner Brooke*.
>
> The calmness and courage with which my colleagues met their final hour was forever an inspiration to the remainder of us in the following years.
>
> The cheerfulness, the keen sense of humour and the ever-ready helping hand endeared the girls to women and children of all nationalities in the camp and as they left us, one by one, the camp became the poorer.
>
> The comradeship and loyalty I received from the girls who came home with me, enabled me to return safely.
>
> Never did their courage falter and it is for them that I am deeply honoured in receiving the Florence Nightingale Medal. May we never let them down.[64]

In her acceptance speech, Bullwinkel acknowledged, honoured and commemorated those who had shared her wartime experiences.

Later in life, Bullwinkel took time to speak to schools about Anzac Day, to explain the meaning of the ANZAC spirit and, according to Manners, 'marched in the commemoration parade until such time as her feet would not permit her.'[65] In 1992 Bullwinkel told an Indonesian gentleman wanting to promote Bangka Island as a tourist destination that she wanted to see a memorial built at Muntok. Subsequently Bullwinkel met a businessman willing to assist with the building of the memorial. Manners records that 51 years after her ordeal Bullwinkel waded into the sea at Muntok and in an act of remembrance arched a posy that tumbled back onto the peaceful surface.[66] Bullwinkel took steps to honour and commemorate those who had died while serving Australia during the Second World War.

Unlike memoirs and biographies dealing with Great War participants, the WWII chronicles lack any mention of Celtic ancestry or denominational origins, although the Rev Broomhead identified himself as 'a Protestant'.[67] This aspect reflects the increased secularism of Australian culture. Although many Australian institutions have ceased claiming any identification with British Australianness and embrace multiculturalism, the individual writings studied concerning the South Australian born, ex-servicemen and women who served Australia in the Second AIF, claimed a blanket identity under an umbrella of the British Empire when dealing with Allies and resonate with a consciousness acknowledging British Australian roots and identity. However, in the cases of memory relating to imprisonment in Changi and Thailand where Australians had a greater chance of survival under Australian leadership, the recollections of ex-prisoners-of-war illustrate a greater awareness of division between British and Australian culture. This awareness mirrors actual statistical records concerning British Empire survival rates from Japanese POW camps in terms of national proportions, and therefore the secondary sources may reflect a combination of memory and known recorded data. Interestingly, in the same way that Australian veterans from the Gallipoli landing added the extra identifying dimension of 'ANZACs' to their personal consciousness of Australian identity, Australian survivors from German and Japanese POW camps during the Second World War include a further identifying factor of an 'ex-POW component' to their sense of Australian identity.

CHAPTER 9

BALANCING THE LEDGER

This story began with a debt, and it seems only fitting that an attempt should be made to summarise any debt repayment by 'balancing the ledger', in terms of acknowledgment of that debt. Any attempt to summarise the state of this particular ledger balance must be an estimate from imprecise data. Even though monetary debt repayment began in South Australia at grass root level in the form of patriotic button days raising money for wounded soldiers in 1915 and continues under the auspices of the Returned Services League as well as the Department of Veterans' Affairs, this exercise will not assess monetary debt repayment. As an alternative, this chapter considers symbolic community acknowledgements of the allegorical debt in the form of material history or cultural artefacts. In 1948, *Back* magazine of the R.S.L. published an article entitled 'Living Memorials: Use Vision When Planning Your War Memorial Make It a Living symbol', saying that 'living memorials' would serve the living while still expressing 'timeless gratitude for unselfish devotion to the defence of our ideals'.[1] This metaphorical ledger sheet sums up the fate of some WWI and WWII 'honour rolls' and monumental soldiers' memorials against the community recognition of 'living memorials' in 2001, as an accounting method designed to discover what South Australians have chosen to remember of the 'debt of honour'.

In 1967, the League conducted a 'Survey of War Memorials situated in the State of South Australia' (League Survey). Additionally, the League maintains a correspondence file begun in the 1980s relating to memorials. 'Australia Remembers', a commemorative programme carried out during the term of the Keating Labor Government in 1995 heightened community awareness of commemoration of war service during the early 1990s. The Howard Liberal Government subsequently launched a further commemorative programme, 'Their Service Our Heritage', (TS-OH), 'to commemorate the service and sacrifice of veterans of all wars and conflicts in which Australia has been involved since Federation.'[2] According to the Department of Veterans Affairs booklet 'Memories & Memorabilia' TS-OH provided Australians with an 'opportunity to acknowledge the debt of gratitude we owe to those who served in the defence of Australia's freedom'.[3] The survey data compiled by the League in 1967 provides a basis to assess community acknowledgement of the original 'debt of honour' after recent 'debt reminders', even though the debt has gravitated in terms of ethics from one of 'honour' to one of 'gratitude'.

The 1967 survey, together with the results of field studies, one conducted in a rural area and a second within the metropolitan area, provides a methodological approach to a system of 'creative' accounting. Whilst this particular accounting model is unlikely to satisfy the audit standards of the National Institute of Accountants, historically it will provide some insight into Anzac culture and material history indicative of South Australian public memory. Memorials figuratively represent Australian collective memory of war dead and war service. Creating significant commemorative sites within local communities partially solved the problem of the absent corpse, not only for Australians but also for the nationals of other countries.

A generation of British Australian children grew up in the 1940s in an ambience of Anzac legend and traditions, part of the evolution of a cultural ritual that stamped the mould of Australian identity. Material history in the form of stained glass windows, soldiers' memorials and honour rolls naming those who enlisted for the two world wars, were part of the landscape of the countryside and the streetscape of Australian towns and cities. A part of life and identity absorbed in the atmosphere of Australian lifestyle, the memorials provided a focus on Anzac Day and Armistice/Remembrance Day for the community respect accorded to the sanctity and sacredness of significant sites commemorating war dead. Not completely duplicating the civic honour rolls, church honour rolls recorded the names of ex-Sunday school scholars and church members who joined the forces. Honour rolls marked the names of those who had died overseas 'to keep Australia free' for those Australians left behind, maintaining the country while others fought. Patriotic duty lay in maintaining the might of the British Empire. The practice of naming war dead on headstones, honour rolls and soldiers' memorials, took place not only in Australia, but also throughout the British Empire, the direct result of burying Empire dead where they fell. American families had the choice of bringing the bodies of their war dead back to America for burial, a practice that only began in Australia during the Vietnam War.[4] Grieving relatives in Australia, particularly at the time of the Great War, wanted the account of their personal sacrifice in the death of loved ones recognised by the community. The narrative inherent in the litany of names on local honour rolls and soldiers' memorials provided a 'stop-gap' measure, an allegorical 'debit note', filling the void of an empty grave. It allowed closure of sorts, enabling local communities to face the future in the belief the names of loved ones would be remembered forever, their deeds and their sacrifice living on in the tangible records of a grateful country.

Tangible records exist in the form of documents in the Australian War Memorial (AWM) in Canberra and the pay and service records of ex-servicemen and women in the Australian Archives. Figuratively speaking, the names listed in official State Memorials exist as symbolic invoices; the AWM provides a list of names in its cloisters itemising a symbolic national account. As older church and civic buildings make way for newer structures, as community assets become part of the narrative that encompasses urban infill and medium density housing, monuments, honour rolls, stained glass windows and soldiers' memorials disappear. Some re-appear in new or different buildings, recycled, having lost their original significance within a different environment. Recent accounting strategies of privatisation, and outsourcing together with policies of urban infill and local council amalgamations, place material evidence of community remembrance of war dead and war serving at risk. The compilation of any record listing the full extent of Australian memorials relating to war service is virtually impossible because local memorials have already been lost, forgotten, moved or destroyed by those elements within religious, local government and commercial organisations that no longer recognise the 'debt of honour'.

Council information gathered in response to the 1967 League Survey was incomplete and contained errors. The League Survey consisted of a request for information from the then existing district councils, city corporations, and town corporations. One city, Port Pirie, four town corporations, those of Burra, Colonel Light Gardens, Murray Bridge and Renmark, together with twenty-four district councils chose not to reply. Those that did reply supplied information relating to 'type of memorial', 'location', 'responsible body' and 'general comments'. Although the information supplied in some cases was imprecise and subject to errors and omissions, it did document an attempt to record existing memorials at a given point of time. Illustrating the imprecise and unreliable nature of the 1967 survey, the Corporation of the Town of Glenelg replied that 'there are no memorials within the Town of Glenelg'.[5]

Even so, documentary evidence exists in the Holdfast Bay History Centre that Glenelg Mayor Hon H. Tassie MLC, did unveil a 'Honour Roll' on Sunday 8 November 1925. The Glenelg Sailing Club had a 1914–1918 'Roll of Honour' and there was a large 'Honour Roll' billboard outside the Glenelg Town Hall, a temporary structure that listed the names of enlisted men from the Glenelg District circa 1940–1941. The billboard supplied the information '[y]ou have to meet your pals when they return' and '[t]here is still room for your name on this Board.'[6] Furthermore, the side wall of the Glenelg Town Hall, recently cracked because of adjacent building construction, is plainly embossed with symbols normally associated with memorials erected to honour war dead. Notwithstanding an acknowledgment that the survey conducted by the League is not one hundred percent accurate, nonetheless it supplies evidence of community recognition regarding commemoration of war dead during the late 1960s at the time of the Vietnam War.

Information relating to the 'Copper Triangle', supplied by the Corporations of the Towns of Moonta, Wallaroo and the District Council of Kadina to the League in October and November 1967 and in the metropolitan area by the Corporation of the City of Port Adelaide in March 1968 differs from field studies conducted in both rural and metropolitan areas in 2001. On 24 October 1967, the Corporation of the Town of Moonta listed one monument at Blanche Terrace Moonta, the responsible body, the RSL. Moonta supplied the further information that the date of erection was 1920 and the monument was 'well looked after'.[7] In October 2001, the pedestal monument erected in 1920, on which stood a representative Digger with slouch hat and rifle, in memory of 'Moonta's Heroes of the Great European War 1914–1919', further supplied the information that it also memorialised:

> [M]emory of the fallen World War 2 1939–1945
> [M]emory of the fallen Malaysia, Korea and Vietnam and of all other Australians who have fallen in the service of their country.
> Australia Remembers 1945–1995[8]

The updated Moonta monument included the fallen from WWII, Asian wars and the 1995 Keating Labor Government 'Australia Remembers' initiative. Community acknowledgement retained and maintained the Moonta memorial situated in the grounds of the bowling club, as community acknowledgement of the 'debt of honour'.

My research in the Moonta area also disclosed items not included in the original survey. Near the bowling club, at the entrance to an adjacent park stood 'The Percy Beaglehole', a slab laid atop two pedestals, one pedestal labelled 'Moonta Soldiers' the other 'War Memorial'. In nearby Moonta Mines, the local museum displayed the 1914–1919 'Roll of Honour for Valour' of the Moonta Mines Public School, while the Moonta Mines Methodist Sunday School Museum also displayed a 'Roll of Honour' for King and Country. Confusingly the spelling on rolls varies between 'honor' and 'honour', nevertheless despite the variation in spelling, the intention to recognise the service of those named on the rolls is in no doubt.[9] In spite of the general decline of community institutions in the Moonta Mines area the school and Sunday school museums maintained rolls relating to the commemoration of former pupils who served Australia in times of war.

The second town of the Copper Triangle, Wallaroo revealed similar care of the town's memorials. The Corporation of the Town of Wallaroo recorded information on 17 October 1967 concerning three types of memorials, all reported to be in good condition. The RSL was responsible for the RSL Club in Elizabeth Street erected in 1919. An arch located outside the Town Hall, erected in 1923 was the responsibility of the Council. A memorial committee was responsible for a park and playground erected in Elizabeth Street in 1963.[10] In October 2001, research conducted at the Soldiers memorial arch, 1914–1919, decorated with the Australian coat of arms, provided the information:

> This Memorial Arch
> Was Erected
> Through the Efforts of
> The Ladies of
> The Wallaroo Cheer Up
> Society and Local Branch
> R.S.S.I.L.A.
> Supported by the Public.[11]

Inside the arch itself, a commemorative plaque remembered men who served Australia during the 1939–45 War, while a side panel commemorated Vietnam and the Corvette HMAS *Wallaroo*. Literally from Gallipoli, a rosemary bush, the herb of remembrance, planted 15 August 1995, recognised the 'Australia Remembers' initiative.[12] A 'living memorial', the RSL Club memorialised the 1939–1945 War, and further advised:

> Life to be sure is not much to lose
> But young men think it is and they were young
> Their name liveth for evermore.[13]

Located opposite the RSL Club, the only resemblance to a park and playground in Elizabeth Street served as a pre-school centre.[14] Wallaroo had retained and maintained the memory of Wallaroo citizens who had served the Australian nation during war. Likewise, it had responded to a national initiative and participated in the 'Australia Remembers' programme. Wallaroo's

Digger Monument, Victoria Square, Kadina

Wallaroo Soldiers' Memorial

memorial arch and 'living memorials' reflected treatment commensurate with community acknowledgement of the 'debt of honour'.

Kadina, the largest community within the Copper Triangle, evidenced maintenance of community memorials, and also exhibited instances of memorial restoration and recycling. On 17 October 1967, the District Council of Kadina advised the League of the existence of four memorials: two monuments, a roll of honour, in good condition, and a 'living memorial', the Kadina Memorial High School. The Kadina District Council was responsible for the monument in Victoria Square, Kadina and the roll of honour in the Kadina Town Hall, whereas the school was the responsibility of South Australian Government and the monument situated at Railway Terrace South, Paskeville came under the jurisdiction of the Paskeville RSL. My field study provided the information the school erected in 1923 'in honour of the men of Kadina and District who served in the Great War 1914–1919', was still in use. With a Digger standing atop the apex, the arch, erected in recognition of those who fell in the Great War, in addition included the names of those who served during the 1939–1945 War. The Paskeville Soldiers memorial in honour of 1914–1919 was unveiled on 16 November 1921. Fascinatingly, the Kadina Town Hall contained not one Roll of Honour relating to 1914–1919, but two. One 'Roll of Honour' for King and Empire suitably decorated with the Union Jack, together with an Australian red ensign and coat of arms, listed those 'Faithful unto death', the second 'Roll of Honour' decorated with the rising sun of the AIF, together with naval and air force insignia presented by T. H. McKay Esq. Also presented by McKay, a roll of honour in memory of servicemen and women who served in Malaysia, Korea and Vietnam. The Kadina Lions Club had restored the rolls.[15] Enquiries elicited the information that the recycled honour rolls had originally been in the RSL Hall.[16] All three communities of the Copper Triangle had maintained and updated memorials, whilst in the largest Council district, a community service organisation had restored and rehung honour rolls in a space available to the whole community illustrating a community desire to remember war dead.

Turning to the metropolitan area for a comparison, the Corporation of the City of Port Adelaide supplied the League with the following information on 27 March 1968. The existence of three halls used as RSL Sub-Branches and situated in Semaphore, Largs North and Rosewater. The Port Adelaide response also listed a number of monuments: a granite monument and clock on the foreshore at Semaphore, a stone monument at Largs North, a granite monument and drinking fountain at Rosewater, and a marble monument on Birkenhead reserve. Lastly, a reserve, a stone memorial with brass plaque, and

Semaphore 'angel of peace'

T.C. Derrick Memorial, Glanville

the Mothers and Babies Health Association Centre, located at the I.C.I. oval, Fletcher Road, Birkenhead.[17] Research conducted in 2001, to discover the fate of memorials dedicated after both the First and Second World Wars to Portonians, persons who grew up in Port Adelaide, confirmed that RSL sub-branches and monuments still exist at Semaphore and Largs Bay, but that changes have occurred at Rosewater and Birkenhead.

The Largs Bay stone monument, together with Semaphore's monumental angel and clock memorial, still honoured the national debt. Lieut.-Colonel L. O. Betts, President of the Semaphore and Port Adelaide Branch of the League officially unveiled and dedicated Semaphore's monumental angel and clock memorial on Empire Day, 24 May 1925. The *Port Adelaide News* reported that in his address to the assembly gathered around the statue of the 'angel of peace', with 'symbolical palm in hand', Betts said:

> He hoped that the story would always be told of the ideals for which their gallant men had given their lives, and of the deeds of heroism and self-sacrifice performed.[18]

Continuing, Betts also remembered the heartache of women waiting for the return of their men and the anguish of those who had lost loved ones because of the war. Since Betts addressed those assembled around that 'angel of peace' Australian culture, particularly in metropolitan areas, has changed. It has become more inclusive, and now provides a space for diverse religions and multiculturalism. Evidence to support the above view exists in the Port Adelaide Enfield Council area, particularly in the suburb of Rosewater and the surrounding working class district. The ways in which the local community has either retained or recycled community assets belonging to Christian churches and the veteran community provides a link between the 'Heroes of the Great War', 'living memorials' and an invigorated community resulting from changing lifestyles and urban infill. Material evidence within the local community indicates changing Australian attitudes to the material evidence commemorating war dead within cultural institutions that form a part of contemporary Australian identity.

As in the case of Glenelg, Moonta and Kadina, the comparative study of Rosewater memorials relating to war dead and war serving provided evidence that more memorials existed than those recorded in 1968 by the local council, both in the form of honour boards or rolls and 'living memorials'. Accounting policies of economic rationalisation and asset sales, put honour boards in former industrial, banking and church buildings at risk. Mergers at Local Government level also resulted in the loss of material history in the form of soldiers' memorials, irrespective of whether those memorials existed as honour rolls, or 'living memorials'. Various honour rolls and 'living memorials' dedicated after both WWI and WWII, with the aim of immortalising the memory of local soldiers who died overseas have not survived into the twenty-first century. Despite renewed interest in Anzac Day, and evidence of memorial updating in rural areas in response to the Federal impetus of the 'Australia Remembers' programme, metropolitan honour rolls and soldiers' memorials continue to undergo removal, recycling and loss.

In the working class suburb of Rosewater, Grand Junction Road provides access to both Port Adelaide and the industrial zones clustered around the port. In 2001, Rosewater still had a number of homes constructed of pressed tin sheeting situated in 'Tin Town', and was the site of the first Housing Trust doubles, or maisonettes, built in 1937. In a short section of Grand Junction Road, are three former community assets. The original function of those particular buildings was as the Rosewater District Council Chambers, the Primitive Methodist Church and the Ottoway Congregational Church.[19] The original use of all three community buildings in Rosewater changed because of subsequent annexure, sale, and leasing arrangements. After the Great War, all three buildings contained memorials recognising the war service of local community members in the form of names listed on honour rolls; two buildings had 'living memorials' in the form of stained glass windows. The fate of the honour rolls and stained glass windows in these three buildings revealed different perspectives in relation to the retention and maintenance of commemorative memorials.

The recent policy of economic rationalism resulting in local council mergers supposedly took place because of fiscal policies designed to reduce costs, but conversely resulted in councils made up of elected members from much wider geographic areas. Councillors are not necessarily conversant with each suburb's local history, yet they have the power to make decisions affecting the loss or retention of material history. In 1899, the Port Adelaide Council annexed the Rosewater District Council.[20] Local residents objected to development plans for the old Rosewater District Council chamber building in 1990. Despite the objections, the re-development resulted in the chamber's division into two-storey home units. The land around the building was the site of a further twenty-one units built as a Strata Corporation project jointly developed as Community Housing by the Port Adelaide Central Mission, The South Australian Community Housing Authority and the City of Port Adelaide Enfield.[21] The transom above the old Council Chamber doorway bore the name and emblem of the Alberton & Rosewater RSS & AILA Sub-Branch, despite its use as home units.[22] As recommended in the Greater Port

Adelaide Heritage Survey 1989, the original building underwent conservation and restoration.[23] There was no place for honour rolls in housing designed to be 'affordable medium density' urban infill, therefore the Port Adelaide Council put the honour rolls belonging to the League Sub-Branch, and the 'Rosewater Womens Memorial 1914–1918 Roll of Honor' [*sic*] into storage.[24]

The same Heritage Survey also recommended the conservation and restoration of the Primitive Methodist Church.[25] In contrast, the story of the former Chapel was quite different. Subsequent denominational unions and mergers eventually ceased in 1977 with the building passing to the Uniting Church. Cement rendering plastered over the foundation stone of the original building, blocked out the chapel's dedication as a religious institution on sacred ground. Research elicited the information that no one connected with the former congregation knew the whereabouts of the honour roll dedicated to the memory of Church members and ex-Sunday School scholars who served in the Great War. The honour roll did exist, because an article recording its existence appeared in the *Port News* of June 1917 stating that thirty-five names were on the roll at that time, and that the photographs of fourteen members of the Sunday School listed on the roll, were unveiled during the Church Anniversary Service.[26] The leadlight and stained glass windows, dedicated at the Church Jubilee Celebrations in 1928, were no longer in the building.[27] Two had been re-used at Wesley House, a home for the aged, and the remainder installed at Trinity Uniting Church, in nearby Alberton.[28] In 1984 the congregations of Yatala, Rosewater and Ottoway Uniting Churches, amalgamated to form Trinity Uniting Church.[29] The Uniting Church policy of amalgamating congregations resulted in parishioners no longer conversant with earlier local parish history. This was evident because the symbolism of windows depicting a cross, intersected with a wreath of leaves bearing the messages 'Greater Love than This Hath no Man' and 'Lest we Forget', the old accounts of 'self-sacrifice', had become recognised by the congregation as a memorial to earlier church members.

The *Port Adelaide News* reported on the Jubilee Celebrations in 1928 when the President of the Conference gave an appropriate address. Mr Fred Pocock, the Sunday School Secretary, presented one of the leaded stained class windows as a memorial 'to the heroes of the Great War'. The church centenary pamphlet listed stained glass windows as dedicated individually to Arthur Jennings and Cecil Pudney, 'killed at war', while Mesdames Weaver, McLaurin, Bottomley, Stephens and Read jointly erected a window in memory of their sons, who 'made the supreme sacrifice in the Great War 1914–1919.'[30] The 1977 Uniting Church merger of the Presbyterian,

Congregational and Methodist Churches was for the Methodists a second merger, the first merger in the early 1900s being that of the Bible Christians, Primitive and Wesleyan Methodists. Mergers, we know, result in surplus buildings, surplus equipment, and surplus officers. After the 1977 merger, the Bosna & Hercegovina Muslim Society SA purchased the defunct Uniting Church Buildings on Grand Junction Road, Rosewater. The Bosnian group subsequently re-sold the building. Parishioners from the old Rosewater Uniting Church believed the honour roll, together with memorial plaques to Church pioneers remained in the building. The subsequent occupier denied any knowledge of their existence.[31] Unavailable to either church members, or the public, the material history encapsulated in the honour roll, and the photographs of 1917, no longer provided evidence of the personal sacrifice of Rosewater 'heroes of the Great War'.

Material history embedded in honour rolls, plaques and memorial windows in former church buildings was, and is, particularly at threat within the Uniting Church because of parish amalgamations. Retention and recycling of some honour rolls and memorial windows does take place. The fate of the congregational assets lies with the individual congregations themselves. The make-up of the Rosewater congregation changed because of the impact of Commonwealth and State Government immigration and housing policies upon that community. In the more affluent district of Parkside, the Epworth Uniting Church building survived with a heritage listing, which preserved its leadlight, stained glass windows, flying buttresses and honour rolls. Other congregations donated honour rolls to historical societies and museums.[32] Unable to display all donated honour rolls because of limited space, some honour rolls became inaccessible to the general community. Research at Rosewater and the Uniting Church Historical Society proved that stained glass windows re-appeared elsewhere, saved for future generations, possibly for their antique value, but also because of their intrinsic value.[33] At the time of the church centenary in 1978, in a booklet produced as part of centenary celebrations, the Rosewater Uniting Church congregation still recognised the original purpose of the memorial windows.[34] By the year 2001, the 'living memorial' windows from the Rosewater Uniting Church had lost their original significance because of their repositioning. 'To fit into the new location', the windows were reconditioned and enlarged either side. The alterations resulted in the dismantling of the dedication panels at the base of the windows. The dedication panel of Pudney's memorial window, installed together with three other dedication panels in Trinity's foyer, provided no clue that specifically identified the window to which it once belonged.[35] Consequently, the parishioners at Alberton were no longer aware of the original reason for the windows' dedication. The significance of some windows erected in commemoration of those killed during war no longer evident, the windows became merely memorials to earlier church workers.

Unlike the forgotten Rosewater Uniting Church honour roll, the beauty of the memorial windows survived, even if the significance of their purpose appeared forgotten. If, in considering the situation at Rosewater, one looks to debates after WWII concerning the benefits of utilitarian memorials versus statuary and names, utilitarian memorials did not guarantee the implied vision of their commemorative purpose remained in the Australian psyche as material history that provided a higher degree of community significance within Australian Anzac culture. The debates after WWII were really a legitimate forum of the arguments for utilitarian memorials that surfaced after the Great War in the form of protests on Anzac Day, when some returned men wanted their memorial to be employment and the promised better life.[36] The Veteran community maintained the traditions of Anzac Day and Armistice Day, now called Remembrance Day. The celebration of Victory Europe and Victory Pacific days palled against the continued significance of Anzac Day. After World War II, some memorials had additional names placed on them, but the proliferation of utilitarian memorials had no place for names.[37] Even so, in established cities and suburbs some Churches continued the tradition of honour rolls.

The number of different memorials where the name of each individual ex-serviceman and woman appeared varied, but in the case of war dead buried overseas the memorial sites multiplied. Take as an example, the first name listed in the *Port News* regarding the photographs unveiled during the Church Anniversary Service in 1917 at the former Rosewater Methodist Church. From Chad Street, Rosewater, W. F. L. Dodson, 10th Battalion AIF, killed in action Wednesday 19 September 1917, aged 29 years, buried Hooge Crater, Belgium.[38] The former lieutenant shares a headstone in Cheltenham Cemetery with his mother; his name appears with others who made the supreme sacrifice on the Rosewater Women's Memorial at Rosewater Oval, a memorial updated by the Veteran Community in the 1990s, with a plaque listing subsequent wars. That particular memorial was also updated at its unveiling. Adjacent, stands a memorial drinking bowl unveiled the same day in 1922, listing the names of those who had died since returning home.[39] Dodson's name appears again, next to that of his brother A. J. Dodson, on the 'Rosewater Womens Memorial Roll of Honor' [*sic*], which names all those who enlisted from the Rosewater District. W. F. L. Dodson's name makes further

Kapunda Fallen Soldiers monument

Memorial Lychgate, church of Saint Margaret of Scotland, Port Road, Woodville

appearances listed at his former school, Alberton Public School, the State Memorial, and on the walls of the cloistered forecourt of the Hall of Memory at the AWM.[40] The lieutenant's name also appears in Appendix III, roll of Honour (Deaths in France) of the History of the 10th Battalion AIF, The Adelaide Rifles, and nowadays, on the Commonwealth War Graves Commission site on the Internet.[41] Metaphorically, local soldiers' memorials and honour rolls serve as debit notes recording the national debt of honour owed to those who died serving Australia in overseas' wars because National memorials took longer to materialise. Dedication of the South Australian State Memorial did not occur until April 1931; the AWM, opened on Remembrance Day 1941, dedication of the Hall of Memory took place, 24th May 1959.[42] Local honour rolls became a tangible reminder of the national debt of honour owed to war dead buried overseas.

Parishioners who oversaw the recording of the debt of honour at Rosewater are themselves dead. Some have burial sites at nearby Cheltenham cemetery, part of the former Council district. Headstones erected to former British Australian pioneers lie in storage at Cheltenham cemetery, the names on the replacement headstones those of the first wave of Middle European immigrants to become part of Multicultural Australia.[43] Population demographics in the former Rosewater District changed noticeably after the two World Wars. Various ethnic groups moved into, and continue to move into, the Rosewater area, the first influx, British migrants, were temporarily housed by the Commonwealth Government in the former Rosewater wool stores. British families moved out from the hostel and purchased land in the surrounding area.[44] Displaced persons from Europe, and later Asian immigrants, also radiated out from Pennington Hostel a few kilometres along Grand Junction Road.

Aptly named, Grand Junction Road displays the invigorated multicultural community at Rosewater as a junction of many cultures. In the days when the carriageway was a link transporting local farm produce between the Adelaide Hills and Port Adelaide the businesses along Grand Junction Road used to be those of Peoplestores Ltd, Graves & Sons Butchers, and the CPS grocery store. In 2001, new signs on the old bank building advertised Bridal Wear. Rosewater businesses were named Saigon Plaza, Wing Chun Kung Fu Academy, Bida France. The local fish and chips shop sold Lebanese sweets. John Gritizalis & Associates prepared tax returns and women in Muslim headwear served in Robin's Deli. A-Dong Restaurant served Thai, Chinese and Vietnamese food; the pillars abutting the car park entrance featured Ming blue, porcelain lions. The Salvation Army still ran a family store but the name of 'Sutton', the family that once owned the local 'Home Service Stores' no longer featured as a business but as a memorial oval to Eric Sutton who died as a prisoner-of-war on the Burma Thailand Railway during WWII.[45] Eric Sutton was a Councillor and Alderman of Port Adelaide before his enlistment in the second AIF The Port Adelaide Council Chambers previously contained a memorial plaque naming Sutton. The plaque read:

In Memory
of
Alderman Eric Erskine Sutton
Who died in Thailand
Whilst a Prisoner of War, on July 14, 1943.
His Duty Nobly Done
Councillor, December 1930 to June 1939.
Alderman, July 1940 to June 1942.[46]

William Henry Gilbert, in the City of Port Adelaide Mayor's Report 1945–1946, wrote:

> I accepted the plaque on behalf of the City Council and said: 'We shall guard it reverently in honour of the faithful and devoted life to whose memory it is erected.'[47]

Removal and storage of the plaque in Sutton's memory took place during building renovations carried out after the merger of Port Adelaide and Enfield Councils in the 1990s. Enquires elicited the information that eventually the merged Council plans to place the plaque in the Rosewater Football Club Buildings on the memorial oval.[48] Resituating the plaque within Rosewater will link the story of Sutton's death in Thailand to the community asset named in his memory.

'Living memorials', advocated by some members of the veteran community as expressions of timeless gratitude, do not guarantee remembrance of war dead in perpetuity any more than monumental soldiers' memorials. Rosewater had retained the Eric Sutton Memorial oval, but in the larger council area of Port Adelaide Enfield, the LeFevre Peninsula Memorial Trust Playground and Health centre commemorating Port Adelaide industrial companies former employees, who gave their lives in WWII, no longer enjoyed its previous significance. The memorial plaque on the former oval known as the ICI Reserve & Playground stated:

> The LeFevre Peninsula Memorial Trust Inc. Playground and Health Centre dedicated to the memory of those employees of the subscribers who gave their lives in World War II 1939–1945.[49]

Harold Moore, Mayor of Port Adelaide in 1950–1951 reporting on Baby Health Centres wrote:

> The other centre at the I.C.I. Reserve, Peterhead, is for the Peterhead Branch, and forms part of a memorial to commemorate employees of Industrial Companies on Le Fevre Peninsula who gave their lives for King and Country in World War II.[50]

The backyard of the Baby Health Centre forming part of the memorial, opened in 1951 by Lady Mawson, did contain some playground equipment.[51] Redeveloped, urban infill replaced the reserve listed as a memorial by the Corporation of the City of Port Adelaide on 27 March 1968, and detailed in a 'Land Evaluation and Need Study 1985'.[52] The plaque attesting the purpose of the memorial survived, shifted to the edge of the housing estate, but was not visible to traffic or pedestrians on Fletcher road where the former Baby Health Centre had a sign advising it was a Child and Youth Health Centre.[53]

The field study conducted in the area now termed 'Greater Port Adelaide', shows that 'living memorials' from the WWII survive, their significance preserved in the memory of those persons who are aware of the historical links. For example, older community members are aware the memorial oval commemorates Eric Sutton who died while a POW.[54] But, until such time as the Port Adelaide Enfield Council actually transfer and rededicate the memorial plaque previously in the Council chamber, there is no material evidence on the memorial site to associate the living memorial with WWII. Likewise, the Baby Health Centre does not conclusively fulfil the vision of a memorial expressing 'timeless gratitude for unselfish devotion to the defence of our ideals, while at the same time serving the living', the statement made in the 1948 League magazine article.[55] Depreciation in terms of community recognition has reduced the value of the reserve as a living memorial.

The final community building in the Greater Port Adelaide field study, the former Congregational Church at Ottoway, now the Junction Community Centre, had a stained glass leadlight window honouring war dead. It contained two church honour rolls both labelled for the 'Heroes of the Great War' even though one was for the First World War and the other for the Second. In 2001, the Community Centre also housed the honour rolls removed from the old Rosewater District Council Chambers. The honour rolls from the former RSL Hall hung in the Junction Community Centre where migrants attended English classes and other ethnic groups, such as Casa Chile, Filipino Seniors, and those attending Vietnamese dance and exercise met.[56] The recycling of these honour rolls took place because of the actions of former Councillors.[57] Members of an older cultural group cared enough to do something about retaining the rolls to ensure that the story they told remained available and a part of the local community. Preservation of the rolls made them part of the new invigorated multicultural community, which incorporated the symbolism of earlier Australian Britons or British Australians, as a dimension of Australian Anglo-Celtic core culture. Councillors who had served an earlier generation with volunteer work in local government, remembered the stories of an even older generation, and took heed of the Rosewater Women's memorials which admonished: 'God Keep their Memory Green' and 'Let those who come after see to it that their names be not forgotten'.[58] Beliefs, memory and commemorative practices forming a dimension of Australian Anglo-Celtic core identity had been recycled as a backdrop to a multitude of cultural activities at the Junction Community Centre.

My research in Greater Port Adelaide provided evidence 'living memorials' from the 1920s in the form of stained glass windows had a partial retention rate, with the symbolism of their original dedication as soldiers' memorials lost. The two 'living memorials' dedicated since 1945, remained extant, but did not wholly reflect the vision of the intended original symbolism. Conversely, Great War rolls of honour from two of the three buildings surveyed had survived, obvious examples of the 'Debt of Honour'. Despite local cost cutting exercises, the ambience of the surviving honour rolls hanging in the Junction Community Centre provided a sense of identity for Australians into the twenty first century. The field study conducted in relation to memorials in the rural Copper Triangle provided evidence that those communities placed more value on their monuments and 'living memorials' than did the institutions operating within multicultural Greater Port Adelaide. The rural communities had responded to the expanding national interest in the debt of gratitude. Nevertheless research conducted in Rosewater also provided evidence that the continued residence of older Australians in suburban areas undergoing processes of increasing diversity in relation to ethnicity, recycling of community assets and urban infill also elicits a positive response from some sections of the Australian community.

My field studies related to the rural Copper Triangle and metropolitan Greater Port Adelaide are but a small indication of loss, recycling, storage and restoration that has occurred in relation to material and 'living memorials' throughout Australia. Letters, telephone calls and visits to local museums resulted in the information that some museums held honour rolls in storage or as part of exhibitions. The Army Museum at Keswick held a number of former Sunday school honour rolls; the National Motor museum possessed a WWI honour roll, whereas the Maritime Museum's catalogue listed a number of rolls in storage.[59] The Historical Society of the Uniting Church in South Australia was another repository storing honour rolls, as was the National Railway Museum.[60] A League file revealed correspondence about forty-two other cases concerning South Australian memorials, some related to the dedication and unveiling of new memorials, but the majority concerned removal, loss, damage, or vandalism. Some memorials suffered removal and subsequent relocation after community lobbying. In the case of one Council, memorial gates mistakenly auctioned, cost a much higher figure to re-purchase and install at a more convenient location. Living memorials in the form of avenues of trees had lost significance when dedication plaques were lost or the intention of their original significance vanished with subsequent replanting of different varieties.[61] The small sample taken within South Australia indicates a loss of material history in connection with the commemoration of war dead throughout Australia, a reduction in local community acknowledgement of the 'debt of honour', particularly in the case of 'living memorials'. In metropolitan areas, some residents no longer remember, and have no connection with, the individual names listed on honour rolls and memorial windows.

However, in contradiction, under the impetus of the 'Australia Remembers' and 'TS-OH commemorative programmes', evidence exists of resurgent national acknowledgement of a debt of gratitude 'to those who served in the defence of Australia's freedom'.[62] In May 1995, Rod Sawford, Member for Port Adelaide unveiled the T. C. Derrick memorial at Glanville. Lt Thomas Currie Derrick V.C., D.C.M., AIF (1914–1945) received the Victoria Cross for gallantry beyond the call of duty. The annual memorial service of the Ex-POW Association of South Australia took place in August 2001 at Prince Alfred College Chapel. Adjacent to the chapel, stood a SA POW memorial relocated from Prospect in 1999.[63] The Hon Trish Worth MP, Federal Member for Adelaide and the Lord Mayor, Mr Alfred Huang, officially opened the Adelaide 'Pathway of Honour' at the rear of Government House on 24 January 2001.[64] Various battalion memorials line the pathway, which runs between King William Road and Kintore Avenue. On 11 September 2001, at Doxiadis Reserve St Agnes, Trish Draper MP unveiled a monument commemorating the men who fought on the Kokoda Track during WWII.[65] At rural Kapunda, the dedication for the Kapunda War Memorial Garden and memorials for World War II Nurses and others that specifically recognised Vivian Bullwinkel, Capt Nancy Wake and Capt Jean Ashton, took place on 23 September 2001.[66] The Church of Saint Margaret of Scotland, located on Port Road, Woodville held a service of rededication for the Memorial Lychgate, 11 May 2002.[67] These South Australian activities represent but a small sample of renewed recognition of the debt of gratitude espoused in the national 'TS–OH' programme. Many more examples throughout Australia are available on the Department of Veterans' Affairs Internet site.[68]

Overall, attempts metaphorically to 'balance the ledger' in relation to the alleged 'debt of honour' resulting from overseas war service by Australian war dead and war serving, demonstrated continuing acknowledgment of an existing debt. Significantly, more memorials seem to have survived a decline in interest in the commemoration of war dead and war serving evident during the Vietnam War, than have been lost. Anzac culture, exhibited in the form of memorials and other commemorative practices, provides material evidence that some Australians still acknowledge a debt owed to those who served the nation during times of war, a debt established by earlier generations of Australians. If one attempts a reckoning capable of representing or recognising the state of the nation's debt for death on overseas battlefields and the war service of Australian citizens, my field studies provide evidence of depreciation to the intrinsic value of 'living memorials' and honour rolls, dedicated at a local community level, in acknowledgement of that debt. This indicates some religious, local government and commercial institutions believe in a reduction of the debt.

Therefore, the premise arises that the Anzac spirit evident in the sense of self-sacrifice for the benefit of the nation no longer occupies the same iconological position it once did in the idiom of Australian identity. Anzac culture has changed to accommodate an evolving sense of Australian identity that now accepts diversity and blending of cultures. Australians who take part in Anzac Day commemorative services paying homage at memorials at the beginning of the twenty first century, are no longer predominately from a British Australian background. Australian British ancestry merges with the ancestry of naturalised Australians from multicultural backgrounds providing Anzac rituals with representation from many cultures in line with the fastest growing ethnic group within the Australian population itself, those acknowledging mixed ancestry. Since the Federal Government 'Australia Remembers' and 'TS-OH' commemorative programmes, acknowledgement of the national 'debt of gratitude' has supplanted local community remembrance of named individuals. Nevertheless, the former 'debt of honour', now 'debt of gratitude', remains a dimension of Australian Anglo-Celtic core culture, an 'investment' in the national 'balance sheet' that still pays a dividend in terms of national identity.

CHAPTER 10

THE 'PILGRIMAGE TRAIL'[1]

Towards the end of the twentieth century, Australian newspaper and television news reports on Anzac Day drew attention to increasing numbers of Australians travelling to Gallipoli for the Dawn Service and to other significant sites at overseas war cemeteries and memorials. Pilgrims make a pilgrimage, in the religious sense of the word, when travelling to a sacred place as an act of religious devotion. Persons travelling overseas for respectful or sentimental reasons, as in the case of parents or loved ones visiting the grave of a son or relation, also make pilgrimages. Some ex-servicemen and women make pilgrimages for nostalgic reasons; revisiting a site of former incarceration as in the case of ex-prisoners-of-war, or to particular battlefields fought in or occupied as part of military service. Australians make a pilgrimage to significant sites such as Gallipoli for nationalistic reasons in the sense of a civil religion. 'Pilgrims' undertaking this quest range from Prime Ministers to ordinary Australians.[2] Travel Agents also label commercial package tours designed to educate the participants, as well as provide a degree of entertainment, as 'pilgrimages'. Some journeys labelled as a 'pilgrimage' more realistically need classification as tourism where the tour merely stopped at a significant site. Nevertheless, with regard to tours travelling to memorials, war cemeteries and various types of 'shrines', there is a degree of spiritualism in the sense that a journey that includes sites venerating war dead is dissimilar from a tour exclusively offering entertainment as a holiday attraction.

These annual pilgrimages, in reality, are only part of an even greater pilgrimage movement that takes place not necessarily on Anzac Day, but also Remembrance Day and other significant anniversaries. At various times in Australia some communists, pacifists and protestors tried to disrupt annual pilgrimages in the form of Anzac processions. Likewise, some clergymen made claims that Anzac Day glorified war, predicting the gradual demise of such commemorative ceremonies, prophesying that they would appeal less and less to younger generations, as the men and women of the generations who lived and played a part during the hostilities died. With nobody left to remember, or mourn the millions who died in what was advocated as a war to end all wars and a war to improve life for following generations, there was no place for battlefield or memorial pilgrimage, whether real or imaged. To date this prophecy has proven untrue.

The pilgrimage 'cult' embraces countries in different hemispheres, encompassing all those who still remember the dead of wars of the last century, as part of what George Mosse termed the 'cult of the Fallen Soldier'. There were so many men slaughtered in the First World War, governments sought to ease the suffering of the bereaved by erecting monuments recognising the patriotism and sacrifice of war dead in both home countries and on overseas battlefields. As detailed earlier, the United States of America gave parents the option of returning the bodies of American dead to the United States, offering the opportunity to conduct pilgrimages to those mothers who chose to leave their son's body in an overseas war cemetery.[3] Where government action was slow in coming, Australian communities erected and made their own memorials. Some communities both intended and depicted those monuments as 'shrines', expecting the occurrence of pilgrimages as iterated by the Governor-General at the opening of the Australian War Memorial. Globally there are monuments erected honouring war dead. In Australia, some Australian monuments record the names of returned ex-servicemen and women as well.[4] Every year, in addition to the thousands travelling to the nearest country town or nearest city to visit the memorials where official ceremonies take place on Anzac Day, there are also 'pilgrimages' made to local cemeteries, to the burial sites of ex-servicemen and women, particularly by school children. Headstones of veterans in local cemeteries are the subjects of individual recognition and not necessarily only on Anzac Day, some forms of memorialisation occur on Remembrance Day or other anniversaries, such as Victory Europe or Victory Pacific Day.

The number of proposed journeys to visit battlefields and war graves makes one want to try to understand the impulse driving the need for overseas pilgrimage. Prime Minister John Howard, has described pilgrimage to Anzac Cove as almost becoming 'a rite of passage as an Australian young man or woman.'[5] It is something that could not have happened to such a great degree if there had been a body to bury in Australia; to place at rest in a grave tended by loved ones. At the time of writing, bodies of Vietnam Veterans brought home for reburial in Australia have not received quite the same treatment or inspired the same behaviour, although some Vietnam Veterans have returned to Vietnam to visit former prisons, war graves and memorials. The extent of Australian mourning and 'pilgrimage' rituals within Anzac culture must be a reaction to the fact that grieving families of the dead from the two World Wars could not conduct a funeral. Unable to achieve closure conducting that last rite of passage, they did all they possibly could metaphorically to lay Australian war dead to rest, to ease the burden of loss. With no survivors from the generation that lost children in the Great War to verify the above theory, later generations can only ponder the reasons and try to understand the compulsion to make a pilgrimage following the trail of war dead, and the erection of multiple memorials to Australian war dead buried in foreign lands. Whatever the cause, whether religious ritual or nationalistic rites of patriotism, evidence supports a desire to 'pilgrimise' and conduct metaphorical last rites repeatedly to ensure remembrance of war dead, irrespective of the location of the actual burial site holding human remains.

With the end of the Great War, European battlefields, where the majority of the war dead lay buried, were a site of 'pilgrimage' undertaken by the relatives of the combatants of both the victorious and the defeated nations.[6] Michelin & Cie., France, produced illustrated guides of the 1914–1918 battlefields, available to British travellers at booksellers, Michelin Stockists, and the Michelin Tyre Co., London.[7] Except for a few individually recorded journeys, the bulk of recorded overseas pilgrimage took place either under the auspices of the RSL and its antecedent organisations or, alternatively, the Australian Government. The support of the Australian Government was, and is, crucial for expediting the supply of required documentation in relation to passports and visas necessary for entry into some overseas countries. Evidence exists that during the interwar period, Australian civilians instigated numerous attempts to visit war graves but there is little evidence that very many reached their goal.

The cost of conducting tours to overseas war graves deterred some Australians who wished to visit Europe, particularly mothers, but in the case of one South Australian, a public appeal defrayed expenses. The *Diggers' Gazette* in March 1921 reported on the planned visit to England of Sammy Lunn, 'a maker of merry rhymes', and credited Lunn, who had collected over £8,000 for Diggers during the war period, with meeting the majority of outgoing and incoming troop transports. Mindful of Sammy's sacrifices on behalf of the Diggers, League representations resulted in Lunn receiving a MBE. Subsequently a public appeal contributed a sum of £425 enabling Lunn, together with Mrs Lunn, to holiday in England and France where 'the Diggers' pal' planned to put a wreath on the grave of every South Australian soldier. This example instances a recurring theme concerning travel undertaken by Australian civilians to overseas battlefields. Lunn's trip was one of dual purpose, for it encompassed travel to burial sites as well as a holiday.[8] South Australian ex-servicemen and women were instrumental in assisting Samuel

Lunn to France for respectful and sentimental reasons.

Evidence reveals that by November 1927 proposed visits to overseas battlefields had received the label of 'pilgrimage'. A letter from the Prime Minister's Department, Canberra addressed to Royston T. Cahir, Esq., Barrister and Solicitor of Chancery House, Melbourne refers to a previous letter of 29 November 1927 regarding a proposed Pilgrimage to Gallipoli. The Department advised Cahir that Turkish Authorities had expressed a willingness 'to grant facilities required in connection with visas for the party.' The letter passed on a warning from the British Ambassador at Constantinople to observe any formalities imposed by the Turkish Government because the St Barnabas Expedition from London to Gallipoli the previous year had been burdened with inconvenience and considerable difficulty despite Turkish Government permission for the pilgrimage. The Turkish Government received advice that the Pilgrimage would depart Australia in April 1928. The British Ambassador at Constantinople was to arrange with the Turkish Government 'for the visa-ing of the Pilgrims passports'. In another example of dual purpose in relation to pilgrims undertaking overseas travel the letter added another warning suggesting that Australian Armenians should be discouraged from joining the Pilgrimage to visit Gallipoli.[9] In the 1920s, the act of conducting a pilgrimage to Gallipoli was fraught with difficulties needing the support of the Imperial Government, the British Ambassador at Constantinople and Turkish Authorities before receiving any necessary visas and 'Pilgrim passports'.

Achieving satisfactory outcomes in relation to touring France and Flanders proved easier for the British Legion than Service bodies in Australia. Archives record the delegation of Captain John F. Robins, RAN, patron of the RS & SILA, as representative for the High Commissioner during a special pilgrimage to France and Flanders arranged by the British Legion in co-operation with the Empire Service League in 1928.[10] However, the 'Battlefields Tour 1929' was advertised as the first opportunity for both New Zealanders and Australians to join an organised tour to the battlefields and cemeteries of Gallipoli, 'although organised tours have been arranged from the old country.' The United Services Association organised the tour through Messrs Burns, Philp & Co, agents in Australia for the London and North Eastern Railway Co. An application form on the back of the information booklet required details of the 'Cemetery Desired to Visit and Particulars', requesting the name, number, cemetery, grave number and other particulars, making this tour one undertaken for respectful, sentimental and nostalgic reasons. On 4 June 1929, Burns Philp wrote to Captain C. E. W. Bean thanking him for 'a considerable amount of information' valuable in finalising 'arrangements for the Party of Pilgrims, leaving Australia on the SS *Baradine*.'[11] A handwritten note supplies the information that from the PM's file it appeared a 1928 Pilgrimage 'fell through' and a pilgrimage consisting of 86 members, 48 women and 38 men took its place. Given the opportunity, Australian women visited war graves for in this case they made up fifty-six percent of the pilgrims travelling to Gallipoli.[12]

Colloquially, Australians referred to the location of the Gallipoli landing as 'Anzac' before the official naming of the site as 'Anzac Cove.' Minutes of the Sixteenth Sub-Branch Conference of the South Australian Branch of the RS & SILA (hereinafter League), recorded in 1933 referred to the desire of the Mypolonga Sub-Branch that the Federal Congress of the RS & SILA consider the practicability of a tour to the battlefields to mark the 25th anniversary of Anzac at 'Anzac,' seven years into the future.[13] Mypolonga Sub-Branch persisted raising the subject again under date 16 January 1935, but received the information both Conference and Congress had considered and disapproved of the proposal; however, the matter was eligible for resubmission to the next Sub-Branch Conference.[14] The prospect of celebrating significant anniversaries at the site of the Gallipoli landing continued to appeal to sections of the Australian community.

Attempting to organise an Anzac Pilgrimage through the auspices of the Australian War Memorial, J. L. Treloar communicated with C. E. W. Bean in January 1935 suggesting a pilgrimage to Gallipoli, Palestine and France as a celebration to mark twenty years since the end of the war. At that time, Treloar was Director of the Australian War Memorial and stationed in Melbourne, for the AWM was still under construction.[15] Concurrently, Bean had yet to complete *The Official History of Australia in the War of 1914–1918*.[16] Treloar advised Bean he used the word Anzac as an indication of the inclusion of New Zealanders. Treloar nominated General Chauvel, Sir Henry Gullett and Bean, as chief guides and speechmakers, adding he hoped for some sort of executive position for himself. Again, the suggestion of dual purpose arose, for Treloar also proposed attending a test match, preferably in Yorkshire or Lancashire to allow barracking, which he considered out of place at Lords! A further suggestion was to visit Germany and 'finally bury the hatchet', while another possibility was that of paying respects to former comrades in Canada, the United States and New Zealand. However, the most critical decision concerned the limiting of the pilgrimage to ex-servicemen and women or including others such as wives and children, mothers and fathers. Realising that particular problem required careful debate, Treloar added that his preference was for ex-servicemen and women, with the possible addition of fathers of fallen soldiers. Treloar's letter did not recognise any need for mothers, wives and children to assuage grief.

Australians 'pilgrimising' overseas had different characteristics from French, Belgian, German and English pilgrims visiting war graves, because secondary features included aspects of going 'home', visiting relatives or attending Empire ceremonies. Although suggested pilgrimages usually advocated observing significant anniversaries in relation to Anzac Day or the Armistice, 1936 provided a different opportunity for a proposed pilgrimage with dual objectives, the King's coronation.[17] The 'Coronation Issue' of the *Official Year book of the Returned Sailors and Soldiers' Imperial League of Australia 1937* reported Battlefield Pilgrims to war graves on French Battlefields numbered approximately 250,000 annually. Reflecting the ease of ability to conduct pilgrimages, French nationals made up 70% of the pilgrims, Belgians 10%, German 6% and British 3%.[18]

The unveiling of the Villers-Bretonneux Memorial provided an opportunity for the League to successfully nominate Mr R. B. Jacob, a former Past President and Vice President of the South Australian Branch, as a representative of the ex-servicemen and women of Australia when His Majesty King George VI unveiled the Australian memorial in France on l July 1938.[19] While RSL sub-branches and officials propose pilgrimages to celebrate various symbolic anniversaries by journeying to overseas battlefields in Europe and the Middle East, particularly Gallipoli, other 'pilgrimages' do not require overseas travel. Thousands of Australians make an annual 'pilgrimage' to attend Dawn Services, to watch or participate in Anzac processions and to memorial services held at the Cross of Sacrifice in Adelaide, the eternal flame in Brisbane, the Shrine in Melbourne, the Cenotaph in Sydney, memorials in Hobart, Perth and Darwin or the tomb of the Unknown Australian Soldier in Canberra.[20]

Intellectually, there has been another category of Anzac pilgrimage in Australia since 1915, a pilgrimage of the mind or psyche. As an example of 'psyche pilgrimage', at the suggestion of the Goodwood Sub-Branch, the League arranged for South Australians unable to travel to France, to attend the screening of a film depicting the inauguration of the Villers-Bretonneux memorial. The League negotiated with the British Empire Service League and obtained a film of the unveiling proceedings from the Imperial War Graves Commission.[21] State President, Mr W. D. Sharland, organised a showing of the film on 1 October 1939 at the York Theatre, Rundle Street. As evidence of the film's popularity, Sub-Branches received an allotment of seats on a pro rata basis. With Australia at war again, the League planned a collection in aid of the Sailors' and Soldiers' Distress Fund.[22]

Organised 'pilgrimages' after WWII were far more likely to be successful than pre-war attempts but there is evidence that, had they been given the opportunity and provided with financial assistance, more mothers and war widows wanted to journey to war cemeteries. League minutes of July 1945 record a letter to the Editor of the *Advertiser* suggesting that the Commonwealth Government provide shipping at reduced rates for veterans.[23] Mr Alec Horne, a South Australian WWI veteran, completed a visit to the battlefields and cemeteries of France and Belgium, a visit reported in *Back*, in August 1947. Horne listed the towns he visited, and described memorials to the Canadians, New Zealanders, and London Scottish. In particular he mentioned the thousands of 'Rising Suns' on the headstones throughout 'the large, well-kept cemetery of Tyne Cot,' the British cemeteries of Belgium, and the Adelaide cemetery at Villers-Bretonneux.[24] Horne paid his respects to dead Allies approximately thirty years after his army service during the First World War, paying particular attention to noteworthy sites of Australian significance. He revisited the sites of former battlefields for nostalgic reasons, inspecting memorials and war cemeteries.

Official delegations journeyed to war cemeteries conducting inspections and commemorative services endowed with Christian ritual, for the Order of Service for a Dawn Service at Gallipoli provides evidence of both secular and religious rites linked to Anzac culture. Lieut.-General Sir Leslie Morshead led an Australian Delegation to Gallipoli for the Dawn Service on Anzac Day and then continued on to Tobruk for the unveiling of the Australian memorial at the Tobruk Siege Cemetery 30 April 1948. The Beach Cemetery, Gallipoli, was the venue for the Anzac ceremony of remembrance during which Sir Leslie gave the address. Judging the purpose of the delegation from the tone of the epilogue leads one to the conclusion the journey to this significant site took place for nationalistic reasons in the sense of a civil religion. However, by interpreting the site of the Beach Cemetery at Gallipoli as a 'sacred place', there were also elements of Christian religious devotion. The rendition of 'The Lord's Prayer' by Sir Leslie Morshead, the Benediction, and the words of 'Anzac Day' wherein the dead are likened to Christ, in that their death enabled other Australians to live redeemed lives, are rites of the Christian faith. Therefore, this journey to Gallipoli had dual purposes for although on the surface, the Delegation's purpose was secular and nationalistic, it used Christian rites as a model to assuage the grief of mourners.

In August 1951, thirty-three years after war service in Europe, Mr A. C. Sharp, member of the 45th Battalion Reunion Committee, wrote to Mr Bob Sinclair, Honorary Secretary, of the 45th Battalion, AIF Reunion Association in

August 1951 describing the 14 day visit to France and Belgium taken with his wife and son while on a trip to Britain. Describing the Menin Gate Memorial, Sharp recorded that he attended the memorial service at the Gate for five evenings giving as a reason for his nightly vigil Laurence Binyon's lines 'At the going down of the sun and in the morning, we will remember them'.[25] Although Sharp's letter does not convey a sense of religious spiritualism by reference to Christ or Christianity, his patriotism informs a civil religion wherein the recitation of Binyon's Ode stimulated a ritual response, 'We will remember them!' During the day, Sharp literally recorded names of the dead in a ritualistic roll of honour, reached a sense of community or communitas with 'his folk' and came away with a sense of journeying to sacred ground. Sharp's letter recorded the names of the Battalion members whose headstones he found and described the numerous war cemeteries he visited such as Clapham Junction, Hooge Crater and 'Sanctuary wood Cemetery where Padre Talbot (Toc H) is buried.' To Sharp Villers-Bretonneux was a credit to the caretaker, South Australian, C. S. Atkin 'who served in the Light Horse in Palestine, 1916–1918'.[26]

In March 1954, Mrs E. J. Harris, a widowed mother asked the League for help with travelling to Malta for the unveiling of a memorial. The State Board deemed her request outside the scope of the League.[27] However, Mr T. C. Eastick's desire to travel to El Alamein for the unveiling of that memorial met with more support. The Board nominated Eastick, who was League President at the time, to Federal Office for appointment as the RSS & AILA representative on the grounds of Eastick's close association with the El Alamein Association and his distinguished service at the Battle of El Alamein.[28] Some journeys referred to as a 'pilgrimage' in League State Board minutes relate to travel to South Australian cemeteries, and interstate journeys on significant occasions. League Minutes recorded South Australians Messrs Joyce and Wilson as 'pilgrims' for the 1955 Gallipoli pilgrimage.[29] The December edition of *Back* magazine of the RSL contained an advertisement for a 'World Commemoration Tour' that incorporated a landing party on the Gallipoli beaches on 25 April 1955 and attendance at the unveiling of a Turkish memorial to war dead. The complete tour extended over five months and visited not only Middle Eastern countries, but also European countries and the United States of America.[30]

In 1955, the Prime Minister's Department became involved with the pilgrimage in an official capacity. The Prime Minister's Department was in a quandary by 24 March 1955 because, officially, they had no knowledge of the RSL Gallipoli pilgrimage. Neagle, General Secretary of the RSL, believed that

General Erdelhun, Chief of the Turkish General Staff, mistakenly thought three Australian Generals were members of the pilgrimage. Consequently, Neagle asked for the appointment of Sir George Holland as Commonwealth representative for the Turkish visit. A letter addressed to the Prime Minister (Robert Menzies) recommended the appointment of Sir George Holland as Commonwealth representative for the visit to Turkey and the purchase of a suitable gift for the Prime Minister of Turkey.[31] Menzies arranged for Holland to present the Turkish Prime Minister with a pair of bronze table type kangaroos.

In 1960, Robert Menzies, Prime Minister of Australia, and W. Nash, Prime Minister of New Zealand, travelled to London and placed wreaths on the Cenotaph on Anzac Day.[32] By July 1960 RSL World Tourists had arrived in London, where Mr Alf Niff, from Royston Park, South Australia, attended a British Legion reception in the company of other members of the 5th Battalion. *Sentry-Go* published a photograph of other World Tourists at Windsor.[33] As in proposed tours during the interwar period, tours after WWII contained an additional element that of visiting sites with important connotations and connection to British history.

Although initially the Australian and British Governments saw visits to war graves as the financial responsibility of the individuals who undertook that quest, Australian governmental policies regarding financial assistance for pilgrimage to significant sites overseas did begin to change in the 1960s. With the fiftieth anniversary of the Gallipoli landing approaching, the RSS & AILA began planning for suitable commemoration procedures to mark the occasion, making a request for financial assistance in the form of a subsidy to meet the expenses of Gallipoli veterans and their dependants or next of kin, for a key feature of the commemoration, a Gallipoli pilgrimage. Acknowledging the organisation of such a pilgrimage as extremely complex and fraught with many difficulties, the RSS & AILA saw it as an event open to all interested parties necessitating a framework of inter-Governmental liaison between Australia, New Zealand and Turkey.[34]

In 1963, the National Secretary of the RSS & AILA, Mr A. G. W. Keys, wrote to the Australian Prime Minister Rt Hon Sir Robert Menzies. The same object of sacrifice in the interest of the nation evident in that letter follows the trend of sermons and addresses given by clergymen to earlier generations of Australians, but in this event, there is no mention of Christ or Christianity. Instead Keys mentioned the high hopes of the RSS & AILA for the development of the pilgrimage 'into a unique demonstration of national feeling.' In touting the Gallipoli pilgrimage as a base upon which to build national feeling, a base for strengthening personal effort and sacrifice, Keys, as National Secretary of the RSS & AILA, advocated patriotism based on Anzac and a national civil religion.[35] Paradoxically, at the time of the Vietnam War, a war accompanied by moratoriums stirred up by issues of unfair conscription policies, veterans of the voluntary first and second AIFs advocated the basis of a civil religion capable of cementing the core of the Australian national identity.

The suggested injection of new life into the Anzac tradition and its supposed impact on young Australians must have resonated within Canberra's corridors of power because, despite the earlier claim that the Government did not financially support pilgrimages, the planned journey's significance was enough to change Governmental policy to the extent of granting a subsidy towards its cost. Further, the Government directed Qantas to grant a 30% group travel concession.[36] In NSW the State Executive agreed 'that the subsidy be devoted to assisting original Anzacs', specifically those unable to meet the cost of the pilgrimage. The Prime Minister's Department gave responsibility for all arrangements and the actual distribution of the provided grant (£20,000) to the RSS & AILA. A special circular dated 25 July 1964 addressed to Secretaries of RSS & AILA Sub-Branches advised that the itinerary included calls at 'Tobruk, Alexandria, Cairo, El Alamein, Beirut and the Greek Islands culminating at Gallipoli on 25 April'. The NSW Returned Servicemen's League elected a committee to investigate the many requests received for assistance.[37] South Australia's allocated proportion of the grant was enough to cover the fares for four persons.[38]

The Government's grant of financial assistance for veterans to return to Gallipoli did not receive unqualified support from all relevant Commonwealth Departments. J. M. Wark, Assistant Secretary, Commonwealth Treasury, advised Treasury rejected any extension of the tour to Second World War battlefields stating that those battlefields had nothing to do with Anzac.[39] The Department of External Affairs expressed misgivings relating to the terminology 'pilgrimage'. Referring to the past behaviour of Australian troops in Arab countries, the Department of External Affairs warned of possible difficulties and endeavoured to change the object of the RSL's 'project' from one of pilgrimage, to that of tourism. A 'confidential' report regarding the RSL Gallipoli Pilgrimage addressed to 'The Minister' signed by J. R. Rowland, Acting Senior Assistant Secretary, Africa and Middle East Section, stated 'memories of our troops in Egypt, for example, may not be entirely happy ones'.[40] Possibly Rowland was referring to 'the battle of the Wassa', which occurred in April 1915, when 'mostly drunk' Australians 'threw furniture into the street and set fire to it.'[41] In the report, Rowland proposed his Department brief the pilgrimage leader, Sir Raymond Huish, Deputy National president of the RSL and State President of the Queensland Branch, together with another possible pilgrim, Sir William Spooner, before their departure overseas.[42] Despite bureaucratic concerns, the 1965 return to Gallipoli proceeded under the leadership of Sir Raymond Huish.[43]

As with other official anniversary pilgrimages, RSL National Office accepted nominations from the South Australian Branch. League minutes record seventeen South Australians taking part in the 1965 Gallipoli Pilgrimage, making particular mention of Messrs P. Auld and J. Gordon.[44] National Office approved the South Australian recommendation of Auld's appointment as the person responsible for the ship's canteen, while Gordon was appointed leader of the South Australian delegation.[45] The same year (1965) the Commonwealth Government offered five couples from each State the opportunity to visit Canberra for the Anzac celebrations.[46] Five South Australian couples, together with a returned sister and war widow, Mrs A. S. Blackman undertook a pilgrimage to Canberra where Anzac Parade, now the site of major memorials, was officially opened as part of the anniversary celebrations.[47] With the help of the Commonwealth Government, Australians marked the 50th anniversary of the Gallipoli Landing by making pilgrimages to overseas WWI battlefields, war cemeteries and the national capital, Canberra. Government attitudes towards veterans and relatives wishing to visit overseas war graves had undergone subtle changes.

Later, in September 1965, the League attempted to arrange for Mrs Jacobs, who was prepared to meet her own costs, to visit Bomana Cemetery, New Guinea, site of WWII war graves.[48] By 1965, pilgrimages to visit the burial sites of dead servicemen of WWI and WWII in overseas war cemeteries had become established practice, part of a national civil religion recognising the valour and sacrifice of Australian volunteers in the service of the British Empire and Australia. At the time of the Vietnam War, various Australian pilgrims ventured to the Middle East, Asia and Europe. Parliamentarians took the opportunity to visit sites connected with Australian prisoners-of-war as well as Gallipoli. South Australians received notice of impending journeys from National Office. In April 1967, national circular 42/67 advised of the 50th Anniversary of the Commonwealth War Graves Commission. The same minutes recorded the proposed tours to Gallipoli of Brig Brown and El Alamein by Mr and Mrs Eastick.[49] One circular related to the dedication of the Ambon War Cemetery and a second tabled for information was the 'Return to Kokoda'.[50] The pilgrimage trail extended to sites of former captivity enabling ex-members of the second AIF to pay respects at the graves of those Australians who had succumbed to malnutrition and the brutal treatment of their captors. As ex-servicemen and ex-prisoners-of-war, some politicians returned to war cemeteries as pilgrims, rather than representatives of Government delegations.[51]

Politicians continued their involvement in overseas pilgrimages and war widows sustained their desire to visit war graves, for in April and May 1968, Mr Les Irwin, Member of Parliament, led a party of WWI Diggers and forty-three war widows on a four-week journey to European battlefields. Secretary-Manager of the Third Division AIF Remembrance Pilgrimage 1968, organised by 9th Brigade AIF Veteran's Association, subsequently thanked the Rt Hon P. M. Hasluck, MP, Minister for External Affairs as joint patron of the 'Remembrance Pilgrimage', which included a private audience with his Holiness Pope Paul VI.[52] The patronage of the Minister for External Affairs allowed the Australian pilgrims the chance to achieve a sense of communitas and ensured the success of their quest.[53]

The Australian Government and its agencies supported the 1968 'Battle of the Somme Pilgrimage' ensuring the journey to France was a considerable success, despite the visit's occurrence at a time when radical students protested in Australia against the Vietnam War. Prime Minister John Gorton, himself an ex-serviceman who served in the Air Force during WWII, published a message stating that the presence of the Australian veterans in Villers-Bretonneux was a reminder that Australians, like the French, had not forgotten.[54] The help of the Minister for External Affairs and the presence of Les Irwin gave the pilgrimage significance at the highest levels of overseas governments in Washington, Paris, Rome and Tel Aviv. Australian ambassadors and staff arranged receptions, and introductions to representatives of official and public bodies, diplomats and media personnel.[55] This pilgrimage included a 'pilgrimise' component in the specific religious sense of the word in terms that 'pilgrimers' journeyed to Rome for private audience with Pope Paul VI. Organised pilgrimage tours recognised other significant events such as the signing of the Armistice. In November of the same year, a combined contingent of one hundred and ninety men from New Zealand and Australia travelled to France and took part in celebrations marking the 50th anniversary of the signing of the Armistice.[56] The Government supported 'Pilgrimage Trail', extended to Europe.

Australian Prime Ministers and Parliamentarians recognised diplomatic and trade benefit resulted from visits to significant sites overseas, becoming increasingly supportive of veteran initiatives to organise tours along what has become a well-worn trail to overseas battlefields and war cemeteries. Eight members of Federal Parliament visited the Gallipoli Peninsular in January 1971. Mr Chris Hurford, MHR, recorded impressions of his visit to Lone Pine, and the New Zealand memorial at 12 Tree Copse. As the Member for Adelaide, Hurford assured veterans and relatives of war dead that the memorials and graves were well cared for. Hurford described the occasion as 'most moving' for he knew his father was at Gallipoli 56 years earlier and he found the name of one of his three great-uncles who died at Gallipoli on a memorial. Labelling the visit as the first official visit from the Australian Parliament to the Turkish Parliament, Hurford found the Turkish people he met during his visit warm and friendly. Hurford also reported that Australia had representatives in Turkey working to ensure a feeling of mutual respect.[57]

Visiting significant sites on specific anniversaries became a feature of future pilgrimages within Anzac culture. Veterans travelled to El Alamein in 1972 for the 30th Anniversary of that battle.[58] April 25 1975 marked the 60th Anniversary, the Diamond Jubilee, of Anzac Day, for which the RSL arranged a pilgrimage to Gallipoli.[59] The *Sydney Morning Herald* reported on 26 April 1975 that this time the veterans met in Turkey, without the backing of their government, one veteran declaring the Australian Government had no part in commemorating the Anzac landing because the Australian RSL alone supported the visit to honour the dead.[60] Historian Patsy Adam Smith, author of *The Anzacs*, joined Australian veterans on a pilgrimage marking the 60th Anniversary of the Armistice, during which Mr Alderman, the Australian Minister for Veterans Affairs, made a speech at Villers-Bretonneux on Armistice Day 1978. A party of eight South Australians toured with this group.[61]

Furthermore, although commemorative Anzac Day observances continued in Britain, Australian Prime Ministers increasingly ventured to Gallipoli and took part in international memorial services. Whereas earlier Australian Prime Ministers William Hughes and Robert Menzies had observed Anzac Day in London, the 75th anniversary of the Gallipoli Landing was notable for the presence of Prime Minister Robert Hawke at Lone Pine, and his speech concerning the re-interpretation of the Anzac tradition.[62] The Hon R. J. L. Hawke, AC, MP, in the presence of 47 original Anzacs, said in his memorial speech on 25 April 1990 that 'the Anzac tradition, forged in the fires of Gallipoli, must be learned anew, from generation to generation'.[63] Continuing, Hawke said:

> In the continuing quest for the real meaning of Anzac, our way is lit by the shining presence here today of the little band of first Anzacs, who have returned.
>
> This is, for all of us here, and for all our fellow Australians at home, an honour, an experience, an emotion, which goes beyond words.[64]

The speech delivered by Hawke referred to a quote from Bean as recognising the meaning of Australian mateship wherein lay the genesis of the Anzac tradition, and at the heart of the tradition a commitment.[65] The Prime Minister's speech recognised the relationship between Anzac culture and Australian identity. However, after stating that the meaning of Anzac only endured as long as each new generation re-interprets it, Hawke delivered a speech that defined the tradition of Anzac as a commitment to mateship, with no reference to women. Unlike Prime Minister Hughes, who recognised the sacrifice of women, and unlike the Anzacs' Australian contemporaries who believed that the 'debt of honour' extended to the relatives and dependants of ex-service personnel. Hawke re-interpreted the Anzac tradition only in terms of the 'cult of the Fallen Soldier', leaving out a large part of the original concept of Anzac culture. Reporting on the makeup of pilgrims who undertook the 1990 Gallipoli Pilgrimage, the RSL Handbook noted the presence of one World War I Nurse with the 58 World War I Veterans who returned to where the Anzac spirit was born, together with eight war widows of World War I Veterans and eight war orphans. Despite the words of Prime Minister Hawke, the RSL remembered to honour all aspects of the original 'debt of honour'.[66]

Also present at Gallipoli in 1990, was an Australian Parliamentary Delegation, which ultimately recommended the maintenance of commemorative services on Gallipoli. The Parliamentary Delegation consisted of Senators M.A. Colston, Leader, D. J. Hamer, Deputy Leader, B. R. Burns, Messrs D. M. Connolly, MP, T. A. Fischer, MP, Leader of the National Party of Australia, L. J. Scott, MP, and P. N. Gibson, MC, Secretary to the Delegation and the Joint Committee on Foreign Affairs, Defence and Trade. The report deemed the presence of the delegation at the Anzac Commemorative service as 'a singular honour and an experience of quite extraordinary dimensions', because the Anzac tradition had related to four generations of Australians of all religious, racial, socio-economic, cultural and political backgrounds; the Anzac tradition said what it meant to be 'Australian'. Using figures from the 1986 census, the report also acknowledged the presence of 37,000 people in Australia who claimed Turkish ancestry, while a second generation calculated at between 80,000 and 150,000 lived mainly in Sydney and Melbourne.[67] Turkish sons and daughters in Australia reciprocated and amplified the presence of Australian sons in Turkey.

Noting the presence of representatives from Turkey, New Zealand, the United Kingdom, Canada, Germany, India and Pakistan who attended the International Ceremony that began with the laying of wreaths, the Delegation expressed appreciation on behalf of the Parliament for the RSL's role in organising the Anzac Service of Remembrance at Gallipoli for many years.[68] Further, the Delegation recommended:

> [T]hat the Minister for Veterans' Affairs take active steps to ensure that the RSL is assisted in maintaining its administrative role in the organisation of commemorative services on Gallipoli in the years ahead. In addition to the Dawn Service organised by the RSL each year, the Delegation sees a need for formal Australian Government involvement, through the Australian Embassy in Turkey, in organising an annual Service of Remembrance at the Line Pine Memorial each ANZAC day. Particularly following the immense national interest generated by the 1990 commemoration at Gallipoli, it is imperative that future arrangements be appropriately and formally supported by the national Government.[69]

Subsequently the Minister for Veterans' Affairs complied with the recommended formal involvement of the Australian Government in the organisation of commemorative services not only on Gallipoli, but also at other significant sites overseas.

Realising that commemorative anniversaries related to war dead and war service would occur repeatedly, the Department of Veterans' Affairs began a small section in 1996 that dealt specifically with a programme known as 'Their Service our Heritage'. The Branch within the Department of Veterans' Affairs deals not only with pilgrimages, but also with school and community education.[70] Members of Parliament and the Australian Prime Minister have continued attending commemorative services as part of Anzac culture. The Deputy Prime Minister, together with the Minister of Veterans' Affairs, Bruce Scott, and a representative group of Vietnam Veterans visited Vietnam, Singapore and Malaysia in 1996.[71] Prime Minister John Howard attended the opening of the Hellfire Pass Museum in Thailand on 24 April 1998. In giving the opening address John Howard's speech recognised that the umbrella of Anzac culture covered both men and women, and the sacredness of land literally imbued with courage and sacrifice intrinsic to the 'cult of the Fallen Soldier'.[72]

Increasing numbers of international pilgrims attended Anzac Day Dawn Services at Gallipoli. Consequently, in the year 2000, a new ANZAC Commemorative Site was inaugurated to provide more space than had been available at the previous location of the Anzac Dawn Service. Prime Ministers John Howard from Australia and Helen Clark from New Zealand, unveiled the Anzac Commemorative Site. Australian Minister for Veterans' Affairs, Bruce Scott, together with the National President of the New Zealand Returned Services Association, Mr David Cox MBE, and the National President, Returned and Services League of Australia, Major General Peter Phillips AO,

MC, took leading roles in the service, as did both the Australian and New Zealand Defence Force Chaplains. The service also recognised indigenous Australians and New Zealanders with a Didgeridoo Calling performed by Robert Slockee, and a Karanga, a Maori Call to Gathering, performed by Corporal Una Tarau.[73] Opposition Leader Kim Beazley was another Australian Parliamentarian present at the Dawn Service.[74] Officially travelling as the Australian Prime Minister, John Howard journeyed from Turkey to France to meet French officials. While in France for the period 26–29 April, even though surrounded by pomp and ceremony, he made a personal pilgrimage to memorials in the WWI battlefields of the Somme, where both his father and grandfather served in the AIF.[75]

Earlier Australian Prime Minsters saw the London Cenotaph as a vehicle for honouring war dead and visits to war cemeteries as a journey for private individuals. Since 1919, more Australian individuals wished to undertake pilgrimages to war graves than had either the opportunity or the financial means to achieve their objective. Parliamentarians and later Prime Ministers recognised overseas war cemeteries as a focus for Australian consciousness or identity. The 'hallowed grounds' of Gallipoli and later battlefields have become the basis of pilgrimage as a rite of passage of an Australian civil religion that recognises sacrifice of Australian blood in the service of the nation.[76] Although Australians used 'pilgrimages' for dual purposes, for part of their 'pilgrimage' related to activities as tourists for purposes of entertainment, travelling from Australia to overseas war graves and battlefields has provided many Australians with a sense of communitas. Having achieved their quest, spiritually moved by emotional experiences once they reached their goal, 'pilgrims' have returned to Australia with a deeper sense of national consciousness and appreciation for the sacrifice of earlier Australians in service of the British Empire and the Australian nation.

Although modern commemorative visits to significant sites are not identical to medieval pilgrimages to a sacred site of religious significance, ritualistic journeys resulting in a psychological, emotional experience do have a spiritual component. Gallipoli, European and Asian battlefields, sites of former incarceration, and Australian war cemeteries overseas have become imbued with a sense of spiritualism in that they are perceived by some Australians as 'sacred ground'. In 1998, Jennifer de Freitas argued that visits to heritage sites are secular pilgrimage.[77] Travelling to sites perceived as sacred or hallowed ground in the context of Australian heritage, pilgrimages to overseas battlefields and burial sites can be interpreted as part of an Australian civil religion that is a dimension of the Anglo-Celtic core culture holding Australians from diverse backgrounds together as a nation. Australian identity and consciousness has achieved redirection away from Britain to Australia via the battlefields of the Middle East, Europe and Asia.

EPILOGUE

In June 2005 I made a pilgrimage of my own. I went on a battlefield journey to the Western Front. I followed in the footsteps of other South Australians: of Sammy Lunn 'the Diggers' pal' in 1921, of League Past President Mr R. B. Jacob who attended the unveiling of the Villers-Bretonneux memorial in 1938, of Mr Alec Horne who journeyed to Tyne Cot cemetery, Adelaide cemetery and the Fifth Australian Division monument at Polygon Wood, Zonnebeke in 1947. I know I followed in the footsteps of other Australians, because everywhere I went there was evidence of an Australian presence claiming a connection with Australian history on the Western Front, evidence showing that the 'debt of honour' was still remembered. Perhaps Mount Barker High School students left some of that evidence during their 2001 Remembrance project?[1]

There was a toy koala hanging from the Digger's rifle strap on the 2nd Division memorial at Mont St Quentin, together with a red poppy behind the dedication plaque. A police badge alongside one name and the symbolic red poppy alongside a few other names high up on the Villers-Bretonneux cemetery wall of the Australian missing that could only have been placed there with the help of a ladder, or the agility of the young. Australian flags and poppy crosses adorned the site of the former grave of the Unknown Australian Soldier in Adelaide Cemetery. Under the broken remains of a German blockhouse supporting the 'Cobbers' memorial at Fromelles, someone had placed remembrance posies and poppies. The Australian Corps Memorial Park at Le Hamel with its black tiled walls and 'Rising Sun' insignia was quite different from the other memorials in France and Belgium. Nevertheless, at the base of the black remembrance stone with its quote from C. E. W. Bean lay more poppy crosses and remembrance posies.

On a small memorial cairn near Bullecourt Australians had placed their own private plaques, poppy wreaths and remembrance posies honouring war dead. Likewise at the base of the nearby Bullecourt Digger and Bullecourt Slouch Hat memorial were more wreaths of poppy and bay leaves. A myriad of small koalas and Australian flags adorned a shelf in the 'Le Canberra' Café

Headstone for W. F. L. Dodson

at Bullecourt. The correspondence displayed at Bullecourt's museum and written by Australians to the museum's curator Jean Letaille, included a letter of condolence on the death of Monsieur Letaille's wife Denise Letaille from Prime Minister John Howard. In Ypres I watched as a member of a RSL sub-branch in Brisbane humbly placed a wreath during a service at the Menin Gate, where members of the Fire Brigade still play the Last Post each evening.

Journeying to Hooge Crater cemetery, I stopped and placed a poppy wreath at the headstone over the 'provisional grave' marked 'believed to be Lieutenant W. F. L. Dodson' who died on the night of 19/20 September 1917, and placed a poppy cross at the foot of the grave of his fellow South Australian, Lieutenant G. H. Leaver killed the same night. But above all my most lasting impression was recognition of the almost overpowering feeling of sacrifice that was embodied in the walls of the names of the missing at Thiepval, and the battle scarred Australian national memorial at Villers-Bretonneux, and on the Menin Gate. The sheer number of names and the corresponding headstones to unknown soldiers is overwhelming. In the visitors' books at the various cemeteries were the signatures of Australians from all over Australia.

God has answered the prayers of Rosewater women and, as asked on the monument in the corner of the Eric Sutton Memorial Oval at Rosewater, kept the memory of Australian veterans green. On Anzac Day and other commemorative days, Australians still acknowledge the undying debt owed to fellow Australians who made the supreme sacrifice and to the men and women who served the nation during times of war.

NOTES TO THE TEXT

Chapter 1 – 'Honouring the Debt'

1. State Ex Service Round Table on Aged Care, (presenter), A Last Debt, A Seminar on Aged Care Needs In the Veteran Community, Funded by Department of Veterans' Affairs. 18 August 2000.
2. *Advertiser*, 'A Debt of Honor', 3 July 1915, p. 13,15; the *Register*, 'Fallen Heroes-Violet Day', 'really a sacred obligation', 2 July, 1915, p. 4; *Advertiser*, 'The Roll of Honor', 3 May 1915, p. 7; *Register*, 'Roll of Honor', 4 May 1915, p. 6.
3. Adelaide City Archives, TCDKT 1915/2964, Arrangements for Anzac Day, 6 September 1915.
4. ACA, 1915/2964, Arrangements for Anzac Day, 6, 24, 29 September, 1915.
5. *Register*, 2,4,5,6,7,8,9,11,12,13 October 1915, p. 2 each day; *Advertiser* 1,2,4,5,6,11,12 October 1915, p. 2 each day.
6. *Register*, 'To-day's Appeal, The Anzac Celebration', 13 October 1915, p. 7.
7. *Register*, 'News of the Day', and 'Labour's Loyalty. Anzac Day Celebration. More than £2,500 Realised', 14 October 1915, p. 4.
8. *Advertiser*, 'Soldiers and Police, Another Serious Riot, Disgraceful Scenes in the City, Two Arrests made', 14 October 1915, p. 9.
9. *Register*, 'First List of Casualties', 3 May 1915, p. 7; *Advertiser*, 'The Roll of Honor', 3 May 1915, 'Statement by Mr Pearce', p. 7; *Advertiser*, 21 May 1915 'The Roll of Honor', p. 8; *Advertiser*, 'General Bridges', 22 May 1915, p. 20; *Advertiser*, 'Lusitania Torpedoed', 10 May 1915, p. 9; *Advertiser*, 'Twenty-fifth Casualty List', 29 May 1915, p. 16.
10. Geoffrey Serle, (gen ed), *Australian Dictionary of Biography* (ADB), Vol 11, (Melbourne: Melbourne University, 1988), Seager, p. 559; Christopher M. Argent, '"For God, King and Country" Aspects of Patriotic Campaigners in Adelaide During the Great War. With Special Reference to the Cheer-Up Society, the League of Loyal Women and Conscription,' BA Honours Thesis, University of Adelaide, 1993, p. 30.
11. ACA, 1915/2048, Cheer-Up Society, 18 June 1915.
12. *ADB*, 1988, p. 559; *Advertiser*, 'Violet Day', 3 July 1915, p. 17; Psalm 23, verse 4, Yea, though I walk through the valley of the shadow of death,/I will fear no evil: for thou art with me,/Thy rod and thy staff they comfort me.
13. *Advertiser*, 'Violet Day', 3 July 1915, p. 17; *Register*, 'In Memory', 2 July 1915, p. 4.
14. *Advertiser*, 'The Governor's Address', 3 July 1915, p. 17.
15. *Advertiser*, 'Australia Day, For our wounded Heroes, Mr Hugh Ward explains a scheme', 2 June 1915, p. 10; 'Preparing for Australia Day', 3 July 1915, p. 15.
16. *Register*, 'A Pageant of Patriotism', 31 July 1915, p. 14.
17. *Advertiser*, 'Australia Day', 2 June 1915, p. 10.
18. Mortlock pamphlet, Zpam 369.294 S731, 1913, W J Sowden, Australian Wattle Day League, Outline history of the wattle blossom celebration in Australia, 1913, pp. 2–3; p. 8; p. 12.
19. John Ritchie, (ed), *Australian Dictionary of Biography, Volume 12, 1891–1939*, (Melbourne: Melbourne University, 1990), Young, pp. 597–598; ACA, 1915/2598.01, Wattle Day Arrangement, Letter from Jeanne F Young to Town Clerk, Adelaide 12 August 1915, p. 1.
20. *Register*, 'Golden Wattle', 7 September 1915, p. 4; 'Wattle Day Preparations', 6 September 1915, p. 4.
21. *Advertiser*, 'A Beautiful Memorial', 8 September 1915, p. 12.

22. *Advertiser*, 'Wattle Day', 8 September 1915, p. 12; *Register*, 'Wattle Day Celebrations', 3 September 1915 p. 4, 'Wattle Day Preparations', 6 September 1915 p. 7; Mortlock Zper 369.29423 A 938 a Wattle Day League (South Australian Branch) Report of the Annual Meeting held at the May Club on Tuesday evening October 5 1915.
23. Minute Book, Inaugural Meetings of RSL 1915–1917, First meeting, 8 December 1915, p. 1; General Meeting 22 December 1915, p. 4.
24. ACA, TCDKT 1916/1145, Anzac Day Commemoration Committee (Brisbane), letter from David J Garland, Hon Secretary, to His Worship the Mayor of Adelaide, S Australia, 28 February 1916.
25. ACA, TCDKT 1916/1145, Anzac Day Commemoration Committee (Brisbane), T J Ryan, Chairman, David J Garland, Hon Secretary Plan of Observance of Anzac Day, Tuesday 25 April 1916.
26. ACA, 1916/1145, Anzac Day Commemoration Committee (Brisbane), Plan of Observance of Anzac Day, Tuesday, 25 April, 1916; Anzac Day Commemoration, 25 April, 1916.
27. Mortlock Library Z Pamphlet Anzac Souvenir 940.425 A637, Anzac Day Commemoration April 25th 1916, pp. 2–46.
28. ACA, 1918/0801, Button Day Returned Soldiers Association – 26 April 1918, Letterhead, Council of Control of Patriotic Street Sales, South Australia, to Town Clerk, Adelaide from Hon Secretary, 5 March, 1918; ACA, 4183 Item 0023.01, Town Clerk's Office Index of Letters received 1916–1917, unpaginated, listed under 'P'.
29. *Advertiser*, 12.4.1916, p. 2; *Advertiser*, 20.4.1917, p. 2. and *Register*, 23.4.1917, p. 8.
30. ACA, 1918/1451, W C Torode – Stone Cross on top of Obelisk Wattle Grove, Memos to Town Clerk and City Gardner, 20 April 1918; Letter to Mr W C Torode, 26 April 1918.
31. *Advertiser*, 'The Meaning of the Grove', 8 September 1915, p. 12.
32. League Minutes, 14 March 1917 adjourned 17 March 1917, pp. 132–134; ACA, 1918/0801 Button Day Returned Soldiers Association, Letter on Council of Control of Patriotic Street Sales letterhead from Fuller, Hon Secretary, to Town Clerk, 5 March 1918; Letter from League dated 23 March 1918, 18 April 1918; Letterhead, The League of Loyal Women of Australia, to Town Clerk 23 April 1918; Letter from League, 23 March 1918.
33. Michael Reardon, 'Anzac Day in Adelaide, 1916–1922 from the first anniversary to a national public holiday', Honours Thesis, University of Adelaide, 1979.
34. ACA, 1918/0801, Special District Order, 20 April 1918.
35. National Archives of Australia, Series number D958/0, Control symbol S1919/5808, Contents date range 1919–1919, Instructions re observance of two minutes silence on Armistice Day, Circular No 570, 10 November 1919; For the history of Armistice Day in Britain, see Adrian Gregory, *The Silence of Memory Armistice Day 1919–1946*, (Oxford: Berg, 1994).
36. *Diggers' Gazette*, Vol II, no 11, 'Human Wreckage', 21 April 1921, pp. 31–37; Vol II, no 12, 'Army of the Dead', 7 May 1921, p. 42; 'The March of the Dead', p. 21.
37. *Diggers' Gazette*, Vol II No 1, 15 Nov 1920, pp. 9–10.
38. *Diggers' Gazette*, Vol III, No 10, 7 October, 1921, p. 10, 26; No 12, 7 November, 1921, p. 1, p. 26.
39. *Advertiser*, 3 July 1915, p. 15; *Diggers' Gazette*, Vol II, No 12, May 1921, pp. 41–42.
40. NAA D959/0, IA1952/817, Tubercular Soldiers Aid Society letterhead, to Controller of Stores GPO, from Miss E Clegget, 1 December 1921; booklet issued by the Tubercular Aid Society, 'The Bedford Call'.

41. NAA D959/0, IA1952/817, correspondence from Miss Clegget 10 February, 12 November 1926; 'The Optimist', with which is incorporated 'The Bedford Call', No 7, March 1929.
42. Hans Mincham, *The Story of the Flinders Ranges*, (Adelaide: Rigby, 1964), p. 287.
43. ACA, 1917/2419.01, Wattle Day League. Planting of Wattle Trees at South Parklands, 17 August 1923; letter from acting Town Clerk, 27 August 1923; *Advertiser* 'Soldiers' Mothers' Band', 27 April 1925, p. 11; 'Soldiers' Mothers', 26 April 1926, p. 11; Des Ryan, words & David Faber, research, 'The forgotten, original Anzac memorial', *City Messenger*, 22 April 1998, p. 6; ACA, National War Memorial 305C, 19.9.68 to 2.10.1975 Pamphlet produced by RSL.
44. *Diggers' Gazette*, Vol II, No 7, 21 February 1921, pp. 43–45.
45. *Advertiser*, 'War Prisoners Reach Britain', 26 April 1943, p. 3; 'Memorable Observance, Dawn Services in City and Suburbs', 26 April 1945, p. 5; *Back*, Magazine of the R.S.L., August 1947, p. 7.
46. League State Board Minutes, (f) Funeral – Miss Clegget, 4 April 1960; SB, (o) Angorichina Hostel, 3 October 1960; SB, TB Soldiers Aid Society, 16 May 1966; SB, TB Assoc, 16 November 1970.
47. RSL Annual Report year ended 31 December 1962, p. 14; A/R 1964–65, unpaginated; Mortlock Library Pamphlet A940.425, Address by Mr W C D Veale, Violet Memory Day, 1 August, 1965, Town Hall Adelaide, p. 8; SB minutes, (f) Violet Memory Day, 18 May 1971.
48. RSSAILA, Annual Report and Balance Sheet, year ended 31st December 1965, no pagination; Annual Report, 1970, p. 17.
49. *Sun Herald*, 'Vietnam Vets weep as nation says thanks', 4 October 1987, p. 2, p. 3; For more information see Peter Haran, *Trackers The Untold Story of the Australian Dogs of War*, (Sydney: New Holland, first published 2000, reprinted 2000, 2001), p. 5 and 195.
50. Information reprinted by the League from the minutes of the Royal Australian Corps of Signals Officers' Association Queensland. Unpaginated; *Advertiser*, 'Impressive Dawn Service', 27 April 1931, p. 8; 'Dawn of Anzac', 26 April 1932, p. 10; 25 April 1933, 'Unley Service at 6.00 am', p. 7; 'Dawn Services Ceremony at State War Memorial', 26 April 1935, p. 18.

Chapter 2 – Sacred Ground

1. Tanja Luckins, *The Gates of Memory, Australian People's Experiences and Memories of Loss and the Great War*, (Fremantle: Curtin University, 2004), p. 159, 161.
2. Compiled by Judith McKay and Richard Allom, *Lest We Forget A Guide to the Conservation of War Memorials*, (Brisbane: Returned Services League of Australia (Queensland Branch), 1984), explains how statues of soldiers carved from white stone, suffer damage when those seeking to renovate the memorials use brown paint, unwittingly destroying symbolism representing an army of dead soldiers.; The author holds photographs of Mt Barker & Kadina 'Diggers'; Mortlock Library, SRG 89, Women's Memorial to the Fallen in the Great War, Letter from Dorothy Gilbert, Hon Secretary, Women's Memorial Fund to Mr Lethaby, 23 August, 1919; Letter addressed to Herbert Baker, 3 September, 1919; Adelaide City Archives, SPF 549A.01 Cross of Sacrifice.
3. G Kurt Piehler, 'The War Dead and the Gold Star: American Commemoration of the First World War', in John R Gillis, *Commemorations: The Politics of National Identity*, (Princeton: Princeton University, 1994), pp. 168–185; the *Advertiser*, 'The Late Major-

General Bridges, The Burial Service', 3 September, 1915, p. 17; 'Funeral Service of the Unknown Australian Soldier, 11 November 1993, Eulogy delivered by the Prime Minister of Australia', in *Journal of the Australian War Memorial*, No 24, April 1994, p. 4.

4. Mortlock, SRG 89, Letter to Imperial War Graves Commission, London, 3 September 1919; Senator G F Pearce, *Where the Australians Rest*, (Aust: Minister of State for Defence, 1920), p. 24, 71, 58, 61, 71.
5. Ken Inglis, foreword, in Annette Becker, *War and Faith The Religious Imagination in France*, 1914–1930, Translated from the French by Helen McPhail, (Oxford: Berg, 1998) p. xiii.
6. Ken Inglis assisted by Jan Brazier, *Sacred Places War Memorials in the Australian Landscape*, (Carlton South, The Miegunyah Press, 1998), Cross of Sacrifice p. 282, 332–3; Memorial Drive p. 138; South Australian National Memorial p. 282, 284, 293–5, 296, 297–8, 445, 446.
7. Uniting Church in Australia Synod of South Australia Historical Society, *The Memorial Hospital Souvenir, 1919;* ACA, 1919/0953 Drive Way around Torrens Lake - War Memorial Drive.
8. Mortlock, SRG 89, copy of Public Notice in the *Register* and the *Advertiser,* 11 March 1919; Typed quarto sheet, 'The Women's Memorial.'
9. ACA, TCDKT 1915/2968, Memorial to Australians at Gallipoli, Memo for Docket, Works & Highways Committee, 13 Sept 1915, Digest Page 461.
10. Mortlock, SRG 89, Letter to Imperial War Graves Commission from D Gilbert, 3 September 1919.
11. Arnold D Hunt, *Methodism Militant Attitudes to the Great War 1914–1918*, (Adelaide: South Australian Historical Society, 1975), p. 14.
12. Vera Brittain, *Testament of Youth*, (Great Britain, Virago Press, 1978), p. 483, pp. 522–527; Jay Winter, *Sites of Memory, Sites of Mourning The Great War in European cultural history*, (Cambridge: Cambridge University Press, 1995), pp. 23–27.
13. Mortlock, SRG 89, Women's Memorial Fund Executive Committee Minute Book March 12, 1919 to July 28, 1920, copy of Public Notice inserted Tuesday 11th March in both dailies *Register* and *Advertiser*.
14. ACA, SPF 549A.01, Cross of Sacrifice, newspaper cutting *Register,* 25 February 1922.
15. ACA, SPF 549A.01, Cross of Sacrifice, Letter to His Worship the Mayor, Town Hall Adelaide, 2 March 1919; Mortlock, SRG 89, Letter to H Baker from D Gilbert, 26 April 1919; ACA, SPF 549A.01, Cross of Sacrifice, Letter to Mayor from D Gilbert, 20 August 1919, handwritten note; Letter from H Baker, 3 July 1919.
16. ACA, SPF 549A.01, Cross of Sacrifice, Letter from H Baker, circa 1919; copy of same letter also in Mortlock, SRG 89.
17. Mortlock, SRG 89, Letter from Sir Reginald Blomfield, R.A., to D Gilbert, 19 May 1920; Letter from Sir Edwin I Lutyens B.A., to Mrs A R Lungley, 10 January 1921; letter to Dr Lethaby from D Gilbert, 23 August 1919; letter to B Mackennal, 3 September 1919; Typed quarto sheet, 'The Women's Memorial.'
18. Mortlock, SRG 89, Executive Committee Minutes, 25 September 1919; Letter to H Baker 29 September 1919; General Committee Minutes, 1 October 1919; ACA, SPF 549A.01, Letter from H Baker circa 1919, copy also in SRG 89.
19. Mortlock, SRG 89, Executive Committee Minutes, 29 January 1920.
20. Mortlock, SRG 89, Letter to H Baker, New Dehli, 29 September 1919; Letter signed by D Gilbert 18 February 1920.
21. Minutes General Committee 15 April 1920.

22. ACA, SPF 549A.01, Letter to Mayor from D Gilbert, 5 March 1920; Letter to Mayor from D Gilbert, 1 April 1920; Letter to Mayor from D Gilbert, 10 April 1920.
23. Mortlock, SRG 89, Executive Committee Minutes, 8 April 1920, 22 April 1920; ACA, SPF 549A.01, Memo from Deputy Town Clerk to Town Clerk, 20 April 1920.
24. Mortlock, SRG 89, Executive Committee, 6 May 1920, Newspaper cutting, *Register,* 'Violet Day', 20 April 1920.
25. ACA, SPF 549A.01, Cross of Sacrifice, Letter to Right Worshipful the Lord Mayor of Adelaide from D Gilbert, 23 April 1920; Enclosure for Town Clerk's Office, Docket number 1437/19, 27 April 1920.
26. Mortlock, SRG 89, Newspaper cutting, 'The Women's Memorial', from 'A Sorrowful Onlooker', pasted in book labelled Minutes of the General Committee, March 12, 1919 to Sept 1, 1920.
27. ACA, SPF 549A.01, Cross of Sacrifice and Mortlock SRG 89, *Register* 25 February 1922.
28. Mortlock, SRG 89, Letter from Bainbridge Reynolds Ltd, to Miss Gilbert, 14 October 1920.
29. Spedding, Q S, (ed), *Returned Sailors and Soldiers' Imperial League of Australia, Official Year Book, 1937 (Coronation Issue),* (Sydney: RS & SILA (NSW Branch) 1937), p. 137.
30. ACA, SPF 549A.01, Letter from H Baker, circa 1919.
31. ACA, SPF 549A.01, Letter from H Baker to Women's Memorial Fund, 3 July 1919; Mortlock SRG 89, Women's Memorial to the Fallen in the Great War, D Gilbert, 18/2/1920.
32. *Advertiser* 1922, 24 April 1922, 'At the Cathedral', 'Service at the Synagogue', p. 10.
33. *Advertiser* 24 April 1922, 'Women's War Memorial Ceremony', p. 9; Mortlock SRG 89 Women's Memorial correspondence from Ethel Wyatt to Rev Father Murphy, 15 February 1922, Reply from J D Murphy to Miss Wyatt 19 February 1922.
34. ACA, SPF 549A.01, Letter to Mayor from D Gilbert, 15 August 1919.
35. Uniting Church Historical Society, 'The Memorial Hospital Souvenir, 1919', p. 4.
36. Uniting Church Historical Society, 'The Memorial Hospital Souvenir, 1919', p. 20.
37. Mortlock, SRG 89, Minutes General Committee, 12 March 1919.
38. Mortlock SRG 89, Letter from RS&SILA, 15 December 1921, Letter from RS&SILA to Miss Clayton, re Unveiling of Women's Memorial, Pennington Terrace, Nth Adelaide, 6 March 1922.
39. *Advertiser,* 'Women's Memorial Unveiled', 26 April 1922, p. 7; 'The Women's Memorial', 26 April 1922, p. 8; ACA, SPF 549A.01 Cross of Sacrifice; newspaper cutting from *Register*, 26 April 1922; Mortlock SRG 89, Newspaper cuttings from *Advertiser*, p. 7,8.
40. ACA, SPF 549A-01, Cross of Sacrifice Pennington Gardens and Mortlock SRG 89, Unveiling Ceremony Women's Memorial to the Men who fell in the War, Order of Service, 25 April 1922.
41. ACA, SPF 549A.01, *Advertiser*, 19 April 1923.
42. ACA, SPF 549A.01, Cross of Sacrifice, Newspaper Cutting from *Register* 'The Women's Memorial to be completed for Anzac Day', 17 April 1923.
43. ACA, SPF 549A.01, Photocopy of articles from *Register* 17 April 1923; Mortlock SRG 89, Letter to Mrs Lendon from G C MacLaren, 13 November 1922.
44. ACA, SPF 549A.01, From City Engineer to Town Clerk 15 May 1923; Mortlock, SRG 89, Letter from Town Clerk to Miss C Clayton, 19 May 1923.
45. ACA, Copy of Minute from Digest, Council Meeting, 21 October 1963, Memo for the Town Clerk, Cross of Sacrifice, Repair and Maintenance (No 1437/19), 2 December 1963.

46. League, State Board minutes, 4, Appeals & Trusts, (c), Services Cem. Trust, 17 April 1972.
47. Photocopy of letter provided by Adelaide City Council, from Director of Parks and Recreation to Mr Hoffman, Secretary, Returned Services League of Australia, dated 3 July 1986 with enclosed diagram, Plan No. G86/P12/092; ACA, SPF549A.01, Letter from Herbert Baker, Delhi to Dorothy Gilbert, Adelaide, undated, refers to letters from Gilbert dated 3.9.19 and 1.10.19.
48. ACA, 1918/3690, Town Clerk Peace Movement, *Advertiser* 'A three Days' Programme', 12.12.18; *Register* 9 April 1919, 'Peace Celebrations'; ACA, 1919/0953, Drive Way around Torrens Lake – War Memorial Drive, Memo from Town Clerk to City Engineer, City Gardener, 7 April 1919; ACA, 1919/0953B, Drive Way around Torrens Lake – War Memorial Drive, Memo 6 November 1925; Memo to City Engineer, 9 November 1925; Typed paragraph for *Register, Advertiser, News*, 'War Memorial Drive', 28 October 1925.
49. ACA, 1919/0953A, Drive Way around Torrens Lake – War Memorial Drive, By Law No XLIV, In respect of traffic on the War Memorial Drive, 30 June 1924.
50. *Diggers' Gazette*, Vol II, No 7, 21 Feb 1921, 'Dishonoring the Dead Neglected Soldiers' Graves', pp. 43–45; *DG* Vol II, No 8, 7 March 1921, 'Anzac Day details of celebrations', p. 15; League 4th State Council, 10 Feb 1921, Soldiers' Graves at West Tce; ACA, 1919/0953, 11 Aug 1920; SB, 28 Sept 1948, AIF Cemetery Trust, SB, 30 March 1953, Lighting Cross, AIF Cemetery.
51. League Annual Report 1972, 'Services Cemeteries Trust'; Commonwealth Department of Veterans' Affairs pamphlets, Bereavement information, Services provided by Office of Australian War Graves; League minutes; League State Board 7 November 1944, p. 380; SB, 16 January 1945, p. 404; SB, Centennial Park Cemetery Inc., 13 February 1945; SB, Enfield General Cemetery, 5 January 1948; SB, World War II Cemetery, 22 January 1951; SB, WWII Cemetery, 13 November 1951; SB, WWII Cemetery, 15 June 1954; *Advertiser,* Melissa King, 'Young and old pay tribute to those who gave their lives children salute our war heroes', 12 November 1999, p. 7.
52. League 24th State Council Minutes, 8 June 1926, pp. 295–297.
53. League 24th State Council Minutes 8 June 1926, p. 296; ACA, 1101/27 Woods, Bagot, Jory & Laybourne-Smith South Australian War Memorial, South Australia. Architectural Competition for a National War Memorial at Adelaide.
54. ACA, 305C, National War Memorial, North Terrace, 19 September 1968 to 2 October 1975, pamphlet produced by the Returned Services League, The State National War Memorial, (Unveiled 25 April (Anzac Day) 1931, circa 1969; 305B, National War Memorial 22 January 1954 to 15 September 1968, the *Advertiser* and *Register*, 22 April 1931, 'Spirit of Sacrifice, Significance of War Memorial, Architect Explains'; Inglis, *Sacred Places*, p. 147, 295, 309.
55. League, 25th State Council Minutes, 12 October 1926, p. 315.
56. ACA, 305A, National War Memorial Reserve, *News*, 16 August, 1948; Minutes Sub-Branch Conference 17 & 18 Sept 1931, p. 432; *Advertiser*, 27 April 1931, 'Youth's Great Tribute to Anzac Heroes', p. 7; League, Fourteenth Sub-Branch Conference 16 & 17 September 1931, p. 427.
57. *Advertiser,* 'Youth's Great Tribute to Anzac Heroes', 27 April 1931.
58. ACA, 305A, National War Memorial Reserve, Letter from Attorney-General Office to Lord Mayor 24 September 1931, reply from Town Clerk 7 October 1931, Hansard, House of Assembly, 4 November 1931, *Advertiser* 6 & 7 November 1931; League, Fifteenth Sub- Branch Conference Minutes 14 & 15 September 1932 p. 447; p. 436.
59. ACA, 305A, Copy of Rough Minutes City Council 24 January 1949.

60. ACA, 305A, C of A, By-Law No. LXIII in respect of the National Soldiers' Memorial, 23 January 1950; ACA, 1101/27 Woods, et al, South Australian War Memorial, Memo for Docket, Parliamentary and Bylaws Committee, 9 October 1951, Digest Page 204, Council Meeting 22 Oct 1951.
61. ACA, 1101/27, Woods, et al, Memo for Docket, Parliamentary and Bylaws Committee, 19 Nov 1951, Digest Page 265.
62. RSL SA Branch Library, 'Unveiling and Dedication of World War II Memorial, 11 November 1956'.
63. ACA, 305B, National War Memorial Reserve, 22.1.54 to 18.9.68, inspection forms.
64. ACA, 305B, National War Memorial, Report, 20 August 1964, memo to Town Clerk, 25 August 1964.
65. ACA, 305C, National War Memorial North Terrace 19.9.68 to 2.10.1975, Services held at National War Memorial, North Terrace, 19 September 1975.
66. Janice Pavils, 'The emergence of South Australian Anzac culture 1915–1925', in *Journal of the Royal Australian Historical Society*, Vol 89, Part 2, December 2003, p. 140.

Chapter 3 – 'The One Day'

1. Michael James Reardon, Honours Degree Thesis, 'Anzac Day in Adelaide, 1916 to 1922: from the first anniversary to a national public holiday', (Adelaide, University of Adelaide, History Department, 1979).
2. *South Australia Official Reports of the Parliamentary Debates, Session 1922, Second Session of the Twenty-Fourth Parliament, From Thursday July 27 to Friday December 15, 1922, Holidays Act Amendment Act,* (Adelaide: R E E Rogers, Government Printer, 1922), p. vi.
3. *Diggers' Gazette*, Vol. II, No 10, 7 April 1921, 'Anzac Day', p. 5; *Holidays Act*, pp. 2306–2307; Alan Seymour, *The One Day of the Year*, (London: Angus and Robertson, 1962), *The One Day of the Year*, A Novel, (London: Souvenir Press, 1967).
4. Maureen Sharpe, 'Anzac Day in New Zealand 1916–1939', *New Zealand Journal of History*, Vol 15, No 2, October 1981, pp. 97–114.
5. National Library of Australia, MS 389, K. Inglis, Box 11, 17.6.1998, File 1921, Statement of different Acts regulating the observance of Anzac Day; Graham Seal, *Inventing Anzac*, Tasmania, p. 115; Q S Spedding, (ed), *RSL Official Year Book, 1937 Coronation Issue*, (Melbourne: RSL Federal Headquarters, 1937), pp. 141–142.
6. Third State Council Minutes, Anzac Day celebrations, 14 September 1920, p. 59.
7. *Diggers' Gazette*, Vol. II, No 7, 21.2.1921, 'Anzac Day', p. 29; Fourth State Council Meeting, 10 February 1921, Consideration of Programme for Anzac Day 1921, p. 71; *Diggers' Gazette*, Vol. II, No 8, 'Anzac Day details of celebrations', p. 15.
8. *Diggers' Gazette*, Vol. II, No 10, 7 April 1921, 'Anzac Day', p. 5.
9. *Diggers' Gazette* 7 April 1921, p. 5.
10. *Diggers' Gazette*, Vol. II, No 11, 21 April, 1921, 'Anzac Day', p. 3.
11. *Diggers' Gazette*, 21 April 1921, p. 3.
12. *Diggers' Gazette*, Vol II, No 12, 7 May 1921, 'The Anzac Celebrations', p. 3.
13. *Diggers' Gazette*, 7 May 1921, 'Annual Re-Union Dinner', p. 7; 'Triumphal Procession', pp. 12–15; 'The Day we Commemorate', pp. 1 9–21; 'Catholic Soldiers' Service' and 'St Peters', p. 27; 'Synagogue Service', p. 31.
14. *Diggers' Gazette*, Vol II, No 10, 7 April 1921, 'The State Elections', p. 9.

15. *Diggers' Gazette*, 7 April 1921, 'The State Elections', pp. 9–11; Vol III, No 2, 7 June 1921, 'Parliamentary Elections', p. 43.
16. *Diggers' Gazette*, Vol III, No 2, 7 June 1921, 'Getting Public Interest', p. 19.
17. Fourth Annual Sub-Branch Conference Minutes, 15 & 16 September 1921.
18. Eighth State Council Minutes, 14 July 1922, Reference to Holidays – Anzac Day, p. 96.
19. John Robertson, *Anzac and Empire*, (Port Melbourne: Hamlyn, 1990), p. 251.
20. *Holidays Act*, p. 2306.
21. *Holidays Act*, p. 2306, 1639; *Holidays Act*, p. 1684, *Australian Dictionary of Biography*, Vol 8, (Melbourne: Melbourne University, 1981), Denny, pp. 287–288; *Holidays Act*, p. 2289.
22. *ADB*, Vol 9, (Adelaide: Melbourne University, 1983), Gordon, p. 51; *Holidays Act*, p. 2290.
23. *ADB*, Vol 7, (Melbourne: Melbourne University, 1979), Bice, p. 285; Vol 10, (Adelaide: Melbourne University, 1986), Mills, 519; *Holidays Act*, p. 2290.
24. *Holidays Act*, p. 2291.
25. *Holidays Act*, p. 2291.
26. *Holidays Act*, p. 2291.
27. *Diggers' Gazette*, Vol II, No 10, 7 April 1921, 'Mr F. M. McMillan', p. 10, Howard Coxon, John Playford and Robert Reid, *Biographical Register of the South Australian Parliament 1857–1957*, (Adelaide: Wakefield Press, 1985), 'McMillan', p. 148; *Holidays Act*, p. 2305.
28. *Holidays Act*, p. 2306.
29. *Holidays Act*, p. 2306.
30. *Holidays Act*, p. 2307.
31. *Holidays Act*, p. 2307.
32. Coxon, *Biographical Register SA Parl*, (1985), Hudd, p. 114; *Holidays Act* pp. 2307–2308.
33. Twelfth State Council minutes, 31 May 1923, p. 124.
34. *Advertiser*, 27 April 1925, 'Anzac Day in England', p. 11; Paul Henderson, *Parliament and Politics in Australia*, (Melbourne: Heinemann Education Australia, Fourth Edition, reprinted 1987), p. 338.
35. *Advertiser*, 27 April 1925, 'Anzac Day in England', p. 11.
36. *Advertiser*, 27 April 1925, 'A Religious Service', p. 11.
37. *Advertiser*, 26 April 1938, 'Celebration in London, Test Men Place Wreath on Cenotaph', 'Bradman Speaks on Anzac Day, Australia Would Again Stand With Empire', p. 19.
38. *Advertiser*, 18 April 1923, 'The question of closing factories', p. 12.
39. *Advertiser*, 20 April 1923, 'Sydney Traders' Shops to Close'; 'Anzac Day in New Zealand', p. 12.
40. *Advertiser*, 20 April 1923, 'Flags to be Half-masted', p. 12.
41. Thirteenth Sub-Branch Conference minutes, 17 & 18 September 1930, By Prospect Sub-Branch, (through Council,) 'That Anzac Day in future be made a close holiday'.
42. Fourteenth Sub-Branch Conference minutes, 16 & 17 September 1931, Anzac Day, by Prospect Sub-Branch, (through Council).
43. State Board minutes, 3 March 1931, item 4, Anzac Day Arrangements; SB, 14 April 1931, 6, Closing of Hotels; SB, 2 May 1933, 27, Closing of Hotels; SB, 16 May 1933 10, State Bank picnic Anzac Day.
44. SB, 16 March 1937, Master Bakers; SB, 6 April 1937, Master Bakers; SB, 20 April 1937, Master Bakers, SB, 18 May 1937, 22, Prospect Sub-Branch, re Sale of petrol on Anzac Day.

45. *Advertiser,* 26 April 1929, 'At Strathalbyn Sports and Concert', p. 15; 26 April 1933, 'State Cycling Record at Renmark', p. 10, 'Sports at Crystal Brook', p. 10; 26 April 1936, 'Anzac Day Sports, Ardrossan', p. 19; 26 April 1939, 'Anzac Services in the Country', p. 6.
46. NAA, B300/1, Control Symbol 6045/15, Parts 1 & 2, Contents date range 1931–1945, Free passes to returned soldiers in connection with Anzac Day South Australia, Letter to Department of the Interior, from Commissioner's Office, dated 11 March 1937.
47. NAA, B300/1, Control symbol 6045/15, Contents date range 1946–1966; 1967–1986 (At the time of research the 1971–1986 files were exempt from public access).
48. NAA, AP39/3/0, Anzac Day Shield 1931, 1933, 1934, 1937, Contents date range 1931–1937, List of towns from where troops travelled to compete in Anzac Day Sports, 25 April 1939; *Advertiser*, 26 April 1938, 'Bleakest Anzac Day March', p. 19.
49. *Advertiser*, 'Stimulating Response to Soldiers' Appeal', 23 April 1938, p. 22; 'Soldiers' Fund £14,603', 25 April 1938, p. 14; <http://www.sa.rsl.org.au/about/history.html> Recent History.
50. NAA, AP39/3/0, Anzac Day Shield 1931–1937; 4th Military District Military & Athletic Competitions Association Annual report year ended 30.6.1938; SB minutes, 20 March 1939, 11, Anzac Day, Pluvius Insurance.
51. NAA, AP39/3/0, Anzac Day Shield 1931 –1937; Pamphlet, Anzac Day competitions Wayville showgrounds, 25 April, 1939, Announcement, to be announced as often as possible up to midday, 22 April 1939.
52. Sixteenth Sub-Branch Conference minutes, 13 & 14 September 1933, p. 484.
53. SB minutes, 12 February 1946, 14, S & S Distress Fund; SB minutes, 26 February 1946, 25, VP Day as annual; SB minutes, 10 December 1946, 29, Anzac Day.
54. SB minutes, 20 January 1948, 16, Anzac Day; SB, 13 April 1948, 17, Legacy Club Appeal; SB, 28 April 1948, 21, Kooyonga Golf Club; SB, 13 April 1948, 17, Legacy Club Appeal.
55. *Advertiser,* 28 April 1953, 'Victoria's Anzac Day Defended', p. 3.
56. *Sentry-Go*, Vol III, No 25, May 1959, 'Here's Why Anzac Day Means So Much to Him', p. 4.
57. *Sentry-Go*, Vol III, No 34, February, 1960, 'Vote carried for half-day', p. 1.
58. *Advertiser*, department store advertisement columns, 25 April 1964, p. 15; 26 April 1965, p. 21.
59. SB minutes, 10 July 1961, 3, Finance (a) Report: Allocation – Anzac Appeal: 1961 Anzac Appeal Allocation lists the following: AIF Cemetery Trust £5,000, War Veterans' Home £2,000, WWII Fund £2,500, WWII Interest payment £750, S & S Distress Fund £1,000; The Annual Report & Balance Sheet for the year ended 31 December 1961, provides the information that "Over the years the racing clubs have contributed more than £110,000, the SA Trotting Club more than £54,000"; SB, 16 April 1962, 14, Anzac; SB, 8 April 1963, (e) Sports Fixtures; 18, General Business, (j) Anzac Reunions, SB, 20.5.1963, (i) Service Stations.
60. Russell Starke, 'Ravings,' One Day every year, *http://www.messenger.net.au/Pulse/htm/starke07.htm*.
61. Alan Seymour, play, *The One Day of the Year*, (London: Angus and Robertson, 1962); Ian Ousby, *The Cambridge Guide to Literature in English*, (Cambridge: Cambridge University, 1993), Alan Seymour, p. 848 and Graeme Davison, John Hirst, Stuart Macintyre, (eds), *Oxford Companion to Australian History*, (Melbourne: Oxford University Press, 1998), Alan Seymour, pp. 582–583.
62. Seymour, play, *The One Day of the Year,* p. 21, 39, 56, 59, pp. 62–64, pp. 76–77, p. 92, 99.

63. Seymour, play, '*The One Day*', p. 78.
64. Seymour, play, '*The One Day*', p. 101.
65. State Board minutes, 16 October 1961, General Business (a), *The One Day of the Year*.
66. SB, 5 March 1962, (f) Football League; SB, 19 December 1966, 17, Anzac (a) Anzac Trotting.
67. SB, 17 April 1972, 9, Anzac-Remembrance; SB, 19 February 1973, 9, Anzac-Remembrance, Opening of Wine & Bottle Shops on Anzac Day; SB, 19 March 1973, (c) Closing of Hotels.
68. SB, 18 May 1971, 16, General Business, (f) Violet Memory Day; SB, 18 October 1971, 4, Appeals & Trusts, (d) Poppy Day.
69. Alan Seymour, *The One Day of the Year*, A Novel, (London: Souvenir Press, 1967), p. 244.
70. For further information on the trauma of war see National Library, MS 389, Papers, K Inglis, Box 3 of 25, Maurice Shadbolt, 'Voices of Gallipoli', in the *Australian* 5.12.1990, p. 11; Jack Kaines, 'The Voice of the Bursting Shell', in the *Advertiser* 25.4.1988, p. 15; Jeff Cook, 'Grandpa what did you do in the War', in the *Advertiser* 26.4.1995, p. 9 and Betty Peters, 'The life experience of partners of ex-POWs of the Japanese', in *Journal of the AWM*, Issue 28, April 1996, *<http://www.awm.gov.au/journal/j28/j28-petr.htm>*
71. SB, 22 April 1974, 15, General Business, (d), English Book, 4th Year High.
72. Philip Kitley, 'Anzac Day Ritual', in *Journal of Australian Studies*, No. 4, June 1979, p. 65; V W Turner in Kitley, 'AD Ritual', *JAS*, p. 66; Kitley, 'AD Ritual', *JAS*, p. 67.
73. State Board minute books held at RSL South Australian Branch. The Anzac Day Commemoration Committee organises Anzac Day and reports to the State Board.
74. SB minutes, 19 April 1960, 7, Appeals (a) Anzac Appeal; League Annual Report 1965, First Girl in a Million Quest, (unpaginated); Annual Report 1964–1965, 'Churchill Doorknock', (unpaginated).

Chapter 4 – 'Diggers and Slackers'

1. *Diggers' Gazette*, Vol I, No 1, 15 November 1919, 'Political', p. 27.
2. G L Kristianson, *The Politics of Patriotism: The Pressure Group Activities of the Returned Servicemen's League*, (Canberra: Australian National University, 1966), p. 255.
3. David Hood, 'Conservatism and Change: the RSL and Australian Society, 1916–1932', Adelaide: University of Adelaide, Doctor of Philosophy in the Department of History, 1994.
4. Marilyn Lake, 'The Power of Anzac,' in M McKernan & M Browne, (eds), *Australia Two Centuries of War and Peace*, (Canberra: Australian War Memorial, 1988), p. 200, p. 222.
5. *Diggers' Gazette*, Vol I, No 3, 15 December 1919, 'Non-Partisan', p. 7; Vol II, No 3, 15 December 1920, 'Outlook for the Future', pp. 32–33.
6. *Diggers' Gazette*, Vol III, No 2, 'Parliamentary Elections', 7 June 1921, p. 43; League minutes Fourth State Council Meeting 10 February 1921, resumed 11 February 1921, Ruling to the Board from Council on policy for approaching State Elections, p. 73; *Diggers' Gazette*, Vol II, No 8, 7 March 1921, '"Slacker" Parliamentary Candidates', p. 5.
7. *Diggers' Gazette*, Vol II, No 10, 7 April 1921, 'The State Elections More Digger Candidates', pp. 9–11.
8. *Diggers' Gazette*, Vol II, No 5, 21 January 1921, 'No Party Politics', p. 10.
9. *Advertiser*, 'Honoring the Anzacs', 26 April 1928, p. 13.
10. *Advertiser,* 'Unemployed returned soldiers', 26 April 1929, p. 13.

11. *Advertiser,* 'Huge Crowd Pay Tribute to Anzac', 26 April 1932, p. 9.
12. 16th Sub-Branch Conference 13 & 14 September 1933, 'Australian War Memorial', p. 472; State Board minutes, 20 June 1933, 31, 'Canberra War Memorial', (Employment), p. 1430.
13. SB minutes, 19 February 1935, 18, Anzac Highway, correspondence and details of scheme submitted.
14. SB minutes, 29 November 1935, 5, Anzac Highway Committee; SB 17 December 1935, 5, Anzac Highway, commencement date 1937.
15. SB minutes 20 April 1937, 14, Anzac Highway, The State Secretary submitted the report of the Anzac Highway Reconstruction Scheme.; 20 July 1937, 10, Anzac Highway, Agreement signed.; 7 September 1937, 15, Anzac Highway, Report on visiting the House during the passage of the Bill through committee stage. Clause concerning preference and maintenance of gardens included.
16. Q S Spedding, RSSILA, *Official Year Book 1937, (Coronation Issue),* 'Preference in Employment', p. 311. Emphasis given.
17. RSSILA, *Official Year Book 1938*, 'You Want a Job?' p. 101.
18. RSSILA, *Official Year Book 1939, Defence Issue*, (Sydney: RSSSILA, (NSW Branch), 1939), p. 132.
19. RSSILA, *Official Year Book 1939, Defence Issue*, 'Employment', p. 247.
20. *Diggers' Gazette* Vol 1, No 20, 'Bonds of Diggerhood', 1 September 1920.
21. RSSILA, *Official Year Book 1939, Defence Issue*, 'Diggers in Parliament', pp. 161–163.
22. RSSILA, *Official Year Book 1939, Defence Issue*, 'Diggers in Parliament', pp. 161–162; Howard Coxon, John Playford and Robert Reid, *Biographical Register of the South Australian Parliament, 1857–1957*, p. 182, p. 196.
23. RSSILA, *Official Year Book 1939, Defence Issue*, 'Preference', p. 250.
24. RSSILA, *Official Year Book 1939, Defence Issue*, 'Grave Nationality Problems', p. 57.
25. SB minutes, 18 April 1939, 21, Membership; 27 June 1939, 24, Membership.
26. Demond O'Connor, *No need to be afraid Italian Settlers in South Australia between 1839 and the Second World War*, (Adelaide: Wakefield Press, 1996), pp. 143–146; pp. 173–174.
27. SB minutes, 9 July 1940, 26.
28. SB minutes, 12 October, 1942, 25.
29. SB minutes, circa 1940–45.
30. Hank Nelson, *Chased by the Sun*, (Sydney: ABC Books, 2002) pp. viii-ix; SB minutes 8 July 1941, 14, Alteration of Name; 19 August 1941, 27, Sisters' Sub-Branch re Change of Name.
31. SB minutes, 20 January 1942, 13, Anzac Day; SB 3 March 1942, 11, Anzac Day, Badge Appeal, re Dawn Services.
32. *Advertiser,* 'Simple but Dignified Anzac Ceremonies, Governor-General at War Memorial Service', 27 April 1942, p. 4.
33. *Advertiser*, 'Anzac Day Services, Quiet, Solemn Commemoration', 26 April 1943, p. 3.
34. *Advertiser*, 'Services in Other States', 26 April 1943, p. 3.
35. SB minutes, 2 March 1943, 13, Anzac Day, Badge Appeal; *Advertiser*, 'Anzac Day Services. Quiet, Solemn Commemoration, Suburban Services', 26.4.43, p. 3.
36. SB minutes, 3 March 1942, 19, Federal Executive Meeting, re Aborigine Question; 29 August 1944, 27, Aboriginal Returned Soldiers.
37. *Back*, March 1947, 'Ex-Service Men and Women', p. 19, emphasis given.
38. *Back*, March 1947, 'Right! You're a Civilian Now', p. 47.
39. SB minutes, 9 May 1944, 11, War Service Homes; SB 18 March 1947, 26, Immigration.

40. *Back*, August 1947, 'Govt. Will Heed R.S.L. Points on Immigration', p. 6.
41. SB minutes, 21 December 1948, Thirteen civilians fined for building without a permit.
42. SB minutes, 8 July 1947, 26, Widows; SB 15 April 1947, A button day for War Widows; SB 24 June 1947, Visit of Viscount Montgomery; SB 5 August 1947, War Widows Craft Guild.
43. *Back*, August, 1947, 'Pig-Slop Pensions To Widows Are Disgrace to Australia,' p. 9.
44. *Back*, January, 1948, 'Living Memorials', p. 17.
45. SB minutes, 13 April 1948, 26, Communists; 19 July 1949, 17, Anti Communist Month.
46. SB minutes, 3 August 1948, 20, Communists; 4 October 1954, 12, Gen Business, (a) Communist Sunday Rallies, Botanic Park.
47. *Advertiser*, 'Anzac March Impresses New Australians', and photo caption 26 April 1950, p. 3.
48. SB Minutes, circa 1951–56.
49. SB Minutes, 30 March 1953, (k) Election Ads in *Back*.
50. SB minutes, 5 January 1953, 15, (u) Turkish Delegation, Anzac 1953; SB 2 March 1953, (h) Federal Executive Meeting; SB 13 April 1953, Visit of Turk, Anzac Period; SB 27 April 1953, 12, Gen Business, (l) Turkish Delegation; SB 8 January 1951, 3, Business arising, (h) German Migration; SB 5 January 1953, (j) Proceeds of Sales, Japanese Embassy; SB 17 March 1980, 3, Hospital Visitation, (b) Hospital Visits.
51. SB minutes, 30 July 1951, 13, Gen Business, (H) Federal Exec. Mtg. 4/9/51; SB 13 April 1953, (c) Citizen rights, Aboriginal ex-servicemen; SB 22 February 1954, 4, Club, (a) Report, Serving of Liquor - Aborigines; SB 20 April 1954, 4 Club, (a) Report, Serving of Liquor, Half & quarter Castes.
52. Charles Duguid, *Doctor and the Aborigines*, (Adelaide: Rigby, 1972) p. 175; SB minutes, 3 May, 1954, 5, Club, (b) Serving of Aborigines – Anzac Day.
53. SB minutes, 31 May 1954, 5, Club (a) Report, Serving liquor to Aboriginals and 'Half Castes'; SB 15 June 1954, 4, Club, (c) Serving of liquor to Aborigines & 'Half Castes'.
54. SB minutes, 16 March 1953, 4, Club, (c) Returned Sisters Sub-Branch; SB 27 April 1953, 12, Gen Business (m) Melbourne Dawn Service; SB 12 December 1955, 14, Gen Business, (r) Female members.
55. *Sentry-Go*, Vol 1, No 1, October-November 1956, p. 2.
56. Annual Report and Balance Sheet, Returned Sailors, Soldiers and Airmen's Imperial League of Australia, South Australian Branch (Incorporated), Year ended 31 December 1960, p. 11.
57. SB minutes, 14 January 1963, Darby & Joan Cottage Scheme listed under 'Committees.'
58. Annual Report 1964, 'Churchill Doorknock', unpaginated; *Advertiser*, 27 April 1964 'Judges Choose S.A. Girl of the Year', p. 3.
59. *Advertiser*, 26 April 1965, 'Homes Fitting Memorial', p. 3.
60. Annual Report 1965, unpaginated.
61. SB, 20 December 1965, League not in favour of returning bodies to Australia of men killed overseas; National Library of Australia, MS 389, K Inglis, Box 4 of 25, *Sydney Morning Herald*, 22 January 1966, 'Policy Changed, War burials'; K. S. Inglis, 'The Digger's Grave', in *Nation*, 19 February 1966, pp. 14–15.
62. Annual Report 1966, unpaginated.
63. Bede Nairn and Geoffrey Serle, (Gen eds), *Australian Dictionary of Biography*, (Melbourne: Melbourne University, 1988), p. 559.
64. SB minutes, 21 April 1981, 14, Gen Business, (z) Mt Barker memorial; SB 19 May

1981, 14, Gen Business, (f) Mt Barker memorial; SB 15 March 1982, 9, Anzac-Remembrance, (b) Invitation to Speak Anzac Day; SB 19 May 1981, 9, Anzac-Remembrance, (i) Anzac Address to school children.

65. SB minutes, 2 September 1957, 15, General Business, (c) Anzac Highway; SB 18 May 1971, 16, Gen. Bus, (d), AH Memorial; SB 9 October 1964, 17, Anzac (f) AH memorial; SB 14 August 1967, 17, Anzac, (b) AH; SB 8 December 1967, 16, Anzac and Remembrance, (a) AH Memorial; SB 16 December 1968, 15, Anzac-Remembrance, (b) AH memorial; SB 15 September 1969, 14, Anzac-Remembrance, (a) AH; SB 17 September 1973, 15, Gen Bus, (n) AH memorial; SB 17 December 1984, 9, Anzac-Remembrance, (b) AH; SB 21 January 1985, 9, Anzac-Remembrance, (a) Anzac Highway; SB 22 September 1986, 8, Anzac-Remembrance, (b) Identification AH; SB 20 October 1986, 8, Anzac-Remembrance (a) Identification – AH; SB 19 November 1986, 8, Anzac-Remembrance, (e) AH Identification; SB 15 December 1986, 9, Anzac-Remembrance (a) AH; SB 18 August 1986, 8, Anzac-Remembrance, (b) Identification of AH; RSL Internet Site, Recent History, http://www.sa.rsl.org.au/about/history.html>.

Chapter 5 – Widening the Ranks

1. John A Moses, 'The struggle for Anzac Day 1916–1930 and the role of the Brisbane Anzac Day Commemoration Committee', in *Journal of the Royal Australian Historical Society*, Vol 88, Part 1, June 2002, p. 55, 58, 59; *Advertiser*, 26 April 1916, Public Notices, RSA, Memorial Parade, p. 2.
2. ACA, TCDKT 1917/1330, RS & SILA letterhead, from A E Tait, Secretary, to the Mayor, dated 12 April 1917; Inaugural Meetings of RSL minutes, Committee Meeting 11 April 1917, p. 147.
3. ACA, 1918/0293, RS & SILA letterhead, 21 January 1918; 1918/0801, RS & SILA, 23 March 1918; 1918/1413, Australian Military Forces, No 22, Memorial Parade Anzac Day; 1918/0801, Letterhead, Council of Control of Patriotic Street Sales, 5 March 1918; AMF, No 23, RS & S Building Fund appeal, 20 April 1918.
4. TCDKT, 1919/0424, RS & SILA, Memorial Hall Appeal, 13 February 1919; *Register*, 26 April 1919, 'Gallipoli Memorial Parade', p. 2; 27 April 1920, p. 2.
5. *Advertiser*, 3 June 1946, 'Victory Day March Arrangements', p. 7; 10 June 1946, 'Nine Million People see Parading Columns, London June 9', p. 1; 11 June 1946, 'Gay Night Scenes, … Memorable March seen by 200,000, Pageant symbolic of S.A. War Effort', p. 1.
6. State Board minutes, 12 February 1946, 20, Anzac Day; SB 12 March 1946, 5, Problems, Anzac Day; SB 26 March 1946, 17, Anzac Day; SB 9 April 1946, 5, Problems, Anzac Day, SB 29 Anzac Day March.
7. *Advertiser*, 25 April 1946, 'March May be Record', p. 1.
8. *Advertiser*, 26 April 1946, 'Adelaide's Finest Anzac Tribute', p. 1.
9. *Advertiser,* 26 April 1946, 'Adelaide's Finest Anzac Tribute', p. 1, 'Moving Scenes as Anzacs March', p 3.
10. National Archives of Australia, D292/5, 18/1/33, Ceremonial General Pt II, Anzac Day 1947–59.
11. *Back*, January 1948, 'News Flashes 50 Australians to Visit New Zealand,' p. 7.
12. SB minutes, 26 November 1946, 28, Greek Ex-Servicemen's Asscn.
13. *Advertiser,* 26 April 1947, photograph, 'Evzone in March', p. 14.
14. SB minutes 18 February 1948, 21, Greek Sub-Branch.
15. SB minutes, 8 January 1951, 5, Report on Federal Executive Meeting, 19.12.50.

16. SB minutes, 16 April 1951, (m) AWAS in Anzac March; SB 19 February 1951, 3, Business arising, (d), Mr V E Hugo – re CMF.
17. *Advertiser*, 26 April 1951, 'Crowds Pay Homage to War Dead', p. 1.
18. RootsWeb: GREAT WAR-L Re: [WW1] 'Old contemtibles', <http://archiver.rootsweb.com/th/read/GREATWAR/2000–02/0950404127>
19. SB minutes, 26 May 1952, (q) Polish Carpathian Brigade; NAA, D292/5, 18/1/33, Ceremonial General Pt II, Anzac Day 1947–59; SB, 21 July 1952, (q), Anzac Ctee. Mtg.
20. *Advertiser*, 27 April 1953. 'Eyes Front'. P. 1; 'Mystery Woman of March', p. 3.
21. SB minutes, 16 March 1948, 16, Anzac Day; SB, 13 April 1948, 15, Anzac Day; SB, 30 July 1951, Anzac Day Committee.
22. SB minutes, 27 April 1953, (p) Children in procession; SB, 3 May 1954, (o) Anzac Celebrations.
23. SB minutes, 5 April 1954, (q) Anzac Day; SB, 31 May 1954, (d) Anzac Day; SB, 1 November 1954, (f) Anzac Day – inclusion Legacy girls in march.
24. SB minutes, 16 May 1955, (K), Anzac Day.
25. NAA, D292/5, 18/1/33, Ceremonial General Pt II, Anzac Day 1947–59.
26. Compiled from NAA D292/5, 18/1/33.
27. *Sentry-Go* Vol l, No 4, April-May 1957, 'New ideas in Anzac march', 1957, p. 1.
28. *Sentry-Go*, Vol 1, No 5, June-July 1957, 'Let's retain march music "grouch" meeting', p. 4.
29. *Sentry-Go*, Vol 1, No 7, Oct-Nov, 1957, 'Why Committee cut March', p. 3.
30. SB minutes, 5 August 1957, 14, Anzac Day, (a) Committee meeting; *Sentry-Go*, Vol 1, No 7, Oct-Nov 1957, 'Why Committee cut March', p. 3.
31. *Sentry-Go*, Vol 1, No 8, December 1957, 'Call for new March Talk fails', p. 1; SB minutes, 30 September 1957, 14, Anzac Day (b) Mr R S Somerville, (c) Mr T G Clark.
32. *Sentry-Go*, Vol 1, No 12, 'Anzac Day Changes', April 1958, pp. 1–3.
33. SB minutes 3 March 1958, 14, Anzac Day, (b) Anzac parade; *Sentry-Go*, Vol l, No 12, April 1958, 'Anzac Day Changes', p. 1; Vol II, No 13, May 1958, 'Thousands watch Anzac Day March', p. 1.
34. AD RSL Assembly Sub Committee File, from 7 Nov 61 to 1 May 69.
35. *Sentry-Go*, Vol III, No 36, April 1960, 'This Year's March', p. 1.
36. *Sentry-Go*, Vol III, No 34, February 1960, 'SA March to be Televised', p. 1; Vol III, No 37, May 1960, 'Anzac Spirit is not Dimmed by Clouds', p. 1; SB minutes, 2 May 1960, 14, Anzac Day (a) Report.
37. SB minutes, 12 December 1960, 14, Anzac (a) Report; SB, 1 May 1961, (c) WWI Sisters.
38. SB minutes, 1 May 1961, 12, Anzac (c) WWI Sisters; AD RSL Assembly SC 22 November 1961 Returned Sisters WWI; AD RSL Assembly Sub-Committee 22 November 1961, South African Veterans; SB minutes, 30 April 1962, 14, Anzac (c) WWII Sisters.
39. John Murphy, 'Vietnam War' in Davison, et al., *Oxford Companion Australian History*, p. 664.
40. AD RSL Assembly SC Anzac Commemoration March 1963 p. 1, p. 5.
41. SB minutes, 13 April 1964, 17, Anzac.
42. NAA, D293/2, 23/4/4, Orders of the Day, 1961.
43. SB minutes, 29 April 1957, 14, Anzac Day (Reports and comments).
44. *Advertiser*, 25 April 1964, 'Cool for Anzac Observance', p. 1.
45. AD RSL Assembly SC Anzac Day March 1964
46. AD RSL Assembly SC, Anzac Day March 1964, newspaper cutting *Mail,* 'Anzac Day incident', 2 May 1964, F W Darley, Mount Gambier.

47. Murphy, in Davison, et al, *Oxford Companion Australian History*, p. 664.
48. AD RSL SC report 1 May 1965.
49. SB minutes 8 February 1965, 17, Anzac (a) Transport – Sth African War Veterans.
50. *Advertiser*, 27 April 1965, 'Marcher Dies At Cross', p. 1.
51. AD RSL Assembly SC report.
52. Compiled from NAA D292/5, 18/1/33, AD RSL Assembly Sub-Committee File. 1961–69 and *Advertiser*, 24 April 1965, 'Anzac Spectacle at Oval', p. 3.
53. *Advertiser*, 26 April 1965, Hannaford Cartoon, p. 2.
54. Murphy in Davison, et al., *Oxford Companion Australian History*, p. 664.
55. Barr Smith Special collections, MSS0049, John Tregenza, Papers 1949–1996, Campaign for Peace in Vietnam, Volume III and the *Advertiser*, 13 June 1998, Jeff Turner, 'Where are those Rebels?' pp. 4–6. For information about the activities of Australian protestors see Kenneth Maddock, 'Opposing the War In Vietnam – The Australian Experience', in John Dumbrell, (ed), *Vietnam and the Antiwar Movement*, (Aldershot: Avebury, 1989), pp. 137–149, and Greg Langley, *A Decade of Dissent, Vietnam and the conflict on the Australian home front*, (Sydney: Allen & Unwin, 1992).
56. Annual Report 1967 (unpaginated).
57. SB minutes, 21 March 1966, 17, Anzac Day (a) Report.
58. SB minutes, 14 June 1966, 17, Anzac (a) Colonel Waite.
59. SB minutes, 20 February 1967, 17, Anzac, (e) Preliminary Co-ordinating Mtg; AD RSL Assembly Sub Committee Report 1967.
60. AD RSL SC Report 1967.
61. *Advertiser*, 24 April 1968, 'Anzac Day Row "Like Spitting in Church"', p. 1.
62. *Advertiser*, 26 April 1968, 'Dust no Bar to March', p. 1.
63. Andrew Rice, 'A forgotten Sacrifice: South Australian National Servicemen returning from the Vietnam War', Adelaide, Honours Degree in History, University of Adelaide, 1985, p. 8, 25, 24.
64. SB minutes, 20 January 1969, 14, Publicity, (a) War Memorial; SB, 21 April 1969, 15, Anzac-Remembrance, (a) Anzac arrangements.
65. SB minutes, 19 May 1969, 14, Anzac-Remembrance, (d) Police Cadets.
66. Annual Report 1969, p. 3.
67. Murphy in Davison, et al, *Oxford Companion*, p. 664; KT, Gorton, John Grey, p. 286.
68. SB minutes, 20 October 1969, 14, Anzac-Remembrance, (b) Dunkirk Veterans; SB, 19 January 1970, Anzac-Remembrance, (b) RAR Assen.
69. SB minutes, 15 December 1969, 14, Anzac-Remembrance, (b) Anzac Ctee; SB, 19 January 1970, 15, Anzac-Remembrance, (a) Anzac Ctee; SB, 16 February, 1970, 14, Anzac-Remembrance, (a) Minutes Meeting A/Day Ctee; SB, 20 July 1970, 14, Anzac-Remembrance, (b) Report.
70. *Advertiser*, 27 April 1971, 'Alone in an Empty City', p. 1; 'Quiet anti-war rally in city', p. 6.
71. *Advertiser*, 27 April 1971, p. 1.
72. Annual Report 1971, p. 14; SB minutes, 18 May 1971, 13, Anzac-Remembrance, (a) Anzac Commemoration; SB, 18 January 1971, 15, Anzac-Remembrance, (a), Anzac Day arrangements.
73. SB minutes, 19 April 1971, 13, Anzac-Remembrance, (b), Legacy participation in March.
74. SB minutes, 17 April 1972, 9, Anzac-Remembrance, (c) Anzac arrangements.
75. SB minutes, 20 March 1972, 9, Anzac-Remembrance, (a) Vietnam Day of Tribute; Annual Report 1972, p. 15.

76. Rice, 'A Forgotten Sacrifice', p. 37.
77. SB minutes, 16 May 1972, 9, Anzac-Remembrance, (a) Anzac Day; SB, 16 October 1972, Anzac-Remembrance (a) Anzac Day march.
78. Annual Report 1973, p. 16.
79. SB minutes, 20.8.1973, Appendix to minutes, Report on Extra-Ordinary meeting of National Congress, ANZAC DAY.
80. SB minutes, 2 September 1974, 9, Anzac-Remembrance, (a) Anzac Bands; SB, 17 June 1975, 9, Anzac-Remembrance, (c) Anzac March; SB minutes, 21 May 1974, 9, Anzac-Remembrance, (a) Anzac Day, letter from Nomis Electronic; SB minutes 20 January 1975, 10, Anzac-Remembrance, (a) Bands; 26 February 1975, 10, Anzac-Remembrance, - Live Bands; Annual Report 1975.
81. SB minutes, 20 May 1975, 9, Anzac-Remembrance, (a) Anzac Day.
82. *Advertiser*, 26 April 1975, 'Princess talks with Veterans, Children', and 'Anzac Day Pull-out at Saigon Embassy', both p. 1; Annual Report 1975.
83. Board minutes, 22 June 1976, 9, Anzac-Remembrance, (b) Anzac March.
84. SB minutes, 20 April 1976, 9, Anzac-Remembrance (a) Anzac arrangements; SB, 18 May 1976, 9, Anzac-Remembrance, (a) Anzac Day; SB, 17 July 1978, 9, Anzac-Remembrance (a) Financial assistance for conduct of Anzac Day; SB, 18 September 1978, 9, Anzac-Remembrance, (b) Anzac Expenses; SB, 21 August 1978, 9, Anzac-Remembrance (a) Anzac Day expenses.
85. SB minutes, 13 September 1976, 9, Anzac-Remembrance, (b) Anzac March; SB, 23 November 1977, 9, Anzac-Remembrance, British Ex-Service Women's Assoc.
86. SB minutes, 18 February 1976, 9, Anzac-Remembrance, (b) Anzac Day Committee; Annual Report 1977.
87. SB minutes, 15 January 1979, 9, Anzac-Remembrance, (a) Requests to March as Units; SB, 22 November 1978, 9, Anzac-Remembrance, (b) SA Women's Ex-Land Army.
88. SB minutes, 21 January 1980, 9, Anzac-Remembrance, (b) British Legion in Anzac March; SB, 20 February 1980, 9, Anzac-Remembrance, (a), Anzac Day, Dambusters.
89. AD RSL Assembly SC file Anzac Commemoration march 1980.
90. *Advertiser*, 25 April 1981, 'Chilly Dawn for Prince', p. 3.; 27 April 1981, 'Prince's Security Worried Police', p. 8.
91. Annual Report 1981, unpaginated.
92. AD RSL Assembly SC File.
93. SB minutes, 19 January 1981, Vice President E H Ainsworth (Mrs); SB, 16 March 1981, 9, Anzac-Remembrance (f) Saluting Base.
94. *Advertiser*, 27 April 1981, 'Women in March Protest: 64 Face Charges', p. 3.
95. *Advertiser*, 26 April 1982, 'Women's Groups Say No', p. 3.
96. *Advertiser*, 27 April 1982, 'Women's Wreaths Taken by Police, Bystanders', p. 16.
97. ACA, 1259/28 Anzac Day Procession, Order of March date stamped, 'rec 24 April 1940.'
98. *Advertiser*, 25 April 1981, 'Anzac Day March Assembly', 'Placing of Wreaths', p. 6.
99. Bill Gammage, (text), David Williamson, (screenplay), Peter Weir, (preface), *The Story of Gallipoli*, (Ringwood: Penguin Books, 1981), p. 5, emphasis.
100. Gammage et al., *The Story of Gallipoli*, p. 10.
101. SB, minutes 28 September 1981, 9, Anzac-Remembrance, (m), Film - Gallipoli.
102. AD RSL Assembly Sub Committee, Orders of the Day, 1982; SB minutes, 18 May 1982, 9, Anzac-Remembrance, (d) 50 Bn Club; SB, 19 April 1982, 9, Anzac-Remembrance, (d) Arrangements – Anzac March, SA Yankalilla 3/9 Light Horse.

103. SB minutes, 20 August 1984, 9, Anzac-Remembrance, (a) Letter from President, ANPI de Liberazione in Australia; SB, 20 February 1985, 9, Anzac-Remembrance, (b), Letter from Associazione Nazionale Partigiani Italiani in Australia; SB, 15 April 1985, 9, Anzac-Remembrance, (b), Anzac Day Arrangements.
104. Ralph Churches, letter to J Pavils, 15 September 2000; For more information see Ralph Churches, *A Hundred Miles as the Crow Flies*, (Adelaide: R F Churches, 1996), Chapter 6, 'Précis of Partisan History', pp. 81–89 and Norman Davies, *Europe*, (London: Pimlico, 1996), reprinted with corrections 1997, p. 1010.
105. SB minutes, 15 April 1985, 9, Anzac-Remembrance, (b) Anzac Day Arrangements, Returned Sisters on Anzac Day.
106. SB minutes, 17 March 1986, 9, Anzac-Remembrance, (a) 1986 Anzac Day; SB, 19 February 1986, 9, Anzac-Remembrance, (a) 1986 Anzac Day progress report; SB, 14 April 1986, 9, Anzac-Remembrance, (a), 1986 Anzac Day; SB, 22 September 1986, 8, Anzac-Remembrance, (a) Letter from The Girl Guides Assn.
107. Annual Report 1986, 3–4 July 1987, unpaginated.
108. SB minutes, 15 December 1986, 9, Anzac-Remembrance, (b) Anzac Day 1987, Demobilised Sailors, Soldiers & Airmen's Assn, Australian Army Training Team Vietnam.
109. Barr Smith Special collections, MSS0049, John Tregenza, Papers 1949–1996, Volume III and *Advertiser*, 13 June 1998, Jeff Turner, 'Where Are those Rebels?' pp. 4–6.
110. AD SC meeting 27.2.2001.

Chapter 6 – Harefield and the Remembrance Connection

1. Ken Inglis, 'Reflections on the Unknown Soldier', in *Journal of the Australian War Memorial*, No 24, April 1994, p. 6.
2. Imperial War Museum, London SA Coo-ee poster, photograph held by J Pavils.
3. Kaye, *English Heaven*, p. 1.
4. Kaye, *English Heaven*, p. 3, 6.
5. Kaye, *English Heaven*, p. 4.
6. Kaye, *English Heaven* p. 5.
7. Senator G F Pearce, Minister of State for Defence, *Where the Australians Rest, A Description of many of the Cemeteries overseas in which Australians – including those whose names can never now be known – are buried*, 1920, p. 58.
8. *Diggers' Gazette*, 'Diggers' Graves at Harefield', 7 July 1921, Vol. III, No. 4, p. 29.
9. The Harefield Calendar 2003, April 2003, 'Anzac Day,' photograph by R G Neil; Slide transparency photographed by J Pavils in November 2000 provides the information: This memorial is erected by/ Sir Francis Newdegate K.C.M.G/ Now Governor of Western Australia/ And formerly of Tasmania/ Honorary Colonel Eleventh Battalion/ Commonwealth Military Forces/ And Charles Arthur Moresby Billyard-Leake Esq/ of Harefield Park/ A.D. 1921.
10. State Board minutes, 12 May 1936, 11, Anzac Day Essays.
11. State Board minutes, 5 January 1937, 25, Mr W J Adey – re Harefield Cemetery.
12. SB minutes, 16 May 1939, 10, Anzac Day, (b) Anzac Essays.
13. W Pearce, letter on Adelaide High School letterhead to J Pavils, dated 14.9.2000; W Pearce, 'A Glimpse of Harefield', in *Adelaide High School Magazine*, August, 1946, p. 26.
14. *Advertiser*, 'Link with England; Village Anzac Service Broadcast', 26.4.1946, p. 3.
15. *Advertiser*, 26 April 1946, p. 3; *Adelaide High School Magazine*, 'News of the School', Harefield and Holland, August 1946, p. 2; *Advertiser* 26 April 1946, p. 3; .*Advertiser*, 'Individual Food Parcels For Britain', 5 June 1946.

16. League State Board Minutes, 18.2.1952, 7.7.1958, 28.9.1964, 16.11.1970, and 17.6.1982.
17. Australian War Memorial, AWM67, 13/63, Suggested Australian Memorial – St Mary's Church, Harefield, England, p. 3; AWM67, 13/62, Minutes of Meeting of the Australian Battlefields Memorial Committee, dated 1 July 1948 give details for Brigadier A E Brown as (Secretary & Executive Member), Secretary-General, Imperial War Graves Commission, (Anzac Agency).
18. *Advertiser*, 26 April 1950, 'Ceremony at English War Cemetery', p. 3.
19. Kaye, *English Heaven*, p. 8
20. *Buckinghamshire Advertiser*, 'Headmaster Dies After Leading Flag Gift Service', 8 December 1950.
21. SB minutes, 31 October 1960, 17, General Business, (d) National Executive; SB, 9 January 1961, 19, General Business, (g) Australian Chapel at Harefield.
22. Adelaide High School Letterhead, 14.9.2000, from William Pearce Hon School Archivist to J Pavils; State Board minutes, 18 November 1981, 14, General Business, (k) Union Jack Replacement.
23. SB minutes, 18 May 1982, 14, General Business, Union Jack.
24. *Advertiser*, 26 April 1986, Kirsten John, 'Our diggers still remembered in a English Village, A faded flag joins hearts in loving memory', photocopy supplied by Adelaide High School.
25. Adelaide High School letterhead, letter to J Pavils from William Pearce, 14 September 2000; RSL Adelaide Library, Video of Anzac Ceremony, Harefield Anzac Cemetery.
26. Letter from Patrick Whiteman addressed to J Pavils, 14 January 2001.
27. Michael McKernan, *Here is Their Spirit A History of the Australian War Memorial 1917–1990*, (St Lucia: University of Queensland, 1991), p. 2.
28. National Archives Australia, Series D958/0, Control Symbol S1919/5808, Contents date range 1919–1919, Title Instructions re-observance of two minutes silence on Armistice Day, Circular No 570, Chief Secretary's Office, Adelaide, 10 November 1919.
29. NAA, Series B300/1, Item 6064, Armistice Day Celebrations, Decode of Cablegram received by H.E. the Governor-General from the Secretary of State for the Colonies, dated London, 2nd November, 1920, 7.40 p. m.
30. Ken Inglis, 'Entombing unknown soldiers', *Journal of the Australian War Memorial*, No. 23, October 1993, p. 4.
31. David Cannadine, 'War and Death, Grief and Mourning in Modern Britain', in *Mirrors of Mortality Studies in the Social History of Death*, Edited by Joachim Whaley, (New York: St Martin's Press, 1981), p. 224.
32. *Diggers' Gazette*, Vol. II, No. 1, 15 November 1920, p. 9.
33. NAA, B300/1, Item 6064, Title Commonwealth Railways, Armistice Day Celebrations, Prime Minister's Department Memorandum for The Secretary, Department of Works and Railways, signed by P E Deane, Secretary, dated 4 November 1927.
34. Thirteenth Sub-Branch Conference minutes, 17 & 18 September 1930, 22, Armistice Night Service; Sixteenth SB Conference minutes, 13 & 14 September 1933, 55, Armistice Day Service and SB minutes, 17 October 1933, 8, Armistice Night Service.
35. SB minutes, 5 February 1935, 31, Armistice Day Services; SB, 7 November 1938, 13, Armistice Day.
36. The Returned Sailors and Soldiers' Imperial League of Australia, *Official Year Book, 1939, Defence Issue*, p. 92.
37. SB minutes, 28 April 1931, 13, Poppy Supplies; The Returned Sailors and Soldiers' Imperial League of Australia, *Official Year Book, 1939, Defence Issue*, p. 92; League Sub-

Branch Conference 17 & 18 September 1930, 59, Poppy Day Sales; SBranch Conference 14 & 15 September 1932, 44, Poppy Day Fund; SB 5 January 1931, 4, Poppy Royalty; SB 23 June 1931, 18, Poppy Sales; SB 31 October 1933, 9, Poppy Day Appeal; SB 5 December 1933, 6, Poppy Royalty; SB 19 December 1933, 9, Poppy Royalty; SB 9 January 1934, 7, Poppy Royalty; SB 23 January 1934, 4, Poppy Royalty; SB 20 February 1934, 3, Poppy Royalty; SB 20 March 1934, 20, Poppy Royalty; SB 3 April 1934, 9, Poppy Royalty; SB 8 May 1934, 5, Poppy Royalty.

38. McKernan, *Here is Their Spirit*, p. 2; NAA, B300/1, 6064, Commonwealth Railways, Armistice Day Celebrations, *Sydney Morning Herald*, 'Armistice Day Plans', 1 November 1941; Prime Ministers Department Memorandum to The Secretary, Department of the Interior, 4 November 1942.
39. NAA, D292/5, Control Symbol 18/1/13, Contents date range 1930–1959, Cabinet Office Department of Defence, 28 October 1939; B300/1, Item 6064, Commonwealth Railways, Armistice Day Celebrations, contains memorandums from Prime Minister's Department, 27 October 1939, 28 October 1940, 3 November 1941, 4 November 1942, 4 November 1943, and newspaper cuttings from *Sydney Morning Herald*, 'Armistice Day Plans 1 November 1941', *Argus* 29 October 1943, 'Armistice Day Observance', *Argus*, 2 November 1944, 'Armistice Day Observance'.
40. *Advertiser*, Monday 10 June 1946, p. 1; *Advertiser*, Tuesday 11 June 1946, p. 1; SB minutes, 4 June 1946, 17, Victory Parade; NAA, D292/5, 18/1/62, Department of Navy, Ceremonial General, Victory Day March & Celebrations, Orders for the Day.
41. NAA, B300/1, Item 6064, Armistice Day Celebrations.
42. B292/5, Item 18/1/73, Ceremonial General, Naval Remembrance Day, Unclassified, From Admiralty to A.G.M. 019A (B1), Typed G.B. 1130K/1/11/46.
43. SB minutes, 7 May 1946, 24, Poppy Day; SB, 16 January 1945, 20, Poppy Day; SB, 27 March 1945, 18, Poppy Royalty; RSL, *Official Year Book 1939, Defence Issue*, Poppy Day Fund, p. 250; SB 4 November 1945, 15, Poppy Day Fund; SB, 20 June 1933, 28, Blanket Appeal; *Back* November 1947, 'Poppy Day on November 7 Will Aid Distressed Families', p. 32.
44. *Back*, November 1947, 'Poppy Day on November 7 Will Aid Distressed Families', p. 32.
45. SB minutes, 5 January 1958, 16, Poppy Day Trust Deed; SB 20 January 1948, 20, Poppy Day Trust.
46. SB minutes, 1 May 1950, 27, Armistice Day; SB, 13 November 1950, 14, Remembrance Day.
47. SB, November 1950, [new League secretary – no item numbers], Remembrance Day.
48. SB, 17 September 1951, Remembrance Day.
49. SB, 15 October 1951, Remembrance Day; SB, 26 November 1951, (z) Remembrance Day observances.
50. NAA, D292/5, Item 18/1/13, Ceremonial General, Armistice Day Ceremonies, Armistice Day and Remembrance Day, Commonwealth of Australia, Department of the Navy, Circular Memorandum No. 80, 3 November 1952.
51. *Back* 'Remembrance Day, November 11', October 1954, p. 4. Emphasis given.
52. SB minutes, 23 June 1952, (o) Serbian Cultural Club; SB 29 September 1952, 12, Gen Business, (n) Legation of Philippines.
53. SB, 20, July 1953, 12, General Business: (c) Service by Ukrainians at War Memorial.
54. NAA, D292/5, 18/1/13, Ceremonial General, Armistice Day Ceremonies, letter dated 18 April 1956 from Consulaat der Nederlanden voor Zuid Australie, to Resident Naval Officer, Department of the Navy, Birkenhead.

55. SB, 12 November 1956.
56. SB minutes, 6 July 1953, 7, Appeals (f) Sale of Crosses, Armistice Period; SB, 15 June 1954, 7, Appeals, (c) Poppy Day publicity; SB, 20 September 1954, 7 Appeals, (e) Use of White Crosses.
57. SB, 3 September 1956, (e) Remembrance Day; *Back*, October 1955, 'The Field of Remembrance – Adelaide', p. 2.
58. *Sentry-Go*, October-November 1956, 'Poppy Crosses to be Lasting Token', p. 2.
59. *Sentry-Go*, December 1959, 'Poppy Day a success', sub-heading 'Migrants,' p. 3.
60. NAA, B300/1, Item 6064, Armistice Day Celebrations, Commonwealth Railways, Anzac and Remembrance (Armistice) Days: Observance of, dated 1 April 1966.
61. NAA, B300/1, Item 6064, Armistice Day Celebrations, Commonwealth Railways, Observance of Anzac and Remembrance (Armistice) Days, 12 May 1966.
62. SB minutes, 19 December 1966, 19, General Business, (f) Remembrance Day; 16 October 1967, 17, Anzac and Remembrance Days, (a) Remembrance Day; 19 October 1970, 14, Anzac-Remembrance, (a) Police Buglers.
63. SB minutes, 1 May 1961, 16, Gen Business, (a) National Aborigines Day; Annual Report 1966, unpaginated.
64. SB 2 September 1974, 15, Gen Business, (e) March by Cyprian Society.
65. ACA, 305C, National War Memorial, North Terrace, 19.9.68 to 2.10.1975, Schedule for information only, not a copy of the original schedule.
66. For more information on the 'cult of the Fallen Soldier' see George L Mosse, *Fallen Soldiers: Reshaping the Memory of the World Wars*, (New York: Oxford University), 1990; See Norman Davies, *Europe A History*, (London: Pimlico, 1996, reprinted with corrections 1997), p. 1009.
67. SB minutes, 20 October 1975, 9, Anzac-Remembrance, (a) Remembrance service; SB, 18 May 1976, 9, Anzac-Remembrance; SB, 22 June 1976, 9, Anzac-Remembrance, (d) Anzac Requiem; SB, 18 October 1976, (b) Anzac Requiem; SB, 19 July 1976, 9, Anzac-Remembrance, (c) Anzac Requiem; SB, 17 November 1976, 9, Anzac-Remembrance, (b) Remembrance Day – wreath placed by students.
68. SB, 21 August 1978, Czechoslovakians.
69. SB minutes, 18 June 1981, 14, Gen Business, (p) IRA & Wreath on Memorial; SB 17 August 1981; 14, Gen Business (l) Use of War memorial 6/8/81; SB 17 August 1981, (r) Polish Veterans; SB 15 March 1982, 14, Gen Business, (a) Wreath Placing War Memorial; SB, 17 June 1982, 14, Gen Business, (f) Proposed erection Ethnic Monument.
70. SB, 16 January 1984, VE & VP Days; SB, 14.11.1984, 9, Anzac-Remembrance, (a) Remembrance Day Services in War Cemeteries; Letter from Peter Young, Director of Australian War Graves – Ceremony for Armistice Day.
71. State Board minutes 20 May 1986, 9, Anzac-Remembrance, (c) Royal British Legion Festival of Remembrance 1986.
72. SB minutes, 14 July 1986, 10, Anzac-Remembrance, Anzac Day – National Day of Remembrance; Various Orders of Service for Anzac Day and Remembrance Day, from both the Australian War Memorial, Canberra and RSL, Adelaide held by J Pavils.
73. SB minutes, 20 January 1986, 9, Anzac-Remembrance, (b) Conduct of Services, State War memorial.

Chapter 7 – God Save Australia

1. *Methodist Hymn Book*, (London: Hazell, Watson and Viney), Australasian Edition, 1904, For the King and Nation, Hymn 971, p. 809, God save our gracious King;/Long live our noble King;/God save the King!/Send him victorious,/Happy and glorious,/ Long to reign over us:/God save the King!
2. *Advertiser*, 'Violet Day, A Tribute to the Dead, Heroic Australians Honored', 3.7.1915, p. 17.
3. ACA, TCDKT 1916/1145, Anzac Day Commemoration Committee, letter dated 28 February 1916 from David J Garland, Hon Secretary to His Worship the Mayor of Adelaide, S. Australia; Anzac Day Commemoration, 25th April, 1916; Plan of Observance of Anzac Day, Tuesday, 25th April, 1916, David J Garland, Hon Secretary.
4. *Advt*, Religious Notices, 25.4.1916, p. 2; ACA, TCDKT, 1916/1145, Letterhead, The Council of Churches of South Australia to His Worship the Mayor of Adelaide, 15.4.1916; Mortlock, Z Pamphlet Anzac Souvenir, 940.425 A637, Anzac Day Commemoration, 25.4.1916, p. 22.
5. *Advertiser*, Religious Notices, 25.4.1916, p. 2
6. *Advertiser*, Public Notices, 26.4.1916, p. 2.
7. *Register*, 'Memorial and Intercession', 1.5.1916, p. 4.
8. *Advertiser*, 'Grandest Day of Them All', 25.4.1938, p. 14.
9. Alberton Circuit of the Methodist Church, Minute Book commencing 2 April 1919, Minutes of the second quarterly meeting of the Alberton Methodist circuit held in Yatala Church on Wednesday evening 2 July 1919, confirmed 1 October 1919.
10. *Diggers Gazette,* Vol II, No 8, 7 March 1921, p. 15.
11. *Advertiser*, 'In Memory of Anzac, Solemn Service, Big Crowd at Elder Park', 24 April 1922, p. 10.
12. *Advertiser*, 'In Memory of Anzac', 24.4.1922, p. 10.
13. *Advertiser,* 'Service at the Synagogue', 24.4.1922, p. 10.
14. League minutes, Ninth State Council Meeting held 12 September 1922, Anzac Day, p. 103.
15. *Advertiser,* 'A United Service', 26.4.1923, p. 11.
16. *Advertiser*, 'Service at the Synagogue', 26.4.1926, p. 11.
17. *Advertiser*, 'Soldiers' Mothers', 26.4.1926, p. 11.
18. *Advertiser*, 'In the Churches', 26.4.1926, p. 11.
19. *Advertiser*, 'Worshippers at Dawn', 27.4.1931, p. 7.
20. League minutes, 7.8.34, Dawn Service.
21. *Advertiser,* 'Service in London', 26.4.1935, p. 18.
22. *Advertiser,* 'We Will Remember Them', 25.4.1935, p. 1; 'Widespread Celebration of Anzac Day', 26.4.1935, p. 18.
23. <*http://homepages* picknowl.com.au/tochsa/about.htm> Toc H South Australia, 19.6.2003, 'What is Toc H? Page 1 of 2; *Advt*, 'Toc H Service at Cross of Sacrifice', 27.4.36, p. 16.
24. *Advertiser*, 'Many Attend Service at Dawn', 27.4.36, p. 15.
25. *Advertiser*, 'Call to Moral Rearmament', 25.4.1939, p. 14.
26. *Advertiser,* 'Requiem Mass at Cathedral', 26.4.39, p. 7.
27. *Advertiser*, 'Premier to March in Anzac Day Procession', 24.4.39, p. 20.
28. *Advertiser*. 'Requiem Mass at Cathedral', 26.4.1939, p. 7.
29. Board minutes, 28.10.1938; 13.3.39; 21.3.39, Villers Bretonneux memorial tree.
30. RSS&SILA, Official Year Book, 'Villers-Bretonneux Memorial', 1939, p. 105.
31. *Advertiser*, 'Gum Tree from France', 26.4.39, p. 7.

32. League minutes, 19.3.1940, Sunday Service.
33. *Advertiser*, 'Suburban Dawn Services', 26.4.1940, p. 27.
34. *Advertiser*, 'Second AIF Honors Predecessors', 26.4.40, p. 21.
35. *Advertiser*, 'Requiem Mass at St Francis Xavier's', 26.4.1941, p. 16.
36. League minutes, 13.5.41, 13, Anzac Day: (b) Procession.
37. *Advertiser,* 'At the Saluting Base', 26.4.1941, p. 16.
38. Richard Ely, 'The First Anzac Day: Invented or Discovered?' in *Journal of Australian Studies*, No 17, November 1985 p. 52.
39. AWM File 623/19, Official opening of the Australian War memorial at Canberra 11 November 1941.
40. AWM, 623/19, Official opening of the Australian War memorial at Canberra 11 November 1941, p. 3.
41. League minutes, 17.2.1942, Dawn Services.
42. Toc H South Australia, <http://hompages.picknowl.com.au/tochsa/about.htm>
43. League minutes, 14.4.1942, 12, Anzac Day, Sunday Service.
44. *Advertiser*, 'Cathedral Services', 27.4.1942, p. 4.
45. *Bible*, authorised King James Version printed by authority, (London: Collins, 1950), New Testament, 2 Corinthians, chapter 5, verse 1, p. 170, emphasis.
46. *Advertiser*, 'Cathedral Services', 27.4.42, p. 4.
47. *Advertiser,* 'Cross of Sacrifice Ceremony', 24.4.1943, p. 1.
48. *Advertiser*, 'Anzac Day Services', 26.4.1943, p. 3.
49. League minutes, 16.3.43, 15, Anzac Day.
50. *Advertiser,* 'Anzac Day Services Tomorrow', 24.4.1943, p. 1.
51. United Nations Documents: The San Francisco Conference (April-May 1945), Truman Presidential Museum & Library, <http://www.trumanlibrary.org/whistlestop/study_collections/un/largesf_conference/>
52. *Advertiser*, 'Solemn Service at Cross', 26.4.45, p. 5.
53. *Advertiser*, 'Dawn Services in City and Suburbs', 26.4.45, p. 5.
54. *Advertiser*, E R Greer, 'An Anzac Day on Malta', 25.4.1945, p. 6.
55. League minutes, 5.2.1951, 17, General Business, (f) Anzac Services.
56. League minutes, 19.2.1951, Speakers for Anzac Celebrations.
57. *Sentry-Go*, Vol l, No 12, April 1958, p. 2.
58. *Sentry-Go*, Vol II, No 17, September 1958, p. 1; League minutes, 9.3.1959, 14, Anzac, (a) Anzac Service.
59. *Sentry-Go*, Vol II, No 22, February 1959. p. 1.
60. AWM 27, 623/20, The Governor-General's address on the occasion of the dedication today of the Hall of Memory, Australian War Memorial, Canberra, 24 May 1959, pp. 1–2.
61. League minutes, 9.7.56, (g) Anzac Sunday Service; 21.9.59, 16, General Business.
62. League Minutes, 6.2.1961, (b) Anzac Sunday Service.
63. John Luttrell, 'Cardinal Gilroy's Anzac Day problem', in *Journal of the Royal Australian Historical Society*, June 1999, v85, il, p. 1, Expanded Academic, Article A55805882, 1999, p. 1 of 14.
64. League minutes, 2.3.1964, 17, Anzac, (a), Report.
65. League minutes, 1.3.1965, (d) Service sheets.
66. League minutes, 26.7.1965, (b) Anzac Commemoration – form of service.
67. Annual Report 1964–1965, Unpaginated.
68. League minutes, 21.3.66, 17, (a), Report.
69. League minutes, 16.10.1967, (b) Anzac Day; 15.1.1968, 16, (b) Anzac Hymn Sheet.

70. League minutes, 19.5.1969, (g) Strathalbyn S/B – Service.
71. League minutes, 20.10.1969, 14, Anzac-Remembrance, Anzac Day Observance – Strathalbyn.
72. League minutes, 18.9.1972, (b) Anzac Hymn Sheet.
73. National Library of Australia, K Inglis, Box 1 of 15, Newspaper clipping, *Sydney Morning Herald*, 'Whitlam's aim for "new" Aust', 4.12.1973.
74. League Minutes, Special Meeting of State Board held 23.4.1931, 7, Song of Australia; RSL Library, Unveiling and Dedication of the World War II memorial, Adelaide Sunday 11 November 1956, Song of Australia (One Verse).; League Minutes, 18.10.1971, (h), 'Song of Australia'.
75. League minutes, 18.6.73, Report extra-ordinary meeting of National Congress, dated 15.8.1973, P. 5; Robert Nicol, *At the End of the Road*, (Sydney: Allen & Unwin, 1994) p. 52; Song of Australia, <http://www.southaustralianhistory.com.au/song.htm>.
76. National Library, MS 389, Papers, K Inglis, Box 1 of 25, *Herald*, 26.4.1974; *Sydney Morning Herald*, provides the words of 'Advance Australia Fair' first performed in Sydney on St Patrick's Day 1878.
77. National Library, MS 389, Papers, K Inglis, Box 4 of 25, *Bulletin*, 11 May, 1974, T F Gleeson, Revesby, NSW, 'Anthem Squabble'.
78. League minutes, 18.11.1974, 9, Anzac-Remembrance, (a) Remembrance Day.
79. National Library, K Inglis, *Bulletin*, 'Gough's order angers Army', 19.4.1975, p. 129.
80. National Library, K Inglis, *SMH*, 26.4.1975.
81. League minutes, 16.4.1984, (b) Report on Anzac Day 1984 arrangement and National Anthem.
82. League minutes, 17.3.1986.
83. Many Australians have written of Anzac 'spirit', 'myth' or 'legend' and of Gallipoli as the beginning of the nation. I include some who have used those particular terms in the titles of articles in a period from 1982 to 1999. Kevin Fewster, 'Ellis Ashmead Bartlett and the Making of the Anzac Legend', in *Journal of Australian Studies*, No 10, June 1982, pp. 17–30; D A Kent, 'The Anzac Book and the Anzac Legend', in *Historical Studies*, Vol 21, No 84, April 1985, pp. 376–390: Jane Ross, 'The myth of Anzac', in 'Reflections, A symposium on the meanings of Anzac', printed in *Journal of the Australian War Memorial*, No 16, April 1990, pp. 55–56; Ken Inglis, 'The Anzacs: Their courage, resourcefulness and comradeship impressed both allies and enemies, and forged a coming-of-age myth for two youthful nations', in *Time International*, 25 Oct, 1999, i43, p48+, Electronic Collection: A57298705, RN: A57298705, p. 1 of 3; Further contributions exist in edited collections relating to Australia and war such as Chapter 17 by Adrian Howe, Anzac mythology and the feminist challenge', pp. 302–310 in *Gender and War*, Joy Damousi and Marilyn Lake (eds), (Cambridge: Cambridge University, 1995).
84. Hank Nelson, 'Gallipoli, Kokoda and the making of national identity', in *Journal of Australian Studies*, June 1997, n53, p157(11), page 1 of 15, InfoTrac Web: Expanded Academic Electronic Collection, A20171122, RN: A20171122.
85. Miriam Dixson, *The Imaginary Australian: Anglo-Celts and Identity – 1788 to the present*, (Sydney, UNSW Press, 1999) p. 63. Dixson writes 'That is to say, civil society and the civic identity model take for granted persisting support from the core culture.' My Honours thesis *'New Australians': Catalysts for a New 'Australian'* found that using representations of Australian identity exhibited in the South Australian centenary and sesquicentenary celebrations that civic support for memorial services recognising 'Anzac' contribution to the nation was one facet of civic identity represented in both

the 1936 and 1986 celebrations. Therefore, I believe Anzac culture to be but one dimension of Anglo-Celtic core culture within Australia.

86. Interview with Simon Berry 30 October, 2001 at 200 Magill Road Norwood, South Australia. 5067. Mr Berry holds slides and a video recording of proceedings in France, Sydney and Canberra relating to the burial of the Unknown Australian Soldier, 11 November 1993 and Neil McPherson, Public Affairs, Australian War Memorial, 'Australia's Forgotten Funeral', in *Australian Funeral Director*, September, 1993, p. 19.
87. Berry, 30.10.2001, and McPherson, *Aust Funeral Director*, September, 1993, p. 19. Also Australian Funeral Directors Association, 'Return home of the Unknown Australian Soldier November 1993', Video produced and directed by Peter Tobin 1993, held by Simon Berry of Charles Berry & Son Pty Ltd, 200 Magill Road, Norwood. 5067.
88. Berry, 30.10.2001, and McPherson, *Aust Funeral Director*, September, 1993, p. 19.
89. Simon Berry, 30 November, 2001.
90. Australian Funeral Directors Association, 'Return home of the Unknown Australian Soldier November 1993'. Video produced and directed by Peter Tobin 1993.
91. Berry, 30.11.2001; Aust Funeral Directors Assoc, 'Return home of the Unknown Australian Soldier November 1993', Video produced and directed by Peter Tobin 1993.
92. Funeral Service of the Unknown Australian Soldier 11 November 1993, Eulogy delivered by the Prime Minister of Australia, the Honourable P J Keating, MP, unpaginated. Copy supplied by Simon Berry.
93. Australian Funeral Directors Association 'Return home of the Unknown Australian Soldier November 1993', Video produced and directed by Peter Tobin 1993.
94. Funeral service for the Unknown Australian Soldier, Australian War memorial, 11.11.1993, Order of Ceremony, unpaginated, Psalm 23, Prayer of Remembrance, Prayer of Committal, Prayer of Dedication.
95. Funeral Service, AWM, 11.11.1993, Order of Ceremony, Unpaginated, A Prayer for Australia, copy supplied by Simon Berry.
96. Ken Inglis in 'Reflections on the Unknown Soldier', *Journal of the Australian War Memorial*, No 24, April 1994, p. 6.
97. Funeral Service for the Unknown Australian Soldier, Australian War memorial, 11 November 1993, Order of Ceremony. Copy supplied by Simon Berry.

Chapter 8 – Australian Britons

1. David Thelen, 'Memory and American History', in *Jnl of American History*, Vol 75, No 4, March 1989, p. 1117.
2. Edwin N Broomhead, *Barbed Wire in the Sunset*, (Melbourne: The Book Depot, 1944); Ralph Churches, *A Hundred Miles as the Crow Flies*, (Adelaide: R F Churches, 1996).
3. Don McLaren, *Mates in Hell: The Secret Diary of Don McLaren, POW of the Japanese 1942–45*, (Henley Beach: Seaview Press, republished 1998). McLaren's original diary held by the Mortlock Library of South Australia.
4. *Advertiser*, 24 July 2000, Peter Hackett, 'Farewell nurse, pal and hero', p. 29; See Betty Jeffrey, *White Coolies*, (Sydney: Angus and Robertson, 1954, Reprinted January 1958) and Norman G Manners, *Bullwinkel*, (Victoria Park, Hesperian Press, 1999).
5. Mortlock pamphlet, Zpam 369.294 S731, 1913, W J Sowden, Australian Wattle Day League, *Outline history of the wattle blossom celebration in Australia*, 1913, p. 12.
6. W J Denny, *The Diggers*, (London: Hodder and Stoughton, 1919), introduction.
7. Denny, *Diggers*, p. 232, 291.
8. Denny, *Diggers*, p. 10.

9. Charles Duguid, *Doctor and the Aborigines*, (Adelaide: Rigby, 1972), p. 60.
10. Duguid, *Doctor*, 1972, Frontispiece, pp. 60–62.
11. Duguid, *Doctor*, p. 63; p 66.
12. Duguid, *Doctor*, p. 68.
13. Duguid, *Doctor*, p. 69.
14. Duguid, *Doctor*, Foreword by Sir Mark Oliphant, unpaginated.
15. Charles Duguid, Violet Day, Adelaide 1931, Memorial Address, "Pro Deo, Pro Rege, Pro Patria", unpaginated.
16. Decie Denholm, (ed), *Behind the Lines One Woman's War 1914–1918 The Letters of Caroline Ethel Cooper*, (London: Jill Norman & Hobhouse, 1982), 22 November 1914, pp. 42–43.
17. Denholm, *Behind the Lines*, 22 August, 1915, p. 95; 12 December 1915, pp. 114–116, Introduction, p. 2, 3.
18. Stella Bowen, *Drawn From Life Reminiscences by Stella Bowen*, (London: Collins Publishers, 1940), p. 63, 49.
19. Bowen, *Drawn From Life*, pp. 58–59.
20. *Advertiser*, Patrick McDonald, 'Passionate war artist blazed a trail for women', 20 July 2002, p. 36.
21. Department of Veterans' Affairs, Bruce Scott MP, Minister for Veterans' Affairs, Media Release, 'Coalition Govt Acknowledges Ordeal of Ex-PoWs of Japan', 22 May, 2001, <http://www.dva.gov.au/media/aboutus/budget/budget01/budget2.htm>
22. Percentages relate to figures given by Lionel Wigmore in *The Japanese Thrust*, (Canberra: Australian War Memorial, 1957), p. 642.
23. Media Monitors, Bill Schmitt, Mornings with Philip Satchell, 891 ABC, 1005, 12.10.2001.
24. Media Monitors, Bill Schmitt, Mornings with Philip Satchell, 891 ABC, 1005, 12.10.01.
25. Media Monitors, Bill Schmitt, Mornings with Philip Satchell, 891 ABC, 1005, 12.10.01.
26. Bill Schmitt to author, 29.10.2001.
27. Don McLaren, *Mates in Hell*, 1998, p. 31.
28. Francis, Execution of 4 POW by Japanese, 2.9.1942.
29. Tim Bowden, *Changi photographer George Aspinall's record of captivity*, (Sydney: ABC Enterprises & William Collins Pty Ltd, 1984), pp. 90–93.
30. McLaren, *Mates in Hell*, 1998, p. 30.
31. McLaren, *Mates in Hell*, 1998, p. 31.
32. McLaren, *Mates in Hell* 1998, p. 112.
33. Guy Baker, *More Lives Than a Cat*, (Strathfield: Consensus Books, 1998), p. 170.
34. Baker, *More Lives*, p. 198.
35. Broomhead, *Barbed Wire*, 1944, pp. 26–27, 146.
36. Broomhead, *Barbed Wire*, 1944, pp. 26–27.
37. Broomhead, *Barbed Wire*, 1944, pp. 32–33.
38. Broomhead, *Barbed Wire*, 1944, pp. 56–57.
39. Broomhead, *Barbed Wire*, 1944, pp. 72–73.
40. 'Land of Hope and Glory', Words by Arthur C Benson, © 1902, Boosey & Co Ltd.
41. Broomhead, *Barbed Wire*, 1944, p. 73.
42. Broomhead, *Barbed Wire*, 1944, p. 176.
43. Broomhead, *Barbed Wire*, 1944, p. 81.
44. Broomhead, *Barbed Wire*, 1944, p. 127.

45. Broomhead, *Barbed Wire*, 1944, p. 128.
46. Broomhead, *Barbed Wire*, 1944, p. 128.
47. Broomhead, *Barbed Wire*, 1944, pp. 146–147.
48. Information concerning Edwin Broomhead's ordination supplied by Rev George Potter, Secretary, The Historical Society of the Uniting Church in South Australia, 29 October, 2003.
49. Rev Edwin N Broomhead, 'Common Folk', in *Back*, April 1947, p. 1.
50. Rev Edwin Broomhead, 'Take a Minute Off for Reflection', in *Back*, November 1947, p. 9.
51. Broomhead, 'Take a Minute Off', *Back*, Nov 1947, p. 9.
52. Handwritten note from Ralph Churches to author December 2001.
53. Churches, *Crow Flies*, 1996, p. ii.
54. Churches, *Crow Flies*, 1996, pp. 92–94.
55. Churches, *Crow Flies*, 1996, pp. 173–174.
56. Churches, *Crow Flies*, 1996, p. 143.
57. Churches, *Crow Flies*, 1996, p. 153.
58. Betty Jeffrey, *White Coolies*, (Sydney: Angus and Robertson, 1954), Reprinted 55,56,57, 1958 edition.
59. Jeffrey, *White Coolies*, 1958, pp. 23–25.
60. Jeffrey, *White Coolies*, 1958, pp. 55–61.
61. Jeffrey, *White Coolies*, 1958, p. 55, 75.
62. Jeffrey, *White Coolies*, 1958, pp. 190–191.
63. Manners, *Bullwinkel*, 1999, p. 198.
64. Manners, *Bullwinkel*, p. 199.
65. Manners, *Bullwinkel*, p. 222.
66. Manners, *Bullwinkel*, p. 224.
67. Broomhead, *Barbed Wire*, p. 32.

Chapter 9 – Balancing the Ledger

1. *Back*, 'Living Memorials Use Vision When Planning Your War Memorial. Make It a Living Symbol', January 1948, p. 17.
2. Ian McGregor, Frances Eltridge and Karen McGregor, Principal Consultants, *Commemorative Program Research*, Project No 4433, prepared for Ms Kerry Blackburn & Mrs Lyn Witheridge, Commemoration Branch, Department of Veterans' Affairs, 26 May 1998.
3. Dr Richard Reid and Dr Gordon Forth, *Memories & Memorabilia*, (Canberra: Department of Veterans' Affairs, undated,) back cover.
4. John R Gillis (ed), *Commemorations: the Politics of National Identity*, (Princeton: Princeton University, 1994), Chapter IX 'The War Dead and the Gold Star: American Commemoration of the First World War,' p. 172; NLA, MS 389, Ken Inglis papers, Box 4 of 25, *Sydney Morning Herald*, 29.6.1965, 'Request on bodies of soldiers'; Box 10 of 25, 22.1.1966, 'Policy changed! War burials'.
5. Department for Environment & Heritage, Government of South Australia supplied a photocopy of *Survey War Memorials Situated in the State of South Australia*, compiled by State Secretary S A Branch, The Returned Services League of Australia, 1967, unpaginated, information supplied by Corporation of the town of Glenelg, Information recorded 25 October 1967.

6. Holdfast Bay History Centre, Brighton, 28–1519–1, Honour Roll – Glenelg, Programme of Unveiling Ceremony, Glenelg Honor Roll, Sunday 8th November, 1925, Mayor; 28–1518–1, Honour Roll, Glenelg Sailing Club, Roll of Honour 1914–1918, (Photo taken when attached to Kiosk on old Jetty); 28–1520–1, Honour Roll – World War II circa 1940, Glenelg District Honour Roll, 28–1520–2, Honour Roll – World War II circa 1941 Glenelg District Honour Roll (To promote enlistment).
7. League survey, Corporation of the town of Moonta, 24 October 1967.
8. Monument, Blanche Terrace, Moonta, October 2001.
9. Photographs taken in Moonta and Moonta Mines, October 2001 held by author.
10. League survey, Corporation of the Town of Wallaroo, 17 October 1967.
11. Arch, Town Hall, Wallaroo, October 2001.
12. Arch and surrounds, Town Hall, Wallaroo, October 2001.
13. RSL Club, Elizabeth Street, Wallaroo, October 2001.
14. Pre School Centre, Elizabeth Street, Wallaroo, October 2001.
15. Photographs of Kadina school dedication plaque, Memorial Arch and Honour Rolls, October 2001, held by author.
16. Information desk, Kadina Council, October 2001.
17. League survey, Corporation of the City of Port Adelaide, 27 March 1968.
18. *Portonian* Vol 19, No 2, 'Semaphore War Memorial', June 1991, pp. 5–6.
19. McDougall & Vines, *Greater Port Adelaide Heritage Survey*, (Norwood: McDougall & Vines, 1989), p. 47, 190, 195, pp. 192–193; Mortlock Library, Z pamphlet, 287.930994231, R818, Rosewater Uniting Church, Rosewater Uniting Church Centenary, 1878–1978, p. 1.
20. Steve Nickolls, 'Mavis Delves into Rosewater History', in Port Adelaide Library, L.H. Ros 1. 9.3.1977.
21. *Portside Messenger*, 'Historic hall to become youth housing', 6 June 1990, p. 7; Theresa Rockley, 'Hall Plan Off', Wednesday 10 October 1990, p. 1; 'Housing plan for RSL Hall "unstoppable"', 17 October 1990, p. 7.
22. SA Land Information System, 12 April 2001, 59 Grand Junction Rd, Rosewater, Strata Corp No 13071; According to site plaque, the project opened 24 February 2000, photograph held by author as is photograph of the Alberton & Rosewater RSS & AILA Sub-Branch transom.
23. McDougall, *Heritage Survey*, 1989, p. 192.
24. Affordable medium density as per Planning, Port Adelaide Enfield Council April 2001; Storage as per former Councillor Rex Serle June 2001.
25. McDougall, *Heritage Survey*, 1989, p. 193.
26. *Port Adelaide News*, Vol 4, No 44, 'Rosewater Methodist Church Photographs Unveiled', 15 June 1917, p. 11.
27. Mortlock, Rosewater Uniting Church Centenary, p. 3; Uniting Church Alberton, Invitation card, Rosewater Methodist Church Jubilee 1878–1928, 17–20 November 1928, Thanksgiving Service, 17 November 1928, Memorial windows will be unveiled during the service; *Port Adelaide News*, Vol 16, No 15, 'Rosewater Methodist Church Jubilee Celebrations', 23 November, 1928.
28. Photographs taken at Wesley House and Alberton Uniting Church in 2001 held by the author.
29. Eric Thompson, *The Uniting Church in Australia, The Origin and First Ten Years of Trinity Uniting Church – Alberton, 30/10/1983 – 30/10/1993*, (Adelaide: Carmel and John Clare, 1993), pp. 1–6, 35–38.
30. *Port Adelaide News*, Vol 16, No 15, 'Rosewater Methodist Church Jubilee Celebrations', p. 2; Mortlock, Rosewater Uniting Church Centenary, p. 5.

31. McDougall, *Heritage Survey*, 1989, p. 193; SA Land Information System, 12 April 2001, 63 Grand Junction Road, A Psorakis.
32. Rosemary Mitchell, *Epworth Uniting Church, Parkside 1884–1984*, (Morphett Vale, Rosemary Mitchell, 1984); In particular, the Uniting Church Historical Society, the Repat Museum at Repatriation General Hospital, Daw Park and the Army Museum of South Australia, at Keswick Barracks, Keswick, Maritime Museum, Port Adelaide.
33. The Uniting Church Historical Society, Memorial Service, Madge Memorial Church, Adelaide, Order of Service, 24.10.1943 for Memorial window dedicated to Leslie John Crowther KIA 24 September 1943, now at Blackforest Uniting Church.
34. Mortlock, Rosewater Uniting Church Centenary, pp. 3, 5.
35. *Outreach*, The Uniting Church in Australia, Alberton Port Adelaide Parish, Vol 15, No 8, 'Windows', p. 15; Vol 15, No 9, October 1985, 'Trinity'; Vol 15, No 10 November 1985, 'Trinity', p. 11; Vol 15, No 11, December 1985, p. 11.
36. *Advertiser*, 26.4.1928, 'Honoring the Anzacs', p. 13; 26.4.1929, 'Unemployed returned soldiers', p. 13.
37. Utilitarian memorials took the form of church halls, lychgates and porches, memorial ovals, memorial hospitals and RSL Memorial Halls.
38. *Port Adelaide News*, Vol 4, No 44, 'Rosewater Methodist Church, Photographs Unveiled,' 15 June 1917, p. 11; WFL Dodson, Lieutenant, 10th Bn., Australian Infantry, AIF, 19 September 1917, <http://yard.ccta.gov.uk/cwgc/register/nsf/wwwcreateservicedetails?openagent&457872>
39. *Advertiser*, 26 April 1924, 'Rosewater Women's Memorial Garden, Dedicated on Anzac Day,' p. 16; *Portonian*, Vol 13, No 3, September 1985, 'Women's War Memorial, Rosewater Reserve,' p. 3.
40. Photographs of Rosewater Womens Memorial Roll of Honor and Alberton Public School held by author.
41. Arthur Limb, *History of the 10th Battalion AIF 1914–1918 Egypt, Gallipoli, France, Belgium*, (London: Cassell and Company, 1919), p. 96: Internet, Commonwealth War Graves Commission as above.
42. *Advertiser*, 'Youth's Great Tribute to Anzac Heroes', 27 April 1931, p. 7; Michael McKernan, *Here is Their Spirit A History of the Australian War Memorial 1917–1990*, (St Lucia: University of Queensland Press, 1991), p. 2; Australian War Memorial AWM 27, 623/17–623/21, 'The Governor-General's address on the occasion of the dedication to day of the Hall of Memory, Australian War Memorial', dated 24 May 1929.
43. Cheltenham cemetery, for example, Section A, Roadway B, Path 4 1st Right (East) Twelve persons buried on the above site between 9th December 1876 and 31st May 1958. Five with the surname 'Garnaut' and seven with the surname of 'Duffield'. Two older headstones replaced by headstones bearing the names Ignacioneck 1/90, Sisa 24/1/90 and Makapoba 5/2/90.
44. Port Adelaide Library Local History folder, LH ROS 1B40001 BU Rosewater Woolsheds, '"Battling Britons" planning reunion', 6.2.1980.
45. Ron Hoskin, *Early Recollections of Ron Hoskin*, (Adelaide: Ronald Bruce Hoskin, 1996), Part 2, Rosewater, p. 9.
46. Port Adelaide Enfield Council supplied a photocopy of the plaque; The Commonwealth War Graves Commission gives E E Sutton's date of death as Sunday, 4th July 1943, age 42. Sutton's burial site is in Thanbyuzayat War Cemetery, Myanmar.
47. William Henry Gilbert, *90th Year, City of Port Adelaide Mayor's Report 1945–1946*, pp. 12–13.
48. Information supplied by Port Adelaide Enfield Council.

49. The memorial listed the subscribers as: 'Adelaide Cement Co Ltd, Adelaide Chemical and Fertilizer Co Ltd, Adelaide Stevedoring Co Ltd, Asbestos Cement Pty Ltd, Caltex Oil (Aust) Pty Ltd, Colonial Sugar Refining Co Ltd, Commonwealth Oil Refineries Ltd, Cresco Fertilizers Ltd, Electricity Trust of South Aust, Ford Motor Co of Aust Pty Ltd, General Motors – Holdens Ltd, ICI Alkali (Aust) Pty Ltd, ICI Employees Social Club Inc, Mothers & Babies Health Assoc, Oldfields Bakery Ltd, Shell Co of Aust Ltd, Sleigh H C Ltd, Vacuum Oil Pty Ltd, Wallaroo – Mt Lyell Fertilizer Ltd. Officially opened 5th May 1951'.
50. Harold Joseph Moore, *95th Year, City of Port Adelaide Mayor's Report 1950–1951*, p. 19.
51. Moore, *95th Year, City of Port Adelaide Mayor's Report 1950–1951*, p. 19.
52. *Portside Messenger*, '$10m housing estate plans for Peterhead', 26 July 1989, p. 5; League Survey, Corporation of the City of Port Adelaide, 27 March 1968; Port Adelaide Library Local History Section, 'Land Evaluation and Need Study 1985, Reserve Plan Folio', LH 711.580994231 27 Vol 3, ICI Reserve & Playground, 37 Trust Tce., Peterhead Sheet 39, DRG no 24.
53. Photograph of plaque May 2001, held by author.
54. Hoskin, *Early Recollections*, 1996, Part 2, Rosewater, p. 9; Rex Serle, June 2001.
55. *Back*, January 1948, p. 17.
56. Pamphlet relating to Junction Community Centre May – July 2001, supplied by Junction Community Centre, Grand Junction Road, Ottoway; Photographs of windows and honour boards taken 2001, held by author
57. Rex Serle and Ron Hoskin to author, 2001; Chris Chereda, Mara Kolomitsev and Kathy Pivetta, *The Building within the Triangle Junction Community Centre Formerly the Ottoway Congregational Church*, (Adelaide, Seaview Press, 2001), p. 16, 34.
58. Rosewater Womens Memorial, 1914–1919 Roll of Honor, photographed 2001, held by author.
59. Site visit Army Museum Keswick; letter from Wolfgang Warmer, Guides Volunteer, National Motor Museum, dated 19 February 2002; Search result, South Australian Maritime Museum Artefact Collection, provided by Bill Seager September 2001, pp. 1–3.
60. Site visit Uniting Church Historical Society, photographs taken at site, letter from Rev'd George Potter, Secretary, The Historical Society of the Uniting Church in South Australia dated 5 February 2002; letter from A D Presgrave, Archivist, National Railway Museum, dated 31 January 2002.
61. Returned & Services League of Australia (S.A. Branch) Inc., Adelaide, Memorial File.
62. Reid and Forth, *Memories & Memorabilia*, back cover.
63. *Advertiser*, 19 February 2000, p. 9; *Barbed Wire and Bamboo*, Vol 52, No 1, February 2000, front cover, Prince Alfred College Prep students celebrate Remembrance Day 1999. Service at the newly located SA POW memorial in College grounds; Bill Schmitt, Secretary, Ex-POW Association of South Australia, March 2000.
64. Media Release, The Hon Trish Worth MP, Member for Adelaide, 24 January 2001.
65. Makin News and Views, Edition Nineteen, August 2002.p. 3; Letter dated from Ben C Martin, St Agnes, addressed to Whom it may concern, dated 21 January 2002.
66. Kapunda Centenary Celebrations, Dedication for Kapunda War Memorial Gardens and World War II Nurses and Others, Sunday 23 September 2001, Hymns & Anthems; photographs held by author.
67. The Anglican Parish of Woodville, Order of Service, The Church of Saint Margaret of Scotland, A Service of Rededication for the Memorial Lychgate, 11 May, 2002; photographs held by author.
68. <http://minister.dva.gov.au/media/speeches>

Chapter 10 – The 'Pilgrimage Trail'

1. DVA, The Hon Bruce Scott MP, Minister for Veterans' Affairs, Media Release, 25/99, 'Sandakan Memorial Opened', 18 March 1999, p. 1 of 2, <http://minister.dva.gov.au/media/media/mar99/memorial.htm>
2. *Canberra Times*, James Grubel, 'A new generation gathers at Gallipoli to pay respects to Diggers', 26 April 2000, p. 1.
3. G Kurt Piehler, Chapter IX, 'The War Dead and the Gold Star: American Commemoration of the First World War', in John R Gillis (ed), *Commemorations: The Politics of National Identity*, (Princeton: Princeton University Press, 1994), p. 177.
4. Ken Inglis assisted by Jan Brazier, *Sacred Places War Memorials in the Australian Landscape*, (Melbourne: The Miegunyah Press, 1998), p. 181.
5. Transcript of the Prime Minister The Hon John Howard MP Veterans' Affairs Policy Launch, Epping, Sydney, p. 4 of 4, 13 October 2001, <http://pandora.nla.gov.au/pan/22107/20011109/www.liberal.org.au/M ... /pmvet-pol13oct.ht>
6. Mosse, *Fallen Soldiers*, p. 152–155.
7. Michelin & Cie, *Ypres and the Battles of Ypres*, (France: Michelin & Cie, 1919), cover.
8. *Diggers' Gazette*, Vol II, No 1, 15 November 1920, 'Sammy Lunn Appeal Fund', p. 21; Vol II, No 9, 21 March 1921, 'Farewell to Sammy Lunn Visit to Battlefields', p. 19.
9. NAA, Series No A1/15, Item No 1934/7024, Pilgrimage to war graves – passport question, Letter from Prime Minister's Department, Canberra to Royston T Cahir, Esq., Melbourne. Undated, but refers to 'my letter to you of the 29th November, 1927.'
10. NAA, Series No A458, Item No L337/7, Defence pilgrimage to France and Flanders, British Legion in co-operation Empire Service, Letterhead, Commonwealth of Australia, Australia House, London, Memorandum to The Secretary, Prime Ministers Department Canberra, from the Official Secretary, dated 2 August, 1928.
11. AWM38, 3DRL, 6673, Item 225, 'Battlefields Tour 1929', Booklet, The Battlefields and War Graves Gallipoli, Reproduced from the BP Magazine.
12. NAA, Series No A1/15, Item No 1934/7024, Pilgrimage to war graves – passport question, handwritten note dated 28/5[1929].
13. League minutes, 16th Sub-Branch Conference held 13 & 14 September 1933, 51, Visit to Battlefields.
14. League minutes, 22.1.1935, 28, Pilgrimage Battle Fields.
15. K S Inglis, 'A Sacred Place The Making of the Australian War Memorial', in *War and Society*, Vol 3, No 2, September 1985, p. 99.
16. Graeme Davison, John Hirst, Stuart Macintyre, (eds), *Oxford Companion to Australian History*, (Melbourne, Oxford University, 1998), p. 66.
17. League State Board minutes, 17 February 1936, 34, King's Coronation Suggested Pilgrimage.
18. Q S Spedding (ed), *The Returned Sailors and Soldiers' Imperial League of Australia (Federal Headquarters), Official Year Book 1937, (Coronation issue)*, (Sydney: NSW Branch, 1937), p. 221.
19. SB, 5 April 1938, 12, and 19 April 1938, 11, Unveiling of Villers-Bretonneux Memorial.
20. Lee Sackett, recognised this aspect of Anzac Day rituals in 'Marching into the Past: Anzac Day Celebrations in Adelaide', in *Journal of Australian Studies*, No 17, November 1985, pp. 20–21.
21. League minutes, 3.1.1939, 26, Goodwood S/B; 22.8.1939, 13, Re Films of War Graves.
22. League minutes, 2.9.1939, 17, and 19.9.1939, 12, Film – Unveiling of Villers-Bretonneux.

23. League Minutes, 3.7.1945, 27, Visit to Battlefields.
24. Alec Horne, 'Flash-Back to France' in *Back*, August 1947, pp. 29–30.
25. AWM 27, 670/2, Description of a visit to Australian Battlefields in France and Belgium by Mr A C Sharp late 'B' Company 45th Battalion AIF, (Extract from letter dated 23 August 1951), p. 1.
26. AWM 27, 670/2, Sharp, Extract from letter dated 23 August 1951, pp. 2–5.
27. League Minutes, 8.3.1954, 12, (h) Unveiling Memorial, Malta.
28. League Minutes, 20.9.1954, (f) Alamein Unveiling.
29. League State Board minutes, 21 February 1955, 14, General Business, (e) Fed Executive meeting, Gallipoli Pilgrimage.
30. *Back*, Advertisement, 'World Commemoration Tour', December 1954, p. 7.
31. NAA, Series No A462/16, Item No 448/12, War and defence – Pilgrimage of ex-servicemen to battlefield at Gallipoli, Prime Minster's Department, The Prime Minister, Gallipoli Pilgrimage, dated 24 March 1955, p. 2.
32. *Sentry-Go*, 'Anzac Observance in London', May 1960, p. 3.
33. *Sentry-Go*, 'RSL World Tourists Arrive in London', July 1960, p. 5.
34. NAA, Series No A463/63, Item No 1963/2297, Part I, Anzac Jubilee 1965 – Pilgrimage to Gallipoli, Letter to the Prime Minister Rt Hon Sir Robert Menzies from A G W Keys, National Secretary, RSS & AILA, dated 11 November, 1963, pp. 1–2.
35. NAA, Series No A463/63, Item No 1963/2297, letter dated 11 November 1963, p. 2.
36. NAA, Series No 1838/1, Item No 1516/6/206, Part 2, Protocol – Visits abroad by Australians – Pilgrimage by the Second, Nineteenth AIF Battalion & others to Gallipoli, marked 'confidential' p. 1 of 3, undated, but refers to other correspondence dated November 1963 and 11 September 1964.
37. NAA, Series No A463/63, Item No 1963/2297, Part I, Special Circular, Returned Servicemen's League (N.S.W.), Circular No. 36/64, File No C60, 92, dated 25 July 1964.
38. League State Board minutes, 25 May 1964, 18, Anzac, Gallipoli Pilgrimage.
39. NAA, Series No A463/63, Item No 1963/2297, Part I, Letterhead Commonwealth Treasury, Reference Number SL 63/4549, addressed to Prime Minister's Department, from J M Wark, Assistant Secretary, dated 6th April, 1964.
40. NAA, Series No 1838/1, Item No 1516/6/206 Part 2, marked 'Confidential' undated, p. 2.
41. Robertson, *Anzac and Empire*, p. 59.
42. NAA, Series No 1838/1, Item No 1516/6/206 Part 2, marked 'Confidential' undated, p. 3.
43. Ken Inglis recorded some of his experiences during the pilgrimage. NLA, MS 389, Box 3 of 25, K S Inglis 'Anzac Pilgrims a Self Portrait', in *Canberra Times*, 25 April 1966, p. 2.
44. League State Board Minutes, 8 February 1965, 19, General Business (q) Mr P Auld; 22 March 1965, (d) Gallipoli Pimgrimage, [sic].
45. League Minutes, 8.2.1965, 19, General Business (q) Mr P Auld; 22.3.1965, (d) Gallipoli Pimgrimage, [sic].
46. SB, 8 February 1965, 19, General Business, (i) Canberra Pilgrimage.
47. League State Board minutes, 22 March 1965, (e), Canberra Pilgrimage; 1965 Annual Report 1964–1965, unpaginated.
48. League minutes, 27.9.1965, Visit to Bomana Cemetery.
49. League minutes, 17.4.1967, 50th Anniversary C'wealth War Graves Commission, national circular 42/67.

50. League minutes, 18.3.68, (d) Dedication Ambon War Cemetery, National circular 69/68; 17.6.68, 18, Gen Business (c) 'Return to Kokoda.'
51. National Library of Australia, MS 389, Ken Inglis papers, *SMH*, 'Cemetery for Island War dead dedicated Ambon', 3 April 1968, Ex POWs and MPs Sir Wilfred Kent Hughes and Mr Thomas Uren; MS 389, Box 11 of 25, 'Stress placed on peace at War memorials abroad', 27 April 1987, Minister for Local Government and Administrative Service Mr Uren.
52. NAA, Series No 1838/362, Item No 25/1/3/25 Part I, France – Battle of the Somme pilgrimage, Letterhead Third Division AIF Remembrance Pilgrimage 1968, Letter to Rt Hon P M Hasluck MP, Minister for External Affairs, from Fred J Cahill, Secretary-Manager, dated 4 June 1968.
53. Brown, *Oxford English Dictionary*, Volume 1, A-M, 1991, community, II, 7, p. 455; For more information on 'communitas' see Jennifer de Freitas, 'Heritage Tourism as Secular Pilgrimage', A Thesis in the Department of Communication Studies Presented in Partial Fulfillment of the Requirements for the Degree of Master of Arts at Concordia University Montreal, Quebec, Canada, May 1998, pp. 27–28.
54. NAA, Series No A1838, Item No 25/1/3/25(I), Message from the Prime Minister of Australia, Gorton, dated 6 May 1968.
55. NAA, Series No 1838/362, Item No 25/1/3/25, Part I, Letter to Hasluck, MP, from Cahill, dated 4 June 1968.
56. NLA, MS 389, K Inglis papers, Box 10 of 25, *Canberra Times*, 'Australians visit France', 19 November 1968.
57. National Library, MS 389, K Inglis papers, Box 4 of 25, 'Visit to Lone Pine', A, 28.1.1971.
58. NLA, MS 389, K Inglis papers, Box 1 of 25, *SMH*, 'Reminders of El Alamein', 18 October 1972.
59. NLA, MS 389, K Inglis papers, Box 4 of 25, *SMH*, 20 April 1974; *Bulletin*, 'A big year for war veterans and their descendants in 1975', 3 August 1974; *SMH*, 'Return to Gallipoli', 12 April 1975.
60. NLA, MS 389, K Inglis papers, Box 1 of 25, *SMH*, 'Anzacs land again without Govt help', 26 April 1975.
61. NLA, MS 389, K Inglis papers, Box 1 of 25, *SMH*, 'Back to their Battlefields', 12 October 1978; 'Memories and Matilda in Northern France', 13 November 1978; 'Patsy Adam Smith', 6 January 1979; League State Board minutes, 16 October 1978, South Australian party to Tour Europe.
62. William Hughes, Mortlock, Z pamphlet 940.425, A637, Anzac Souvenir and *Advertiser* 24 April 1916, 'Australian Heroes honoured in London', p. 7; Robert Menzies, *Sentry-Go*, May 1960, p. 3.
63. RSL Library, Adelaide. The Parliament of the Commonwealth of Australia, Report of the Australian Parliamentary Delegation, 75th Anniversary Commemoration of the Landings at Gallipoli, April 1990, p. 4.
64. RSL Library, Adelaide, C of A, Delegation to the 75th Anniversary Commemoration of the Landings at Gallipoli, April 1990, Canberra, Appendix 1, Speech by the Prime Minister, Hon R J L Hawke, AC, MP, Lone Pine Memorial, Gallipoli Peninsula, Turkey, 25 April 1990, pp. 35–36.
65. RSL Library, C of A, Appendix 1, Speech by the PM, Hawke, Lone Pine, 25 April 1990, p. 37.
66. *RSL Handbook*, 75th Anniversary Issue, 1991, A publication of the Returned and Services League of Australia Limited, (Sydney Macarthur Press, 1991), p. 9.

67. RSL Library, C of A, Report of the Australian Parliamentary Delegation to the 75th Anniversary Commemoration of the Landings at Gallipoli, April 1990, Canberra, p. iii; p. 4; p. 7.
68. Report of the Australian Parliamentary Delegation, Gallipoli, April 1990. p. 18.
69. Report of the Australian Parliamentary Delegation, Gallipoli, April 1990. p. 30.
70. Interview with Mr Healey, Department of Veterans Affairs, Canberra, April 2000.
71. Veterans' Affairs Media Releases, Press release, Sept96-vietna1.htm, Vietnam Veterans visit strengthens Australia-Vietnam relationship, 93/96, 11 September 1996. <http://minister.dva.gov.au/media/press/sept96/vietna1.htm>
72. Hellfire Pass Museum Opening, The Prime Minister The Hon John Howard MP, Address at the Opening of the Hellfire Pass Museum, 24 April 1998, <http://www.pm.gov.au/media/pressrel/speech/1998/musmed.htm>
73. ANZAC 2000, Dawn Service-Order of Commemoration, pp. 3–5 of 7, <http://www.embaustralia.org.tr/anzac/anzac2k.htm>
74. *Canberra Times*, James Grubel, 'A new generation gathers at Gallipoli', 26 April 2000, p. 1.
75. Dennis Shanahan, Villers-Bretonneux, 'Howard Anzac trip a personal pilgrimage', *Weekend Australian*, April 29–30, 2000, p. 8.
76. Prime Minister of Australia News Room, Transcript of the Prime Minister The Hon John Howard MP Speech at the National RSL Congress, Melbourne, 5 September 2001, p. 2 of 3. <http://Pandora.nla.gov.au/pan/10052/20020221/www.pm.gov.au/news/spec ... /speech1217.ht>
77. de Freitas, 'Heritage Tourism as Secular Pilgrimage', 1998.

Epilogue

1. See *Journey of Remembrance: An account of Mount Barker High School's Remembrance 2001 project*, compiled by Julie Reece, (Mount Barker: Julie Reece, 2002).

SELECT BIBLIOGRAPHY

ARCHIVAL SOURCES

Adelaide City Archive
Australian War Memorial Research Centre
Barr Smith Special collections
Holdfast Bay History Centre, Brighton
Mortlock Library
National Archives of Australia: Canberra
National Archives of Australia: Collinswood
National Library of Australia
Port Adelaide Library Local History Files
Returned & Services League of Australia (S.A. Branch) Inc. Library, Adelaide
The Uniting Church Historical Society

PRIMARY SOURCES

Broomhead, Edwin N, *Barbed Wire in the Sunset*, (Melbourne: The Book Depot, 1944).

City of Port Adelaide, Mayor's Report 1945–1946, William Henry Gilbert, 90th Year. Mayor's Report 1950–1951, Harold Joseph Moore, 95th Year.

Denny, Captain W J, *The Diggers*, (London: Hodder and Stoughton, circa 1919).

Francis, Dick, 'Execution of 4 POW by Japanese, CPL Brevington, Pte Gale (Both AIF) and 2 English ORs, September 2nd 1942'. Bill Schmitt's handwritten copy of Dick Francis, Sergeant, 8th Division Headquarters report hidden in Changi, Singapore, retrieved at the end of WWII.

Gellert, Leon, *Songs of a Campaign*, (Sydney: Angus & Robertson, 1917), Third and enlarged edition with pictures by Norman Lindsay.

Keating, P J Honourable, MP, Eulogy delivered by the Prime Minister of Australia, Funeral Service of the Unknown Australian Soldier, 11 November 1993.

Methodist Church, Alberton Circuit, Minute Book Commencing April 2 1919.

Michelin & Cie, *Ypres and the Battles of Ypres*, (Clermont-Ferrand: Michelin & Cie, 1919).

Pearce, G F Senator, *Where the Australians Rest: A description of many of the Cemeteries overseas in which Australians-including those whose names can never now be known-are buried.* (Australia: Minister of State for Defence, 1920).

Rogers, R E E, *Anzac Day Commemoration April 25th 1916*. (Adelaide: Government Printer, 1916).

South Australia Official Reports of the Parliamentary Debates, Session 1922, Second Session of the Twenty-Fourth Parliament, From Thursday, July 27, to Friday, December 15, 1922, Holidays Act Amendment Act, (Adelaide: R E E Rogers, Government Printer, 1922).

Tobin, Peter, (Producer and Director), *The Return of the 'Unknown Soldier', November 1993*, Australian Funeral Directors Association, Video, Loaned by Charles Berry & Son Pty Ltd.

Published Sources

Australia

Australian Funeral Director.
Back, Magazine of the RSL.
Barbed Wire and Bamboo Official Organ Ex-Prisoners of War Association of Australia.
Makin News and Views.
Outreach

Port Adelaide News.
Portonian
Portside Messenger.
RSA Magazine.
Sentry-Go, News-Magazine of the SA RSL.
Stand-to.
Advertiser.
Age.
Canberra Times.
City Messenger.
Courier-Mail.
Diggers' Gazette.
Herald Sun.
Register.
Sunday Herald.
Weekend Australian.

United Kingdom

Buckinghamshire Advertiser.

Ephemera

Pamphlets

Australian War Memorial
Commonwealth Department of Veterans' Affairs.
Junction Community Centre May-July 2001.
Rosewater Methodist Church Jubilee 1878–1928, An Invitation.

Radio Interview

Schmitt, W H, A M, Secretary, Ex-POW Association of South Australia Incorporated, Mornings with Philip Satchell 891 ABC 1005, 12.10.2001, (Adelaide: Media Monitors, 2001).

Unpublished Materials *(Correspondence, etc)*

Adelaide High School. ex W Pearce, Honorary School Archivist.
Charles Berry & Son Pty Ltd, Norwood. Slides, video and photocopies relating to Funeral of the Unknown Australian Soldier ex Simon Berry.
Churches, Ralph.
Department for Environment & Heritage, Government of South Australia.
Makin Office, Martin, Ben C.
Myhill, Helen, correspondence re Rosewater Methodist Church Honour Roll.
National Motor Museum.
National Railway Museum.
Port Adelaide Enfield Council.
Port Adelaide Historical Society.
SA Govt, SA Land Information System.
South Australian Maritime Museum, Search Result Artifact Collection, Supplied by Curator, September 2001, List of Honour Boards held in collection.
Worth, Trish, MP, Media Release, 24 January 2001.

Unpublished Theses

Argent, Christopher M, 'For God, King and Country: Aspects of Patriotic Campaigners in Adelaide During the Great War, With Special Reference to the Cheer-Up Society, the League of Loyal Women and Conscription', Honours Degree of Bachelor of Arts in History, University of Adelaide, 1993

de Freitas, Jennifer, 'Heritage Tourism as Secular Pilgrimage', Master of Arts Thesis, Concordia University, Montreal, Quebec, Canada, 1998.

Hood, David, 'Conservatism and Change: the RSL and Australian Society, 1916–1932', Doctor of Philosophy in the Department of History, University of Adelaide, May 1994.

Reardon, Michael James, 'Anzac Day in Adelaide, 1916 to 1922: from the first anniversary to a national public holiday', Honours Thesis, Department of History, University of Adelaide, 1979.

Rice, Andrew, 'A forgotten Sacrifice: South Australian National Servicemen Returning from the Vietnam War,' Honours Degree in History, University of Adelaide, 1985.

SECONDARY SOURCES

Allchin, Frank M M, Lt-Col, *Purple and Blue The History of the 2/10th Battalion, AIF (The Adelaide Rifles) 1939–1945*, (Adelaide: The Griffin Press, 1958).

Australian Dictionary of Biography, Nairn, Bede & Serle, Geoffrey, (eds), Vol 7, (Sydney: Melbourne University Press, 1979).

Vol 8, (Melbourne: Melbourne University Press, 1981).

Vol 9, (Adelaide: Melbourne University Press, 1983).

Vol 10, (Adelaide: Melbourne University Press, 1986).

Serle, Geoffrey, (ed), Vol 11, (Melbourne: Melbourne University Press, 1988).

Ritchie, John, (ed), Vol 12, (Melbourne: Melbourne University Press, 1990).

Baker, Guy, *More Lives than a Cat*, (Strathfield: Consensus Books, 1998).

Becker, Annette, *War and Faith The Religious Imagination in France, 1914–1930*, (Oxford: Berg, 1998).

Benson, Arthur C, 'Land of Hope and Glory' (1902), in *Boosey's Community Song Book*, (London: Boosey & Co Ltd), 1927.

Bowden, Tim, *Changi Photographer: George Aspinall's Record of Captivity*, (Sydney: ABC Enterprises & William Collins Pty Ltd, 1984).

Bowen, Stella, *Drawn From Life*, (London: Collins Publishers, 1940).

Brown, Lesley, (ed), *New Shorter Oxford English Dictionary*, (Oxford: Clarendon Press, 1991).

Brittain, Vera, *Testament of Youth*, (Great Britain, Virago Press, 1978).

Chereda, Chris, Kolomitsev, Mara & Pivetta, Kathy, *The Building Within the Triangle Junction Community Centre Formerly the Ottoway Congregation Church*, (Henley Beach: Seaview Press, 2001).

Churches, Ralph, *A Hundred Miles as the Crow Flies*, (Adelaide: R F Churches, 1996).

Coxon, Howard, Playford, John & Reid, Robert, *Biographical Register of the South Australian Parliament 1857–1957*, (Adelaide: Wakefield Press, 1985).

Curthoys, Ann, 'Expulsion, Exodus and Exile in White Australian Historical Mythology', (Critical Essay), *Journal of Australian Studies*, Dec 1999 p1, Expanded Academic Electronic Collection: A57387441 RN: A57387441, Full Text Copyright 1999, University of Queensland Press.

Damousi, Joy and Lake, Marilyn, (eds), *Gender and War Australians at war in the twentieth century*, (Melbourne: Cambridge University, 1995).

Davies, Norman, *Europe*, (London: Pimlico, 1996, reprinted with corrections 1997).

Davison, Graeme, Hirst, John, Macintyre, Stuart (eds), *Oxford Companion to Australian History*,

(Oxford: Oxford University, 1998).

Denholm, Decie, (ed), *Behind the Lines One Woman's War 1914–1918 The Letters of Caroline Ethel Cooper,* (London: Jill Norman & Hobhouse, 1982).

Dixson, Miriam, *The Imaginary Australian: Anglo-Celts and Identity – 1788 to the present*, (Sydney: UNSW Press, 1999).

Duguid, Charles, 'Pro Deo, Pro Rege, Pro Patria', Violet Day Adelaide 1931, Memorial Address.

Duguid, Charles, *Doctor and the Aborigines*, (Adelaide, Rigby, 1972).

Dumbrell, John, (ed), *Vietnam and the Antiwar Movement: An International Perspective*, (Aldershot: Avebury, 1989).

Dunstan, Keith, 'Our Life with the V.C.', *Independent Monthly*, July 1989, pp. 14–16.

Ely, Richard, 'The First Anzac Day: Invented or Discovered'? *Journal of Australian Studies*, Vol 17, November 1985, pp. 41–58.

Fewster, Kevin, 'Ellis Ashmead Bartlett and the Making of the Anzac Legend', *Journal of Australian Studies*, Vol 10, June 1982, pp. 17–30.

Gammage, Bill, (text), Williamson, David, (screenplay), Weir, Peter, (preface), *The Story of Gallipoli*, (Ringwood: Penguin Books, 1981).

Gillis, John R, *Commemorations: The Politics of National Identity*, (Princeton: Princeton University, 1994).

Gregory, Adrian, *The Silence of Memory Armistice Day 1919–1946*, (Oxford: Berg, 1994).

Haran, Peter, *Trackers: The Untold Story of the Australian Dogs of War*, (Sydney: New Holland, 2000, reprinted 2000, 2001).

Henderson, Paul, *Parliament and Politics in Australia*, (Melbourne: Heinemann Education Australia, Fourth Edition, reprinted 1987).

Hoskin, Ronald Bruce, *Early Recollections of Ron Hoskin*, (Rosewater: R B Hoskin, 1996)

Hunt, A D, *Methodism Militant Attitudes to the Great War 1914–1918*, (Adelaide: South Australian Historical Society, 1975).

Inglis, K S, 'The Digger's Grave', *Nation*, February 19, 1966, pp. 13–15.

Inglis, K S, 'A Sacred Place: the Making of the Australian War Memorial', *War & Society* Vol 3, No 2, September 1985, pp. 99–126.

Inglis, K S, 'Gallipoli pilgrimage 1965', *Journal of the Australian War Memorial* No 18, April 1991, pp. 20–27.

Inglis, Ken, 'Entombing unknown soldiers', *Journal of the Australian War Memorial,* No 23, October 1993, pp. 4–12.

Inglis, Ken, 'Reflections on the Unknown Soldier', *Journal of the Australian War Memorial,* No 24, April 1994, pp. 6–7.

Inglis, K S, Assisted by Jan Brazier, *Sacred Places War Memorials in the Australian Landscape*, (Melbourne, The Miegunyah Press, 1998).

Inglis K S, 'The Unknown Australian Soldier', *Journal of Australian Studies,* March 1999 p 8, Expanded Academic, Article A56457691.

Inglis, Ken, 'The Anzacs: Their courage, resourcefulness and comradeship impressed both allies and enemies, and forged a coming-of-age myth for two youthful nations. (Australian and New Zealand Army Corps)'. *Time International,* Oct 25, 1999 i43 p48+, Expanded Academic Electronic Collection: A57298705 RN:A57298705. Full Text Copyright 1999 Time, Inc.

Jeffrey, Betty, *White Coolies*, (Sydney: Angus and Robertson, 1954, Reprinted January 1958).

Jordens, Ann-Mari, *Alien to Citizen: Settling Migrants in Australia*, 1945–75, (St Leonards: Allen & Unwin, 1997).

Kaye, Patricia, *Under an English Heaven*, (Harefield: Patricia Kaye, 1993).

Keating, Paul, Eulogy delivered by the Prime Minister of Australia, 'Funeral Service of the Unknown Australian Soldier', *Journal of the Australian War Memorial,* No 24, April 1994, pp. 4–5.

Kent, D A, '*The Anzac Book* and the Anzac Legend: CEW Bean as Editor and Image Maker', *Historical Studies*, Vol 21, No 84, April 1985, pp. 376–390.

Kitley, P, 'Anzac Day Ritual', *Journal of Australian Studies*, Vol 4, June 1979, pp. 58–69.

Kristianson, G.L., *The Politics of Patriotism: The Pressure Group Activities of the Returned Servicemen's League*, (Canberra: Australian National University, 1966).

Langley, Greg, *A Decade of Dissent: Vietnam and the conflict on the Australian homefront*, (Sydney: Allen & Unwin, 1992).

Limb, Arthur, *History of the 10th Battalion A.I.F. 1914–1918 Egypt, Gallipoli, France, Belgium*, (London: Cassell and Company, 1919).

Luckins, Tanja, *The Gates of Memory: Australian People's Experiences and Memories of Loss and the Great War*, (Fremantle: Curtin, 2004).

Luttrell, John, 'Cardinal Gilroy's Anzac Day problem', *Journal of the Royal Australian Historical Society*, June 1999 v85 i1 p1, Expanded Academic, Article A55805882.

Manners, Norman G, *Bullwinkel*, (Victoria Park, Hesperian Press, 1999).

McDougall & Vines, *Greater Port Adelaide Heritage Survey*, (Norwood: McDougall & Vine, 1989).

Port Adelaide Centre Heritage Survey 1993–1994, (Norwood: McDougall & Vines, 1994).

McGregor Tan Research, *Their Service Our Heritage Commemorative Program Research, Project No 4433*, Prepared for Commemorations Branch, Department of Veterans Affairs, (Adelaide: McGregor Tan Research, 1998–1999).

McGregor, Ian, Eltridge, Frances and McGregor, Karen, Stage 1, Situation Analysis, 26 May 1998.

McKay, Judith and Allom, Richard, *Lest We Forget A Guide to the Conservation of War memorials*, (Brisbane: Returned Services League of Australia (Queensland Branch), 1984).

McKernan, M & Browne M, (eds), *Australia: Two Centuries of War and Peace*, (Canberra: Australian War Memorial, 1988).

McKernan, Michael, *Here is Their Spirit A History of the Australian War Memorial 1917– 1990*, (St Lucia: University of Queensland, 1991).

McLaren, Don, *Mates in Hell*, (Adelaide: Seaview Press, 1998).

Methodist Hymn Book, (London: Hazell, Watson and Viney), Australasian Edition, 1904.

Mincham, Hans, *The Story of the Flinders Ranges*, (Adelaide: Rigby, 1964).

Mitchell, Rosemary, *Epworth Uniting Church Parkside 1884–1984*, (Morphett Vale: Rosemary Mitchell, 1984).

Moses, John A, 'The Struggle for Anzac Day 1916–1930 and the role of the Brisbane Anzac Day Commemoration Committee', *Journal of the Royal Australian Historical Society*, Vol. 88, Part 1, June 2002, pp. 54–74.

Mosse, George L, *Fallen Soldiers: Reshaping the Memory of the World Wars*, (New York: Oxford University, 1990).

Nelson, Hank, 'Gallipoli, Kokoda and the making of national identity', (Fatal Shores), *Journal of Australian Studies*, June 1997 n53 p157 (11), Expanded Academic, Electronic Collection: A20171122.

Nelson, Hank, *Chased by the Sun*, (Sydney: ABC Books, 2002).

Nicol, Robert, *At the End of the Road*, (St Leonards: Allen & Unwin, 1994).

O'Connor, Desmond, *No need to be afraid: Italian Settlers in South Australia Between 1839 and the Second World War*, (Kent Town: Wakefield Press, 1996).

Ousby, Ian, *Cambridge Guide to Literature in English*, (Cambridge: Cambridge University Press, 1993).

Pavils, Janice, 'The emergence of South Australian Anzac culture 1915–1925', *Journal of the Royal Australian Historical Society*, Vol 89, Part 2, December 2003, pp. 123–144.

Peters, Betty, 'The life experience of partners of ex-POWs of the Japanese', *Journal of the*

Australian War Memorial, Issue 28 – April 1996, <*http://www.awm.gov.au/journal/ j28/j28-petr.htm*>

Reid, Richard and Forth, Gordon, *Memories & Memorabilia*, (Canberra: Department of Veterans' Affairs, undated).

Robertson, John, *Anzac and Empire: The Tragedy & Glory of Gallipoli*, (Port Melbourne: Hamlyn, 1990).

Ross, Jane, 'The myth of Anzac', *Journal of the Australian War Memorial*, No 16, April 1990, pp. 55.56.

Sackett, Lee, 'Marching into the Past: Anzac Day Celebrations in Adelaide', *Journal of Australian Studies*, Vol 17, November 1985, pp. 18–30.

Seal, Graham, *Inventing Anzac: The Digger and National Mythology*, (St Lucia: University of Queensland Press, 2004).

Seymour, Alan, *The One Day of the Year*, (London: Angus and Robertson, 1962).

The One Day of the Year: A Novel, (London: Souvenir Press, 1967).

Sharpe, Maureen R, 'Anzac day in New Zealand: 1916 to 1939', *New Zealand Journal of History*, Vol 15, No 2, October 1981, pp. 97–114.

Thelen, David, 'Memory and American History', *Journal of American History*, Vol 75, No 4, March 1989, pp. 1117–1129.

Thompson, Eric, *The Uniting Church in Australia, The Origin and First Ten Years of Trinity Uniting Church – Alberton*, (Alberton: Carmel and John Clare, 1993).

Whaley, Joachim (ed), *Mirrors of Mortality: Studies in the Social History of Death*, (New York: St Martin's Press, 1981).

Cannadine, David, 'War and Death, Grief and Mourning in Modern Britain', pp. 187–242.

Wigmore, Lionel, *Australia in the War of 1939–1945, Series One, Army, Volume IV, The Japanese Thrust*, (Canberra: Australian War Memorial, 1957).

Winter, Jay, *Sites of Memory Sites of Mourning The Great War in European cultural history*, (Cambridge: Cambridge University Press, 1995).

Internet Sites

ANZAC 2000, Dawn Service-Order of Commemoration <*http://www.embaustralia.org.tr/anzac/anzac2k.htm*>

Commonwealth War Graves Commission <*http://www.cwgc.org/cwgcinternet/casualty_details*>

Department of Veterans' Affairs, < *http://minister.dva.gov.au/media/speeches*>

Governors, Sir Francis Alexander Newdigate Newdegate 1920–1924, <*http://www.ccentre.wa.gov.au/html/prems_govenors/governorsh … / alexandernewdegate.htm*>

Prime Minister <*http://www.pm.gov.au/media/pressrel/2000*>

RSL Recent History, <*http://www.sa.rsl.org.au/about/history.html*>

Song of Australia, <*http://www.southaustralianhistory.com.au/song.htm*>

Starke, Russell, 'Ravings', One Day every year, <*http://www.messenger.net.au/Pulse/htm/starke07.htm*>

The Winston Churchill Memorial Trust, <*http://www/churchilltrust.com.au/*>

Toc H South Australia, People Caring for People since 1925, <*http://homepages.picknowl.com.au/tochsa/about.htm*>

United Nations Documents: The San Francisco Conference (April-May 1945), Truman Presidential Museum & Library, <*http://www.trumanlibrary.org/whistlestop/study_ collections/un/large/sf_conference/*>

Index

A

Absent corpse, 21, 23, 156
Account Rendered, 17, 18, 129
Accounting policies, 157, 163
AD Committee, 81, 82, 83, 85, 86, 89, 90, 94, 98, 130
Adelaide, 5, 13, 16, 19, 21, 22, 23, 39, 47, 50, 54, 64, 70, 71, 79, 95, 107, 114, 120, 121, 125, 133, 136, 139, 141, 145, 180
Adelaide High School, 99, 100, 101, 102, 103, 104, 116
Adelaide Oval, 2, 3
Adey, W. J., 101
Advance Australia Fair, 132, 133, 134, 137
AIF cemetery, 18, 120, 125
Ainsworth, E. H., 75, 94, 96
Albany, 19
Alberton, 119, 126, 164, 165, 169
Alderman, Mr, 187
Alice Springs, 54
Allen, Major-General, 127
Allison, R., 134
America, 129
Angorichina, 16, 17
Anzac Day Committee, 2, 18, 77
Anzac Highway memorial, 64, 76
Anzac Parade, 185
Armbruster, C., 82
Armistice Day, 13, 14, 15, 18, 35, 39, 51, 98, 99, 104, 105, 107, 108, 109, 110, 111, 118, 127, 139, 147, 167, 187
Army of the Dead, 1, 14, 15
Arnold, Lynn, 88, 97
Ashton, J., 151, 173
Atkin, C. S., 182
Auld, P., 185
Australia Remembers, 155, 158, 159, 164, 173, 174
Australian American Association, 113
Australian Funeral Directors' Association, 135
Australian Natives Association, 8, 120
Australian Parliamentary Delegation 1990 Gallipoli, 188
Australian War Memorial, 22, 63, 102, 104, 108, 115, 127, 130, 133, 134, 135, 143, 157, 169, 176, 179
Australian War Museum. *See* Australian War Memorial

B

Bagot, E.D.A., 65
Baker, G. T., 145
Baker, Herbert, 28, 31, 35, 40, 41
Balance sheet, 174
Baltic Council, 113, 114
Barrett, Lord Mayor & Lady Mayoress, 126
Barwell, Sir Henry, 49
Baxter, C., 109
Bean, C. E. W., 178, 179, 188, 192
Beazley, K., 190
Bedford Park, 16
Beersheba, 126
Benskin, Rev F. G., 121
Beovich, Most Rev Dr M., 127
Bernstein, Rabbi I. A., 121
Berry, S., 135, 136
Betts, Lieut-Colonel L. O., 163
Bice, J. G., 47
Billyard-Leake, C., 99, 101
Binyon, L., 148, 182
Birdwood, 97
Birkenhead, 125, 161, 163
Blackman, A. S., 185
Blinman, 16
Blomfield, Sir Reginald, 22, 28
Bottomley, Mrs, 165
Bowen, S., 139, 143
Bradman, D. G., 52
Breavington, Corporal E. E., 144
Bridges, General, 4, 22, 44
Brighton, 121, 123, 125
Brinkworth, 71
Brisbane, 10, 133, 180, 193
Brisbane ADCC, 10, 11, 19, 43, 77, 118
Broomhead, Rev E. N., 139, 145, 146, 147, 148, 149, 150, 151, 152, 153
Brown, Brigadier, 102, 185
Bruce, Stanley, 53
Buaby, N. F., 112
Bulbeck, Rev A. L., 125, 129
Bullecort Mayor, 135
Bullwinkel, V., 139, 151, 152, 153, 173
Burgess, J. H., 127
Burma, 129
Burnside, 123
Burra, 5, 157
Bute, 5
Butler, C. P., 46
Butler, Mr, 38

C

Cahir, R. T., 178
Campaign for Peace in Vietnam, 89
Campbell, Miss, 96
Canada, 129
Canberra, 22, 44, 54, 63, 94, 108, 127, 130, 133, 135, 136, 157, 178, 180, 184, 185
Cantwell, Rev Father W., 127
Carleton, C., 132
Carr, E. B., 142
Cathedral Memorial Committee, 28, 30, 36
Centennial Park cemetery, 28, 74
Chauvel, General, 179
Cheer-Up Society, 4, 8, 11, 12, 17, 29, 30
Cheltenham, 37, 167, 169
Chittleborough, J., 88, 97
Christian, A. W., 65
Churches, R. F., 96, 139, 150, 151
Civil religion, 175, 181, 182, 184, 185, 190
Clarence Park, 78
Clark, Helen NZ Prime Minister, 189
Clark, T. G., 82
Clayton, Rev P., 124
Clegget, Miss, 15, 16, 17
Colonel Light Gardens, 157
Committee for Vietnam Protest, 89
Commonwealth War Graves Commission. *See* Imperial War Graves Commission
Communist Party, 71
Communitas, 182, 186, 190
Cook, Sir Joseph, 51, 52
Coomb, R., 136
Cooper, C. E., 139, 142, 143
Corcoran, James Desmond, 92
Cosgove, General Peter, 76
Cox, D., 189
Crawford, Rev N., 124
Creswell Gardens, 2
Cross of Sacrifice, 20, 23, 24, 28, 29, 31, 33, 35, 36, 37, 41, 42, 79, 83, 84, 85, 87, 89, 90, 92, 93, 94, 95, 96, 97, 98, 124, 125, 126, 127, 128, 129, 130, 131, 149, 180
Cudmore, C. R., 65
Cult of the Fallen Soldier, 114, 123, 129, 135, 176, 188, 189
Curtin, John, 108, 109, 127
Cyprian Society, 113
Czechoslovakian Society, 113
Czechoslovakians, 114

D

Dalziel, A. H., 51
Darley, F. W., 86
Darwin, 180
Davies, Rev E. A., 123
Debit notes, 156, 169
Debt of Gratitude, 1, 15, 18, 136, 155, 172, 173, 174
Debt of Honour, 1, 3, 8, 15, 17, 18, 20, 24, 55, 61, 62, 65, 66, 98, 111, 125, 129, 155, 156, 157, 158, 161, 169, 172, 173, 174, 188
Debt reduction, 174
Debt reminders, 156
Debt repayment, 1, 4, 13, 33, 66, 99, 120, 155
Denny, W. J., 39, 46, 47, 49, 65, 139, 140, 141, 142
Department of Veterans' Affairs, 1, 37, 155, 174, 189
Depreciation, 88, 171, 174
Derrick Garden of Remembrance, 28, 37
Derrick, Lt T. C., VC, DCM, AIF, 173
Desecration, 38, 39, 41, 88, 173
Dick, Flight-Lieut G. T., 103
Dividend, 174
Dodson, A. J., 167
Dodson, J. L., 76
Dodson, Lieutenant W. F. L., 167, 193
Draper, T., 173
Dryburg, M., 130
Duguid, Dr C., 72, 139, 141, 142
Duguid, R., 141
Duguid, W., 141
Duke of Kent, 135
Dunk, A. S., 69
Duntroon, 22, 44

E

Eastick, Mrs, 185
Eastick, T. C., 72, 89, 91, 131, 182, 185
Edwardstown, 111, 125
Egnar, W., 75
Egypt, 49
Eight Hours Day, 2, 3, 19
Elder Park, 44, 46, 90, 120
Eliott, L. C., 52
Enfield, 37, 170
Erdelhun, General, 183
Eudunda, 123

F

Fascist Party, 66, 67
Finnis, Rev H. P., 124
Flinders Ranges, 16, 17
Floyd Shannon, Rev W., 123
Forster, Governor-General Lord, 21
Forster, Rev J., 120
Forsyth, Brigadier-General J. K., 13
France, 49

Francis, H. R., 144, 152
French community in South Australia, 117

G

Gale, Private V. L., 144
Galleghan, Lieut-Colonel, 139, 144, 145
Gallipoli Dawn Service, 175, 181, 189, 190
Gallipoli Day, 12, 13, 77
Galway, Sir Henry, 5, 36
Gandon, Rev A., 104
Gawler, 5, 9
Gaza, 126
Gellert, L., 1
George, Sir Robert, 40
German migrants, 112
Germany, 129
Gilbert, D., 25, 30
Gilbert, W. H. Mayor, 170
Gladstone, 54
Glanville, 173
Gleeson, Bishop, 131
Glenelg, 5, 64, 76, 130, 157, 158, 163
Glover, C. R. J. Lord Mayor, 36
Glover, Lady Mayoress, 24, 25
God Save the King, 118, 120, 147
God Save the Queen, 130, 132, 133, 134
Goodwood, 123, 180
Goolwa, 54, 71
Gordon, D. J., 48
Gordon, J., 185
Gorton, John, 90, 186
Gowrie, Governor-General Lord, 108, 127
Great Britain, 129
Greek Association, 116
Greek Community, 115
Greek Consul, 113
Greek Orthodox community, 113
Greenham, Mr, 101
Greer, E. R., 129
Gregory, R., 103
Gullett, Sir Henry, 179

H

Hackham, 76
Hackworthy, Rev H. G., 128
Harcourt, G. C., 89
Harefield, 23, 99, 100, 101, 102, 103, 104, 116
Harris, E. J., 182
Harwood, Dr B., 124
Hasluck, P. M., 186
Hawke, Robert, 187, 188
Henley Beach, 109
Hindmarsh, 121
Hirsh, Rabbi, 121
Hobart, 133, 180
Hoff, R., 38
Hoffman, K. W., 59, 89, 133
Holland, Sir George, 183
Holmes, Lieut-Colonel E. B., 145
Hopkins, Major General, 58
Hore-Ruthven, Sir Alexander, 54
Horne, A., 181, 192
Horton, Arch Deacon B., 137
Howard, John, 1, 19, 176, 189, 190, 193
Huang, A. Lord Mayor, 173
Hudd, H. S., 46, 50, 65
Hughes, William, 11, 15, 119, 187, 188
Huish, Sir Raymond, 185
Human Wreckage, 1, 14
Hungarians, 111
Hurford, C., 187
Hurst, L. M., 85

I

Imperial War Graves Commission, 21, 28, 35, 102, 180, 185
Indigenous ex-servicemen, 61, 68, 72, 73
International Women's Day Collective, 94
Investment, 174
Invoices, 157
IRA, 114
Irwin, L., 186
Islington, 46, 47, 139
Italy, 129, 148, 152

J

Jacob, R. B., 180, 192
Jacobs, Mrs, 185
Jamestown, 54
Jeanes, W. H., 52
Jeffery, E. F., 100
Jeffrey, E. A. (Betty), 151, 152
Jennings, A., 165
Jerusalem, 126
Johnson, Councillor, 39
Jose, Rev G. H., 118, 119
Joyce, Mr, 182

K

Kadina, 5, 9, 158, 161, 163
Kain, Rev A. E., 124
Kapunda, 9, 173
Katherine, 78
Keating, Paul, 134, 136
Kelly, Lieutenant, 141
Kelson, B., 134
Kensington, 125
Kerr, Sir John, 133
Kersbrook, 92

Keswick, 13, 55, 76, 172
Keys, A. G. W., 183, 184
Kiek, Rev, 124
King George V, 11, 14, 104, 105
King George VI, 108, 125, 180
Kipling, R., 31
Kokoda, 134
Kooyonga, 56
Korean and South East Asian Forces Association, 115

L

Lambert, W. E., 84
Largs North, 161, 163
Laura, 5
Lawrence, A. A., 51
Laybourne Smith, Mr, 38, 40
League of Loyal Women, 12, 24
Leaver, Lieutenant G. H., 193
Leckie, F., 82
Ledger sheet, 155
Lee, J., 16
Legacy, 56, 80, 86, 91, 96
Letaille, D., 193
Letaille, J., 193
Liability, 3
Libya, 129
Light Oval. *See* AIF cemetery
Linger, C., 132
Lion Mound, 12, 24
London, 136
London Cenotaph, 23, 31, 35, 39, 51, 52, 105, 107, 109, 123, 183, 190
Long, G., 102
Look, Corporal-Bugler K., 124
Lundie Gardens, 17
Lunn, Mrs, 177
Lunn, S., 177, 178, 192
Lutyens, Sir Edwin, 28, 31, 33, 125
Lyons, J. A., 65

M

Mackay, G. M. Councillor, 125
MacLaren, G. C., 35
Maitland, 131
Malta, 129
Maltese Council, 113
Mannum, 49
Martin, H. Councillor, 126
Mawson, Lady, 171
McCabe, S., 52
McCann, W. F. J., 53
McCrae, Colonel John, 14, 149
McFarlane, W. H., 16
McIntosh, M., 39
McKay, T. H., 161
McLaren, M. D. (Don), 139, 144, 145
McLaurin, Mrs, 165
McLeay, J., 65
McMillan, I., 46, 49, 65
McPhee, Colonel J. C., 119
Meincke, J., 9
Melbourne, 15, 39, 70, 73, 121, 133, 179, 180, 188
Memorial Drive, 23, 24, 31, 35, 36, 37
Memorial Hospital, 24, 31, 33
Menin Gate Memorial, 182, 193
Menzies, D., 51, 53
Menzies, Robert, 75, 183, 187
Merry, T. B., 2
Michael, H. D., 65
Milera, H. J., 68
Millie, 15
Mills, W. G. J., 48
Mitcham, 11, 142
Mitchell, Captain Padre, 148
Monash, General, 49
Montgomery, Viscount, 70
Moonta, 54, 158, 163
Moonta Mines, 158, 159
Moore, H. Mayor, 171
Morphettville, 76, 142
Morrissey, C. K., 95
Morshead, Lieut General Sir Leslie, 181
Mount Barker, 5, 69, 75, 192
Mount Gambier, 31, 130
Multicultural, 41
  Americans, 80, 81, 87, 96, 127
  British, 73, 79, 80, 81, 84, 87, 93, 109
  Canadians, 79, 81, 87
  French, 81, 87, 125
  Greeks, 79, 81, 87
  Italian ex-servicemen post Mussolini downfall, 96
  Italian WWI, 66
  Maltese, 87
  New Zealanders, 79, 81, 87, 109
  Polish, 80, 81, 87, 115
  Serbian, 81, 87, 96
  South Vietnamese, 96, 98
  Turkish, 71, 72
  Yugoslavian, 84
Munro Ferguson, Sir Ronald, 9
Murphy, Rev Father, 31
Murray Bridge, 157
Mypolonga, 179
Myrtlebank, 15, 17, 58

N

Nash, NZ Prime Minister, 183
National Aborigines Day League, 113
National account, 157
National debt, 163
Neagle, Mr, 182, 183
Netherlands Consul, 111
New Australians, 71, 111, 112
New South Wales, 21, 44, 52, 54, 65, 94, 99, 103, 184
New Zealand, 43, 52, 66, 79, 104, 116, 118, 147, 148, 179, 183, 186, 187, 188, 189
New Zealanders, 13, 116, 151, 178, 179, 181
Newdegate, Sir Francis Newdigate, 100, 101
Nicholl, Sir Robert, 126
Niff, A., 183
North Adelaide, 46, 128, 142
North Africa, 129
Northern Territory, 65
Norwood, 125, 135
Nuriootpa, 75

O

O'Brien, D., 84
O'Connor, Mr, 46
O'Doherty, Rev Father J. P., 124
Obelisk, 9, 12, 13, 14, 16, 21, 83
Oliphant, Sir Mark, 142
Orroroo, 54
Ottoway, 164, 165, 171

P

Pacific Islands, 129
Palembang, 151
Palestine, 129
Palsovannis, Dr C., 128
Parachilna, 16, 54
Paris Arc de Triomphe, 123
Parkside, 118, 119, 166
Paskeville, 161
Paterson, 'Banjo', 20
Pathway of Honour, 173
Pearce, G. F., 3, 22, 100, 119
Pearce, W., 102
Pennington, 169
Perry, Rev, 125, 129
Perth, 180
Petersburg, 9
Philippines Legation, 111
Phillips, Captain Mark, 92
Phillips, Major General Peter, 189
Playford, Sir Thomas, 65, 69, 71, 74, 110, 124, 126
Pocock, F., 165
Pope Paul VI, 186
Poppy Day, 18, 56, 59, 98, 107, 109, 116
Port Adelaide, 5, 48, 126, 130, 158, 161, 163, 164, 165, 169, 170, 171, 172, 173
Port Adelaide Enfield, 163, 164, 170, 171
Port Augusta, 54
Port Lincoln, 95
Port Pirie, 157
Port Wakefield, 9
Pound, D., 143
Powell, L. J., 2
Pratt, Captain O., 126
Prince Charles, 93
Princess Anne, 92
Prisoners-of-war, 17, 129, 130, 139, 143, 144, 148, 151, 152, 170, 175, 185, 186
Pritchard, A. C., 83
Prospect, 53, 54, 56, 173
Protests, 63, 65, 78, 86, 88, 89, 90, 91, 94, 95, 97, 111, 113, 114, 115, 167, 186
Pudney, C., 165, 166

Q

Queen Elizabeth II, 130
Queensland, 44, 54, 65, 185
Quorn, 54

R

Read, Mrs, 165
Reid, Dr R., 134
Remembrance Day, 14, 17, 24, 37, 40, 41, 99, 110, 111, 112, 113, 114, 115, 116, 117, 133, 134, 136, 138, 149, 156, 167, 169, 175, 176
Remembrance Sunday, 79, 98, 108, 109, 110
Renmark, 157
Reynolds, F. E., 128
Reynolds, Mrs, 128
Richards, Justice, 126
Richards, R. S., 68
Rigney, G., 129
Rite of passage, 176, 177, 190
Robin, Right Rev B. P., 127
Robins, Captain J. F., 178
Rosewater, 123, 124, 126, 161, 163, 164, 165, 166, 167, 169, 170, 171, 172, 194
Rowland, J. R., 184, 185
Royal Consulate of Greece, 113
Royston Park, 183
Rudall, R. J., 65

S

SA Hiroshima Committee, 114, 115
Satchell, P., 144

Save our Sons movement, 88, 91
Sawford, R., 173
Schmitt, W. H., 144
Schumann, J., 88, 97
Scott, B., 189
Seager, A., 4, 5, 10, 30, 75
Seager, F. L., 2
Semaphore, 123, 124, 125, 126, 161, 163
Serbian Cultural Club, 111
Shannon, A., 123
Sharland, W. D., 180
Sharp, A. C., 181, 182
Sicily, 129
Simpson, A. A. Mayor, 24, 39
Sinclair, B., 181
Slockee, R., 190
Smedley, Adjutant, 126
Smith, C. J. D., 65
Smith, E. H., 85, 132
Smith, Mr, 46
Smith, P., 90, 91
Smith, Sir Ross, 120
Soldiers' Memorial, 4, 5, 12, 13, 24, 79, 83, 118
Solomon, W. J., 121
Somerville, R. S., 82
Somme Prefect, 135
Song of Australia, 40, 130, 132
South Australia, 21, 50, 53, 57, 65, 66, 107
Sowden, W. J., 1, 8, 10, 16
Spence, C., 9
Spooner, Sir William, 185
State Memorial, 18, 19, 23, 24, 37, 38, 39, 40, 41, 54, 79, 82, 83, 88, 89, 90, 93, 94, 107, 111, 112, 113, 114, 115, 116, 117, 123, 124, 125, 130, 131, 136, 169
Stephens, Mrs, 165
Stone of Remembrance, 20, 33, 35, 92
Strathalbyn, 49, 54, 131
Street, Lieutenant Governor Justice, 133
Sutton, E. E., 170, 171, 194
Sydney, 38, 52, 58, 133, 135, 180, 188
Symonds, T. Councillor, 126
Symons, Sir Josiah, 25

T

Talbot, Padre, 182
Tarau, Corporal U., 190
Tasmania, 44, 65, 100, 103, 132
Tassie, H. Mayor, 157
Tel Aviv, 126
Their Service Our Heritage. *See* TS-OH
Thomas, C., 82
Tidswell, L. A., 85
Tobin, P., 136
Toc H, 124, 127, 182
Toole-Mackson, Rev K. T., 102
Torode, W., 9, 12
Treloar, J. L., 179, 180
Trembath, Mr, 130
TS-OH, 155, 173, 174, 189
Tubercular Soldiers Aid Society, 15, 16, 17

U

Ukrainians, 111
Undying debt, 194
Unknown Australian Soldier, 22, 99, 134, 135, 136, 180, 192
Unknown Warrior, 14, 104, 105, 134
Unley, 9, 12, 19, 64, 121, 123, 125, 130
Upper Sturt, 25

V

Vaughan, Crawford, 11, 119
Vaughan, J. H., 62
Venning, Mrs, 101
Victor Harbor, 54
Victoria, 5, 44, 54, 57, 65
Victoria Square, 2, 88, 92, 94
Victory Europe Day, 115, 167, 176
Victory Pacific Day, 56, 115, 167, 176
Vietnam Crisis, 88
Vietnam Moratorium Campaign, 90
Villers-Bretonneux Mayor, 136
Villers-Bretonneux, Adelaide Cemetery, 22, 135, 181, 192
Villers-Bretonneux, Australian National War Memorial for the missing in France, 31, 125, 180, 192, 193
Von Bibra, Major, 103

W

Waite, Colonel, 88
Wake, N., 173
Wallaroo, 9, 158, 159
Walton, R., 103
Ward, H., 8
Wark, J. M., 184
Wattle Day League, 8, 9, 11, 12, 16, 21, 83, 120, 140
Wayville, 9, 54, 55
Weaver, Mrs, 165
West Terrace cemetery, 14, 17, 28, 37
West Torrens, 64
Western Australia, 44, 65, 100
Western Desert, 129
Whereat, Padre, 131
White, Rev A. E., 19
Whitlam, Edward Gough, 132, 133, 134
Whitman, O. P. Q., 104

Wilson, Mr, 182
Wilson, N. D., 57
Women against Rape in War, 94
Women's Memorial, 21, 23, 24, 29, 31, 33, 35, 41, 43, 121
Women's Memorial Fund, 24, 25, 28, 29, 30, 31, 33, 35, 36, 40, 41
Wood, Rev T. P., 49, 51, 121
Woods, Bagot, Laybourne-Smith and Irwin, 40
Woodside, 72
Woodville, 125, 173
Woolloomooloo, 21, 135
Worth, T., 173
Wylde, H., 124

Y

Yankalilla, 95
Yatala, 165
Yeatman, Lieut.-Colonel, 100
Yorketown, 31, 53
Young, J. F., 9
Young, P., 115
Ypres Mayor, 136